RELIGION

RELIGION

The Classical Theories

JAMES THROWER

GEORGETOWN UNIVERSITY PRESS
Washington, D.C.

For my daughter Annabel

© James Thrower, 1999

Georgetown University Press
Washington, D.C. 20007

Typeset in Goudy Old Style
by Norman Tilley Graphics, and
printed and bound in Great Britain
by The Bath Press

Library of Congress Cataloging-in-Publication Data

Thrower, James, 1936-
    Religion: The classical theories / James Thrower.
      p.   cm.
    Includes bibliographical references and index.
    ISBN 0-87840-751-0 (pbk. : alk. paper)
    1. Religion—Philosophy.   I. Title.
BL51.T54   1999
200—dc21   99-18216
                                   CIP

Contents

Preface   vii

1. Introduction   1

Part I
RELIGIOUS THEORIES OF RELIGION

2. Religion as Revelation   9
3. Religion as Experience   49
4. Religion as Philosophy   74

Part II
NATURALISTIC THEORIES OF RELIGION

5. Religion as Human Construct: Some Greek and Roman
   Theories of Religion   93
6. Religion as Primitive Error   99
7. Religion as Psychological Construct   126
8. Religion as Social Construct   161

9. Conclusion: What is Religion?   202

Index   206

Preface

In his book *Real Presences* George Steiner calls attention to the tidal wave of secondary literature that threatens to overwhelm the humane disciplines. Commenting on the grotesque situation which exists in the Academy today, he writes:

> Commentary is without end. In the worlds of interpretative and critical discourse, book ... engenders book, essay breeds essay, article spawns article. The mechanics of interminability are those of the locust. Monograph feeds on monograph, vision on revision. The primary text is only the remote font of autonomous exegetic proliferation. The true source of Z's tome are X and Y's works on the identical topic.[1]

This, I am afraid, is just such a meta-text as Steiner deprecates, yet it is one, I believe, that is needed by contemporary students of religion. Ideally, of course, if Steiner is right – and on the whole I think that he is – it should consist simply of a bibliography directing students of religion to the primary texts where they might engage directly with those whose creative genius led them to formulate enduring insights into the nature of religion. Yet most of these texts were written for a more leisurely age and an engagement of what Steiner calls 'immediacy' with even the most central texts would take more time than most students have at their disposal. A guide, therefore, is needed which will sift, sort and summarise these works in the hope that an initial second-hand acquaintance with the thinking that informs them will lead the student to become acquainted with at least some of them at first hand. This is the purpose of this book and I take comfort from some further words of Professor Steiner when he notes earlier in the same essay that 'for many a tentative reader, the pedagogic-critical shepherd can be invaluable'.[2] It is this role that I try to fulfil in the pages which follow.

A number of people have had a hand in the production of this book and it is my pleasant task here to acknowledge and thank them. First and foremost I would like to thank my students over the years at Aberdeen, and at other universities where I have taught, if only briefly, for forcing me to confront, and to confront again, the question 'what is religion' and who have refused to let me rest, as I have been all too inclined to, in the agnosticism of the fifth-century BCE Greek thinker Protagoras who, in his treatise *On the Gods*, wrote: 'I cannot feel sure either that the gods are or that they are not, nor what they are like … for there are many things that hinder certain knowledge, the obscurity of the subject and the shortness of life.' It is, however, because I have had and still have no firm answers of my own to offer – or at least none in which I have much confidence – that I have directed them, as I direct the reader now, to those more confident than myself who have offered what have become the classic answers to the question 'what is religion?'

I would also like to thank the University of Aberdeen for giving me a term's sabbatical leave to complete work on this book. My colleagues Malise Ruthven and Helen Bond read parts of the manuscript in draft and made useful suggestions for the improvement of its style and content. I alone, of course, am responsible for what is presented to the public. I must also thank the secretaries in the Department of Divinity with Religious Studies at Aberdeen, Theresa Clark and Helena Thomas, for continuing to supply me with the tools of the trade – paper, toner, photocopying, coffee and refreshing conversation. The commissioning editor at Edinburgh University Press, Jane Feore, has been helpful and encouraging throughout and has had a faith in my ability to 'deliver' not always shared by myself. Finally, I would like to thank SandyM1234, whose interruptions on the Internet provided diversion and enjoyment during the latter part of the writing of this book, and Mary Tesmer, of Greencastle, Indiana, for quite literally saving my life on an otherwise uneventful Spring evening in April 1998 on the beautiful campus of Depauw University. Without her timely assistance, and the subsequent help of Greencastle Operation Life, of the doctors and nursing staff at Putnam County Hospital and at Methodist Hospital in Indianapolis, this book would never have been completed.

James Thrower
King's College, the University of Aberdeen

– NOTES –

1. George Steiner, *Real Presences*, London: Faber & Faber, 1989, p. 39.
2. Ibid., p. 23.

CHAPTER 1

Introduction

We live today with an awareness of the phenomenon and phenomena of religion denied to previous generations and any theory purporting to explain religion must, if it is to have credibility, reflect this. However, the knowledge that we now possess of the history and the geography of religion both helps and hinders attempts to explain it. Such knowledge helps because it is now possible to test such explanations as are or have been advanced against a wider body of evidence than has previously been possible – a procedure which demonstrates the often limited and culture-bound nature of many of the explanations which have held Western intellectuals in thrall. Yet, at the same time, such knowledge hinders attempts to explain religion because our increased awareness of the variety of religious expression found in the world makes it well nigh impossible to formulate a comprehensive theory of religion that will encompass this variety: counter-examples proliferate.

But if we are the first generation to possess such a significant volume of knowledge about religion, we, or at least those of us who live in western Europe, are also the first people to live in a predominantly non-religious, or post-religious, culture, and this too has consequences for attempts to explain religion, for it allows us to see religion from a perspective denied to previous generations – a perspective that allows us to both contemplate and experience secular ways of living that would hardly have seemed possible even a century ago. Dostoevsky and Nietzsche who, more than any other nineteenth-century writers, explored the atheistic existential alternatives to religion did so only in their imaginations. Today we are confronted by the real thing and can begin to make a preliminary assessment of how living without a religious outlook on life is working out. Yet, as Peter Berger has noted, when looked at in a global perspective, the predominantly secular culture of western Europe is a unique phenomenon even in today's world. The assumption made by sociologists a generation ago that modernisation would lead inevitably to secularisation has not, in fact, proved to be the case.[1]

Previous introductions to theories of religion have concentrated almost exclusively on sociological and psychological explanations and have, for the most part, ignored what theologians, philosophers and religious believers have said about religion.[2] They have thus been organised around the explanations of religion offered by thinkers such as Tylor, Frazer, Marx, Nietzsche and Freud, all of whom were hostile to religion. My own approach is somewhat different in that, whilst I shall not ignore these important and influential thinkers, I shall also consider what religious believers themselves have said about religion. However, the principle around which this work is organised is not primarily biographical but typological and, whilst individual thinkers play a prominent part in what I have to say, what I am seeking to introduce are not just the thoughts of individuals but the different types of explanations of religion which have been advanced primarily, but not exclusively, from within the Western tradition. My hope in organising my material in this way, and by looking at both religious and non-religious explanations of religion, is that what I have to say will result in a more comprehensive account of theories of religion than has been offered hitherto and that it will, for that reason, appeal not only to undergraduate students of theology and religion – for whom it is primarily intended – but also to the educated lay person looking for an overview of the kinds of answer which have been given to the question, 'what is religion?'

The book is divided into two parts. In the first part I shall look at what the religions of the world have said about religion whilst in the second I shall look at explanations, most of them – although not all – hostile to religion, which have been advanced from within the disciplines of anthropology, psychology and sociology. The conclusion offers a brief comment on the future of theorising about religion in the rather different situation which exists today compared to the situation which obtained when the classic theorists went about their work.

But before I move on to discuss the theories which have been offered to account for the phenomenon of religion I would like to recall some words of Goethe, who has reminded us that:

> All theory ... is grey,
> But green is life's glad golden tree.

To no area of enquiry are these lines from *Faust* more apposite than to second-order enquiries into religion, and this for the reason that religion has its *raison d'être* within a shared form of life, and to stand outside that form of life and theorise about it is a very grey business indeed. As the eleventh-century Muslim philosopher and mystic al-Ghazzali so graphically expressed it: to understand the causes of drunkenness is not the same thing as to be drunk. And William James at the conclusion of *The Varieties of Religious Experience* likened the difference between the theory and the practice of religion to the difference between a menu and a four-square meal. There is a very real sense in which religion looks different when viewed from the standpoint of the believer than when viewed from that of the spectator.

Yet some words of another German thinker which also speak of 'greyness' will, I think, explain why it is that, from about the middle of the eighteenth century, explanations of religion have come to preoccupy thinking men and women in the Western world as never before in the history of Western thought. In the concluding paragraph to the preface of his *Philosophy of Right* Hegel wrote: 'When philosophy paints its grey on grey, then a form of life has grown old. And by this grey on grey it can only be understood, not rejuvenated. The owl of Minerva flies only at dusk.' Hegel's words about the role of philosophy are particularly relevant to the business of explaining religion, for it is only when religion has ceased to be at the living heart of a culture, that is, when its status has become problematical, that explanations to account for its existence come to the fore.

Explanations of religion fall into two broad categories according to whether the subject-matter of religion is regarded as an ontologically primary or as an ontologically secondary phenomenon. These I shall call, respectively, religious explanations of religion and naturalistic explanations of religion. A religious explanation of religion takes the transcendental discourse of religion as *sui generis* and holds that such discourse can not be reduced to any other form of discourse. A naturalistic explanation, on the other hand, rejects, or radically reinterprets, the overt claims of religions, and seeks to reduce religious discourse to the more amenable because, so it is claimed, more empirical discourse of the disciplines of psychology and sociology. According to the accounts of religion put forward from within these disciplines religion can be exhaustively accounted for in terms of individual or social psychology, often allied to an account of its social function. Although explanations of religion fall more or less into one or other of these two broad categories, these categories are not necessarily mutually exclusive, and we find among the explanations that have been put forward to account for religion a number of ways of combining the two, a particularly common way being that put forward by those who offer a religious account of their own religion and a reductive account of the religions of others.

This broad distinction has much in common with the distinction drawn by the French thinker Paul Ricoeur, between what he terms 'a hermeneutics of recollection' and 'a hermeneutics of suspicion'.[3] For Ricoeur, a 'hermeneutics of recollection' is a hermeneutics which is sympathetic to religious claims in that it is inclined to accept that religion is in touch with something objective, real and ultimately other than the consciousness of the individual religious believer, something which can be retrieved or 'recollected'. Those who practise a 'hermeneutics of suspicion', on the other hand, seek, through a suspicious reading of an untrustworthy surface, to uncover the hidden meaning in a mode of discourse or a way of life – for example, for Marx, that of the determining socio-economic forces; for Nietzsche, the uncovering of the will to power; and, for Freud, the revelation of unconscious desires concealed beneath the surface of everyday life. These 'masters of suspicion', as Ricoeur calls them, find a particularly happy hunting ground in the field of religion.

Whilst a definition is not an explanation, no theoretical enterprise can get off the ground without defining its terms. The term 'religion', however, is notoriously difficult to define. This is in large measure due to the wide variety of religious beliefs and practices found in the world and which appear, *prima facie*, to have little in common. Yet this need not, I think, worry us for no less a thinker than Wittgenstein has extolled the merits of concepts with what he termed 'blurred edges' and in his *Philosophical Investigations* he devised a method of 'family resemblances' specifically to do away with Procrustean generalisations which rely on the lowest common denominator or on an invariable set of defining qualities, replacing such generalisations by the notion of 'family resemblances' in which the members of a group or class are taken to share a number of common characteristics without any of these being essential for membership of the group or class in question. Wittgenstein offered several arguments for using this notion of 'family resemblances'. In *Philosophical Investigations* §67, for example, he wrote: 'the strength of a thread does not reside in the fact that some one fibre runs through its whole length, but in the overlapping of many fibres', and in §71, writing of the advantages of 'a concept with blurred edges', he asked, 'Is it even always an advantage to replace an indistinct picture by a sharp one? Isn't the indistinct one often exactly what we need?' The relevance of this method of proceeding – 'along different roads through the same country', to use another of Wittgenstein's analogies – in looking at something as varied and complex as religion will, when confronted by the variety of religious expression found in the world, be obvious. In this respect it is also worth calling to mind some words of Eric Sharpe, who wrote that: 'To define religion is … far less important than to possess the ability to recognise it when we come across it.'[4]

Yet Wittgenstein's reference to 'family resemblances' also serves to remind us that religions, despite evidence to the contrary, do have certain things in common – not the least being the fact that all, without exception, see human life within a wider context than naturalism is prepared to admit. However, if we are to recognise religion when we see it, some criterion of recognition is necessary and I would suggest, with Sharpe, that

> the only tenable criterion is that of the firm conviction on the *believer's* part (not the observer's) of the actual existence of a supernatural, supersensory order of being, and of the actual or potential interplay, through a network of sacred symbols, of that order of being with the world in which [men and women's] normal life is lived. The interplay may take place on the individual or on the corporate level; it may involve rules of conduct or it may not; it may rest on an intensely personal experience or it may not; it may be intellectually worked out or it may not. But dismiss the supernatural order from the picture altogether, and you are left with sacred symbols which refer to nothing in particular. What you are left with may be moral, inspiring, intellectually or aesthetically satisfying … but it will not be religion, and some other word ought to be found to describe it.[5]

The contemporary Christian theologian John Hick offers a not dissimilar definition of religion in his book *God and the Universe of Faiths* when he writes that religion is: 'an understanding of the universe, together with an appropriate way of living in it, which involves reference beyond the natural world to God, to gods, or to a transcendental order or process.'[6]

These substantive definitions of religion take us, I believe, to the heart of what is distinctive about religious understandings of the world in a way that functional definitions do not. Functional definitions, as Kolakowski has pointed out, are not really definitions at all, but theories of religion and they will be considered as such at the appropriate place in this book. Kolakowski wrote:

> However ingeniously developed and however efficient in organising the mythological material, they cannot possibly be suggested by, let alone inferred from, the empirical material of an anthropologist. We need more than this material to assert that when people speak of God or the gods, of invisible forces purposely operating behind empirical events, of the sacred qualities of things, they are *in fact*, and without knowing it, speaking of something entirely different: they are expressing thereby social conflicts, or sexual inhibitions, or that they seek to produce a system for codifying natural phenomena etc. Nobody would deny that people creating their myths say of themselves more than they intend to. This is true of all human products, whether material or spiritual. Yet from this common-sense generality we may not conclude that what can be discovered behind religious beliefs – their unquestionable usefulness in various 'secular' areas of life – makes up their genuine meaning. The latter assertion is arbitrary and not empirical.

And he concluded: 'The questions I am going to examine will be discussed on the shallow assumption that what people mean in religious discourse is what they ostensibly mean.'[7]

It is on just such an assumption with regard to the meaning of religion that this book is predicated. Whether such an assumption is justified is, of course, another question.

– Notes –

1. C.f. Peter Berger, 'Against the Current', *Prospect*, March (1997), pp. 32-6.
2. E.g. J. Samuel Preus, *Explaining Religion: Criticism and Theory from Bodin to Freud*, New Haven: Yale University Press, 1987; Donald A. Crosby, *Interpretative Theories of Religion*, The Hague: Mouton, 1981; Daniel L. Pals, *Seven Theories of Religion*, New York: OUP, 1997.
3. Paul Ricoeur, *Freud and Philosophy: An Essay in Interpretation*, trans. Denis Savage, New Haven: Yale University Press, 1970, pp. 28-36.
4. Eric Sharpe, *Understanding Religion*, London: Duckworth, 1983, p. 47.
5. Ibid., p. 48.
6. Hick, *God and the Universe of Faiths*, London: Collins/Fontanta, 1977, p. 133.
7. Leszek Kolakowski, *Religion*, London: Collins/Fontana, 1982, pp. 15-16. Robin Horton is also critical of symbolist and functionalist interpretations of religion. C.f. Horton, *Patterns of Thought in Africa and the West*, Cambridge: CUP, 1994, pp. 19-49.

PART I

Religious Theories of Religion

CHAPTER 2

Religion as Revelation

By far the oldest and most widespread theory of religion is the conviction held by those who stand within a particular religious tradition that the beliefs and practices of that tradition are the outcome of an act or a series of acts of divine revelation, and although the manner and content of revelation differs from tradition to tradition, the belief that a particular religion has, in some sense or other, been 'revealed' is a conviction found among the adherents of all of the world's religions.

The belief that supernatural beings – gods, goddesses, ancestral spirits, demons – speak to men and women was widespread in the ancient world, as indeed it still is among those peoples whom a previous generation of social anthropologists and historians of religion regarded as 'primitive'. Whilst one can encounter those in the Western world for whom this belief is still very much alive, the role that such belief plays in Western culture today is marginal to say the least and its disappearance from large areas of contemporary thought is often regarded as the hallmark of modernity.

The most common word in the English language for the recipient of revelation is 'prophet', a word which comes from the Greek *prophetes* and means 'one who speaks for another'. The Greeks, however, as Professor E. R. Dodds informs us in his book *Pagan and Christian in an Age of Anxiety*, had a number of words for such people: only for believers in their powers were they *prophetai* – spokesmen for the supernatural – or *entheoi* – people filled with god. For those who did not believe that such people were the recipients of a revelation from the gods they were *daimonontes* – demon-ridden – and regarded as being little different from epileptics and para-noiacs. The Greeks also used the neutral term *ekstatikoi* for anyone in whom the normal state of consciousness was temporarily or permanently suspended. The vulgar term for such people was *engastrimuthoi* – belly-talkers. The Greeks, like other peoples among whom divine inspiration was widely claimed, rarely accepted such claims without question.[1]

The Hebrew word translated into English as 'prophet' is *nabi'*, and is similar in meaning to the Greek *prophetes*, for *nabi'* also refers to a person who, it was believed, spoke for God. Later generations of religious believers, both within Judaism and Christianity as well as, in a limited way, within Islam, came to believe that certain of these Hebrew prophets were the bearers of an authoritative revelation from God – that they were, in the striking phrase of the fourth-century Christian thinker Athanasius, 'the sacred school of the knowledge of God and of the spiritual life for all mankind',[2] although Christians and Muslims also believe that this earlier revelation came to fruition only in the definitive revelation given to the prophetic founders of their own religions.

The claim to be the recipients of a divine revelation is not, however, a claim that is found only in Judaism, Christianity and Islam. It is also found in the religions of the Indian tradition and in what today are known as 'primal' religions. It is, in fact, the very ubiquity of such claims that makes any explanation of religion in terms of revelation difficult to accept. Too many people have claimed to be the recipients of divine revelation, and the disagreement over what is believed to have been revealed is so great that if revelation is to be accepted as an explanation of a religion then some criterion for deciding which, if any, of the myriad claims to revelation is authentic must be found. Yet finding such a criterion has proved notoriously difficult and when formulated in this way – as the search for a criterion which will allow a choice to be made between differing traditions all claiming to have been revealed – there is, perhaps, no satisfactory solution. At the close of this chapter we shall be looking at some of the ways in which religious thinkers have reformulated the problem of religious plurality.

– THE PRIMAL TRADITION –

Before we come to look at the idea of revelation in the world's major religious traditions, it will be instructive to look first at its meaning in those forms of religion which pre-date the rise of the great world religions and which historians of religion today call 'primal' – a word which, unlike the earlier term 'primitive', indicates, in the words of Professor Andrew Walls, this form of religion's 'historical anteriority and [its] basic, elemental status in human experience'.[3]

Although, following convention, I have headed this section 'the primal tradition', those peoples whom historians of religion regard as having a 'primal' outlook on the world represent a great diversity of cultural and religious adaptations scattered widely over time and space. However, whether found in the distant or in the recent past, and in whatever part of the globe, people living in small-scale, non-literate, and, for the most part, tribal societies have a sufficient number of features in common for us to consider them as having a common world-view – a world-view which lies at the base of all known cultures and which has not entirely disappeared from the outlook of men and women in the Western world today.

One of the most significant features of primal societies is that they are organic, in the sense that all the major elements in their society and culture are interlocking. This is nowhere more evident than in the relationship that exists in such societies between culture and religion, for religion in primal forms of society is not, as it is in contemporary Western society, a cultural option, but an integral aspect of an organic way of life. Further, little, if any, distinction is made in such societies between 'natural' and 'supernatural', for anything at any time can become the vehicle through which what the Western tradition has come to call 'the supernatural' might manifest itself. This means that such societies do not, in fact, have what we would call a 'religion' for, as Wilfred Cantwell Smith has shown in *The Meaning and End of Religion*, the way in which the term 'religion' has come to be used in the Western world from the late Middle Ages onwards is new and is not found in societies outwith the Western world except in so far as those societies have come under the influence of that world.[4] The difference between the way in which the term 'religion' was used in pre-modern cultures and the way in which 'religion' is used in contemporary Western culture is, says Smith, that in pre-modern cultures the term 'religion', where the word exists at all, is a term which can properly only be applied to the culture considered as a whole. In modern Western cultures, by contrast, it is used to designate a belief-system that is optional and thus may or may not be espoused by those living in that culture. It is the holistic nature of primal societies that is the basis of the appeal that these societies have for many in the fragmented societies of the Western world today.[5] It is the attraction of a not dissimilar, if somewhat idealised, perception of a one-time holistic Islamic society that is driving many contemporary Muslims to seek to revive what they believe to be traditional Islamic society in contrast to what they see as a socially and morally disintegrating West. It should also be noted that it was the promise of re-creating just such a society that was the source of the appeal that both German National Socialism and the International Communist movement had for many of those who responded to their message.

The greatest single difference, however, between modern Western men and women's way of looking at the world and the world as seen through 'primal' eyes lies in the fact that whereas modern men and women see the world as impersonal, as an 'It' set over against them, in the primal apprehension of the world the world is experienced as personal, as a 'Thou' which confronts men and women as a living presence. As the historian of ancient cultures Henri Frankfort remarked with reference to Edward Tylor's animistic theory of the origin of religion which we will be looking at in Chapter 6: 'Primitive man simply does not know an inanimate world and for this reason does not [as Tylor's theory presupposes] personify phenomena.'[6] At certain times, says Frankfort, the 'natural' world which confronts men and women in primal societies confronts them as one which is alive as they are alive and they have, therefore, only one mode of discourse – the personal. Their relationship to the world is, therefore, a dynamic and reciprocal one. Frankfort sums up the primal apprehension of reality as follows:

> The world appears to primitive man neither inanimate nor empty but redundant with life; and life has individuality, in man and beast and plant, and in every phenomenon which confronts man – the thunderclap, the sudden shadow, the eerie and unknown clearing in the wood, the stone which suddenly hurts him when he stumbles on it on a hunting trip. Any phenomenon may at any time face him not as an 'It' but as a 'Thou'. In this confrontation, 'Thou' reveals its individuality, its qualities, its will. 'Thou' is not contemplated with intellectual detachment; it is experienced as life confronting life, involving every faculty of man in reciprocal relationship. Thoughts, no less than acts and feelings, are subordinated to this experience.[7]

Mary Douglas makes a similar point. Writing of what she prefers to call the 'primitive' world-view, she says that:

> A primitive world view looks out on a universe which is personal in several different senses. Physical forces are thought of as interwoven with the lives of persons. Things are not completely distinguished from persons ... the universe responds to speech and mime. It discerns social order and intervenes to uphold it.[8]

And a contemporary theologian, Keith Ward, writes: 'A consideration of primal religions suggests that it is natural for human beings to see themselves as parts of a fundamentally spiritual reality, a world of spirits, of acting and responsive powers and values.'[9]

The primal world is one which is inhabited by gods, goddesses, ancestral spirits, demons and a host of other non-human powers who interact with men and women and who can aid or hinder, for whatever reason, their health, wealth and general well-being. This is not to say that men and women in such societies – either in the distant or in the recent past – understood the world wholly in this way. As Malinowski noted of the Trobriand Islanders of the South Pacific, and as innumerable monographs on similar peoples bear witness, whilst such peoples certainly attribute good and bad fortune to the activity of supernatural beings, they also rely on a rudimentary knowledge that we today would call 'scientific'. In a passage in his essay *Magic, Science and Religion*, Malinowski pointed out that magic and religion come into play in Trobriand society because the Trobriand Islander's experience has taught him 'that in spite of all his forethought and beyond all his efforts there are agencies and forces which one year bestow unwonted and unearned benefits of fertility … and another year again the same agencies bring ill luck and bad chance, pursue him from beginning till end and thwart all his most strenuous efforts and his best-founded knowledge'.[10] It is both to explain these happenings and to influence those agencies on whom good or bad fortune is believed to depend that those living in primal societies and, we might add, large numbers of people living in Western societies today have recourse to magic and religion. I shall be returning to this point when I come to look at Malinowski's theory of religion in Chapter 6. At the level of self-conscious reflection primal societies pose and answer the question asked by Socrates in Plato's dialogue *Phaedo*, when, dissatisfied with the explanations of events in the world given by the science of his day, Socrates says that he wants to know not *how* events in the world come about, but *why*.[11] It is a question which, as Robert Segal has shown, is beginning to re-emerge in contemporary sociology of religion.[12]

But if it is incorrect to see the primal way of conducting the affairs of life entirely in terms of magic and religion, it is also incorrect to see people living in primal societies as governed by fear of the supernatural forces which they believe surround them, for through priests, prophets, mediums, diviners and other specialists, they have, so they believe, ways in which they can establish channels of communication with these supernatural beings and so become informed of what it is that such beings require of them and, conversely, how these supernatural beings might be influenced. The figure of the shaman is central here. The word itself comes from Ural-Altaic peoples of Siberia, but it is increasingly being used today, by both social-anthropologists and historians of religion, as a word for anyone, in whatever society, who acts as a medium or conduit between the spirit world and the world of men and women. Such people are found in all primal societies and are not, of course, unknown in the contemporary Western world. As a prominent feature of what, today, is known as the 'New Age', shamanism appears to be returning to Western society, if in fact, it ever totally disappeared from it. Certainly this and many other elements of the primal outlook survived into so-called 'Christian' Europe well into the medieval period, as a reading of the early chapters of Keith Thomas's

Religion and the Decline of Magic makes plain.[13] There is also an increasing recognition among contemporary historians of religion of the continuity that exists between the shaman and the founders of the great prophet religions.

The shaman is believed, through a variety of techniques, of which the state of trance is the most notable, to be able to travel in spirit, or through the medium of a familiar animal, such as a bird, to the spirit world to converse with and even control the various spirits active within the world of men and women. Alternatively, the shaman may become possessed by a spirit and through word and gesture convey the spirit's message to the people.[14] The task of the shaman is, therefore, to maintain or, where such has been broken, to re-establish harmony between the spirit world (including the land of the dead) and the world of men and women and so avert or rectify misfortune and cure illness. He or she also has the oracular function of conveying the will of the spirits with whom he or she is in contact to the people. It is in the ecstatic visions of the shaman that many historians of religion claim that prophecy as the vehicle of revelation began.[15]

But if the shaman represents the case of the specialist intermediary between the world of spirit and the human world, for ordinary people it is in dreams that they most frequently feel they are in contact with the spirit world, although it may well be necessary for the interpretation of a dream for ordinary people to have recourse to the shaman or some other religious specialist. The 'classic' dream theory, as found among innumerable different peoples, holds that the soul leaves the body during sleep and that its experiences in the world of the spirits, or in the land of the dead, is what is recorded in dreams.[16] Alternatively, it might be claimed that the spirits, including ancestral spirits, visit persons in their dreams. Either way dreams are regarded as vehicles of communication between the spirit world and the living.

Apart from dreams, the spirit world also interacts in primal societies with ordinary people in their everyday intercourse with the world: strange natural phenomena, illness, untoward happenings, good and bad fortune – all can be attributed to the activity of spirits even where the 'natural' causes, as we would call them, are perfectly well understood. The question, as we have noted, which people living in primal societies put – and it is a question which is also put by many living in the modern world in the face of events such as sickness and ill-fortune – is not 'how?', but 'why?', 'why has this happened to me?' This seems to lead inevitably to the further question: '*Who* has done this to me?' It is at this point that the person living in primal society has recourse to the shaman who will consult the spirit world to ascertain which spirit is responsible and what must be done to appease such a spirit. Untoward events might equally in primal societies be attributed to witchcraft or black magic and the question then is, 'who has been working such magic or witchcraft?' This again will often mean recourse to the shaman.

It must be noted that shamans undergo a lengthy and rigorous training in their craft from older shamans, a training in which they are taught, among other things, how to induce trance, see visions, recognise and interpret what is seen, and how to cure sickness. Although in primal societies the function of the shaman is largely conservative, in that shamans play a vital role in legitimating and re-enforcing the values and the social structures of the societies in which they live by upholding the belief that these are in accord with the will of the gods and the ancestral spirits, there is always the possibility that individual shamans will break free from the constraints of tradition and change or develop it under their own particular genius or as the result of divine inspiration, and this, many believe, is what happened in the religions of the Semitic tradition.[17]

– THE SEMITIC TRADITION –

There is a good deal of evidence to show that ancient Hebrew culture exhibited many of the features of the primal response to the world and although I shall focus in what follows on the prophetic tradition – as the claimed bearer of revelation – this should not be taken to imply that this was the only aspect of the understanding of the world that the early Hebrews shared with primal peoples.

In the scriptural tradition which has come down to us from ancient Israel the first reference to 'prophets' (nabi'im) is found in the Book of Samuel, a book which reflects the situation in Israel immediately prior to the establishment of the institution of monarchy around the turn of the first millennium BCE. After Samuel, the spiritual leader of the Israelites, had anointed Saul as king over Israel, he enumerated a number of signs which would indicate the Israelite god Yahweh's agreement with this commission. One was that Saul, on coming to the 'hill of God' (the sacred sanctuary), would 'meet with a band of prophets coming down from the high place with harp, tambourine, flute, and lyre before them, prophesying'. Then, says Samuel, 'the spirit of Yahweh will come mightily upon you, and you shall prophesy and be turned into another man'.[18] The Hebrew verb used in this passage literally means 'to prophesy ecstatically' and, as the passage indicates and as Saul's behaviour on a subsequent occasion – when he is seized with 'prophetic ecstasy' and strips off his clothes and lies naked in a stunned condition for a day and a night – shows, prophecy, at least in the period to which the story of Saul refers, was linked in Israel with ecstatic states, the main medium in primal forms of religion through which communication with the gods takes place.[19]

The Hebrews had three methods of communicating with the supernatural: dreams, the sacred dice known as *Urim* and *Thummin*, and prophesy. The last, as the biblical scholar Bernard Anderson has noted, was more suited to interpret the will of its god, Yahweh, for being possessed by his spirit, so it was believed, the prophet was able to interpret the providential meaning of political events and so proclaim the will of Yahweh in concrete terms.[20] This important political and social function allowed certain individuals to establish for themselves an authority and a reputation which impressed not only their contemporaries, but subsequent generations of religious believers, both in Israel and the Christian church as well as in Islam, with the authenticity of their claim to be proclaiming the will of God.

In his book *Belief in God*, Charles Gore, a former Bishop of Oxford – and in his day (the early part of the twentieth century) a noted Christian theologian and apologist – raised the question whether the Divine Mind or Spirit, whose existence, so Gore believed, could be established by rational argument, had 'taken action, like a person, on His side to disclose or reveal Himself'. His answer, which may be taken as representative of that traditionally offered by the Christian religion, was that:

> The Religion of Israel, on which Christianity and, in a different degree, Mohammedanism [sic] are based, claims that such a revelation has been given. It has persuaded the whole Western, and in a sense the Mohammedan, world over long centuries of the truth of this claim. And what is more important, the strength of our morality has been drawn from the belief in the self-revealing God. The belief has obvious power … Thus the claim deserves at least the attention of every rational man.[21]

Gore believed that it was 'supremely' in the proclamations of the Hebrew prophets, beginning with Amos and ending with Malachi, that the core of that revelation of the nature and will of God which he believed came to fulfilment in the person and redeeming death of Jesus of Nazareth was to be found. Gore was aware that prophecy did not come into being with Amos, but he, like many since, sought to distinguish the shamanistic activity of the early prophets from those whose proclamations have come down to us in the sacred literature which bears their names. Muslims make a similar claim with regard to the prophet Muhammad, seeking to distinguish his prophetic activity from the activities of the Arabian prophets and soothsayers who were as much a part of the life of the Arabia of his day as they were of early Hebrew society. Gore articulates this claim as follows:

> Here then [in the period from Amos to Malachi] we find a succession of wonderful men, mostly conscious of profound unpopularity in their contemporary world, who nevertheless, even in face of the most determined hostility of courts and people, delivered a message which we feel to be self-consistent and to involve the same great principles throughout, about God – His nature, His will, His purposes – and about human nature – its dignity, its responsibility, and its sin; a message which they declare, with the fullest conviction, to be derived not from their own reasoning or speculation, nor from tradition (although they would have indignantly denied that they were its first recipients), nor from any external source at all, but from God, the God of Israel, speaking in their own souls, so intensely and clearly that there could be no mistake about it.[22]

Gore was not alone in this belief. The nineteenth-century Jewish historian of Islam Ignaz Goldziher was similarly impressed by the Abrahamic monotheistic tradition which came to its supreme expression, he felt, not in Christianity, but in Islam.[23] Goldziher, who had had a traditional Jewish education as well as a Western secular education at the University of Budapest, where he had read and assimilated both the philosophy of Hegel and German higher criticism of the Bible, came to see Judaism (rather as did Gore) as essentially the monotheism of the prophets: law and ritual, he believed, came later and were the product of particular times and places. It was thus necessary, he believed, to separate what was essential from what was temporal and unessential in the life not only of Judaism, but of other religions as well. It was whilst he was living and working in Damascus and Cairo during 1873–4 that he became impressed by the austere and uncompromising monotheism of Islam. It was this, he came to believe, which lay at the heart of all true religion. As he wrote in his diary:

> My way of thought was thoroughly turned towards Islam, and so was my sympathy ... I was not lying when I said that I believed in the prophetic missions of Muhammad ... my religion was henceforth the universal religion of the prophets.[24]

Henceforth, outwith the scholarly study of Islam, Goldziher came to see his mission as that of bringing Judaism (and other religions) back to the uncompromising monotheism which he believed constituted their essential truth. The core of his thinking on this matter can be got from a series of lectures which he wrote for delivery during a proposed visit to the United States in 1907, but which illness prevented him from delivering. Entitled *Introduction to Islamic Theology and Law*,[25] Goldziher sought in these lectures to fit Islam into a theological framework derived from the German

Christian theologian Friedrich Schleiermacher, whose views we shall be considering in the next chapter. Beginning from Schleiermacher's view that religion derives from a core feeling of absolute dependence, Goldziher contended that this core feeling works itself out differently in different religions. Albert Hourani has summarised Goldziher's explanation of religion as follows:

> Goldziher saw the development of Islam as being broadly similar to that of other prophetic religions, as viewed by the scholars and theologians of his time: first came the prophet, then the prophetic revelation was fixed in holy writ, then the theologians tried to defend it and legal scholars to draw out its practical implications. During this process, however, the lure and hazards of the world lay all around. For Muslims the Word of God, the Qur'an, revealed His will for mankind, and the elaboration of the *Shari'a*, the 'holy law' or system of ideal morality, was therefore an essential and central part of the process by which Islam was articulated into a system, but it had its dangers: it could stifle the desire for holiness which lies at the heart of all religions.[26]

In seeing religion as originating in desire for what he termed 'holiness', Goldziher anticipates the work of the German theologian Rudolf Otto, whose understanding of religion will be dealt with in the next chapter.

Keith Ward, although more aware than were Gore and Goldziher of the claims made in religious traditions other than in the Semitic, also makes what is essentially the same point as Gore when he writes:

> Belief in the total moral demand of God does not come from speculation alone. It comes from the experience of the prophets, and from perception of the mighty acts of deliverance which show God's purposes in history. In accepting this revelation, one accepts the prophetic experiences, the historical records of Israel, and the inspired nature of the laws of Israel. In these three respects, one can see the development and transformation of some major themes of earlier religious traditions. The shamanistic vision-quests of primal religion develop into the prophetic experiences of the God of Israel as a being of moral demand and love. The magical spirit-manifestations of primal religion develop into a perception of the mighty acts and wonders of a God who delivers from evil and oppression. The spirit-possessed oracular utterances of primal religion develop into the Spirit-guided teachings of the Divine Wisdom.[27]

Thus, for Ward, does revelation develop into what he, and the Christian tradition in which he stands, regards as a more intellectually and morally satisfying understanding of the will of God than that found, for instance, in the theism of the Indian religious tradition.

But to return to Gore. What so impressed Gore, as it had impressed Goldziher and those within the Jewish and Christian traditions down the ages, was not just the message itself, but the integrity and consistency of that message over a long period of time. The message, however, was not entirely new and Gore's statement that the message of the prophets did not come from tradition needs considerable qualification, for the basic content of the prophetic message had been formulated at least two centuries earlier by an unknown writer – whom biblical scholars today call 'the Yahwist' – who, on the basis of yet earlier traditions, had given the Hebrews their national epic – an epic that defined the destiny of the nation and its special, covenant relationship with its God.

This epic is embedded in, and runs through, the first five books of the Hebrew Bible – known to the Jews as the Torah. It was composed about the beginning of the first millennium before the common era as a response to Israel's espousal of monarchy, an event which for those who stood within the tradition which 'the Yahwist' espoused was thought to compromise the Hebrews' unique relationship with their God. Taking oral traditions which were circulating more or less independently of each other at various cultic centres, the Yahwist reworked these traditions into a comprehensive history of Yahweh's dealings with men and women from the creation of the world to the Hebrews' entry into the Promised Land of Canaan. The purpose of this account was to remind the Hebrews of their covenant relationship with Yahweh, established, so they believed, through Moses at Mount Sinai, and of the obligations which this placed upon them and which made them different from all the other nations of the earth. However, the Yahwist did not create the content of Israel's faith: this he regarded as having been revealed by Yahweh to Moses at Sinai and to be enshrined in the Torah, which the people of Israel believed to have been written by Moses. The Torah, as well as containing the law by which the people of Israel believed that they should live, also tells of the mighty acts of God towards them in history – the deliverance from Egypt, the establishment of the Covenant, the giving of the Law by which they, as the Chosen People, should live, and the settlement in Canaan. The core tradition of this belief the author of the Yahwist epic took from oral tradition, the essence of which is preserved in Deuteronomy 26:5–9:

> A Syrian ready to perish was my father and he went down into Egypt and sojourned there, few in number; and populous: and the Egyptians evil entreated us, and laid upon us hard bondage: and we cried unto the Lord, the God of our fathers, and the Lord heard our voice, and saw our affliction, and our toil, and saw our oppression: and the Lord brought us forth out of Egypt with a mighty hand and with an outstretched arm, and with great terribleness, and with signs, and with wonders: and he hath brought us unto this place, and hath given us this land, a land flowing with milk and honey.

This recital of Yahweh's saving acts, which constituted Israel as a nation, the author of the Yahwist epic worked into a theological setting which combined the Mosaic tradition of the establishment of the nation with stories concerning primeval history in such a way as to present an unfolding drama of God's dealings with men and women from the creation of the world to the Hebrew conquest of Canaan. The Yahwist's purpose was to remind the Hebrews of their unique God-given destiny at a time when this appeared to be endangered by the espousal of monarchical government which, for those who stood within this tradition, was seen as compromising Israel's unique relationship with its God.[28]

It was this traditional faith, together with the obligations which human beings owed to both God and their fellow men and women, that was reaffirmed and enriched by the prophets and which has been seen as the core of the revelation which Christians and Muslims believe was given to the Hebrews, and which they further believe was brought to fulfilment in the life and teaching of their own Prophet. Whatever the peculiar destiny which the Hebrew prophets believed their nation to possess in the councils of their God, what possessed them was a sense of the overriding unconditional obligations owed by the nation of Israel (and indeed by all men and women) to God their creator. Morality, for the Hebrew prophets, was not a set of rules necessary for social cohesion, nor a prescription for maximising the greatest happiness of the greatest number, nor a bare sense of duty; it was something set within the context of the will and purpose of God as expressed in history – past, present and to come. It spoke of hope, a hope which would eventually become the Messianic hope which Christians would see as having been fulfilled in the life, death and resurrection of their own Prophet, in the redemption which he wrought, and in the kingdom which he came to establish. For the Jews it was the hope of a community of justice and peace which God, using Israel as his chosen instrument, would, in his own good time, bring into being on earth. It is a powerful vision and one which has sustained the people of Israel through some of the darkest moments of their history. It is also, it should be noted, a faith rooted in time and history and one which asserts the ultimate value of life in this world. As such it is very different from the a-historical understanding of human destiny enshrined in the religions of the Indian tradition.

An important stage in the process of the institutionalisation of revelation in religious traditions or, to use Max Weber's phrase, in 'the routinisation of charisma', is when what is believed to have been revealed is recorded in writings that come to be regarded as sacred scripture, although, even when the canon and the text of such scriptures has been finalised, problems remain in all traditions with scriptures regarding who is entitled to offer the authoritative interpretation of such scriptures. It is at this point that revelation becomes a social reality, a reality which is kept in being by all the mechanisms of social consensus and social control so transparently disclosed in the work of Peter Berger and Thomas Luckmann.[29] Yet important as an understanding of these processes is for the student of religion, the student of religion must also keep in mind the claim made, from within religious traditions, that the process of formulating a canon of scripture is held to have been divinely inspired and in view of the place that 'the Bible' has in Christian churches today, it will be necessary to look in some detail at how the scriptural canon came to be established .

In Judaism the canon of books making up the Hebrew Bible was not finalised until after the destruction of the nation of Israel by the Romans in 70 CE, an event which gave the final impetus to discussions about the extent of the scriptural canon. The loss of the Temple, Judaism's vital centre, posed the threat that the tradition would be distorted by outside, and particularly by Hellenistic, influences, and that Jews, who were then beginning to emigrate from the land of Israel in large numbers, would begin to loose their sense of identity. A major role in the reorganisation of Judaism and in the finalising of the canon of scripture was played by the academy of Jabneh on the coast of Palestine. Founded shortly after the fall of Jerusalem by Rabbi Jonathan ben Zakkai, the Jabneh Academy soon became the leading centre for Pharisaic Judaism. The closing of the Jewish canon is usually held to have taken place during discussions at Jabneh around 90 CE, although, as the Jewish scholar Samuel Sandmel has warned, we must not think of the discussions at Jabneh as in any way comparable to the councillor meetings called to define Christian faith in the third and fourth centuries. The canon, he writes, 'was a matter of the evolution of opinions which converged over a period of decades, 90 being the likely terminal date, but far from a definite one'.[30] The final acceptance of the Hebrew canon requires, as later did the acceptance of the Christian canon, a belief in the continuing inspiration (or providential guidance) of God during the processes of formulating and finalising that canon.

The core of the Hebrew canon – the Torah – had, of course, been established centuries before the discussions at Jabneh took place. The Torah, which comprises the first five books of the Hebrew Bible (the Pentateuch), and traditionally believed by Jews to have been composed by Moses, was promulgated by Ezra as the basis for the life of the Jewish community after their return from exile in Babylon in 538 BCE. Sometime after 200 BCE the prophetic books were added to this core canon so that by the time we reach the period of the rise of Christianity 'the Law and the Prophets' had become the common designation for Hebrew scripture.[31] The fluidity of the Hebrew canon outwith the Law and the Prophets can be seen by comparing the books found in the standard text of the Hebrew Bible, known as the Masoretic Text and finalised in Palestine in the early years of the common era, with the rather wider number of books found in the Septuagint which was compiled and translated into Greek by Egyptian Jews in Alexandria under the aegis of Ptolemy II between 285 and 246 BCE.

One of the points at issue during the discussions regarding the Hebrew canon at Jabneh (and subsequently in the Christian church) was the status of what in Hebrew were known as *Kethubim* (The Writings) and which include such texts as The Wisdom of Solomon, Ecclesiasticus, and I and II Maccabes. The principles that were used to determine what should be included and what should be excluded from the canon were, first, harmony with the written Torah and, second, the doctrine of prophetic inspiration. A view which was widely accepted in the Judaism of the first century of the common era held that prophecy had ceased in the post-exilic period, that is after the time of Ezra. According to this view Haggai, Zacharia and Malachi were the last of the prophets. With their death, the Rabbinic tradition held that 'the Holy Spirit had departed from Israel'. On the principle that only writings which were the outcome of prophetic inspir-ation could be accorded a place in the canon of sacred scripture, only writings which could be dated before the cessation of prophetic inspiration could be included. Books which were undoubtedly composed after the death of Malachi, and in particular those composed during the Hellenistic period, such as The Wisdom of Ben Sira and I and II Maccabees, thus fell outside the canon. Although the Rabbis meeting at Jabneh had serious doubts about the Song of Songs and Ecclesiastes, these were accepted on the grounds that they were written by Solomon – something which histori-cal scholarship has now shown not to be the case. Books written in Greek, such as the (supposed) Wisdom of Solomon were automatically excluded despite their having been attributed to great figures of the past.

This uncertainty about the extent of the accepted writings between Palestine and Alexandria continued into the Christian church to the extent that the early Christian Fathers were, in fact, unclear about what exactly constituted what they came to regard as the 'The Old Testament'. The great Latin Father of the Church, Jerome (342–419 CE), who translated the Hebrew and Christian Scriptures into Latin – a translation which became known as 'The Vulgate' – was inclined to follow the Masoretic tradition and to relegate the extra writings in the Septuagint to a lower place, but his contemporary, Augustine (354–430 CE), insisted that the Old Testament include all the books found in the Septuagint on the grounds that this was the established usage of the Christian church. This division of opinion has continued up to the present day in the Christian church with Protestants largely following Jerome and the Roman Catholic Church following Augustine.

The issue came to a head within Western Christendom in the sixteenth century when the Reformers, who sought to get 'back to the Bible', called for the elimination from the canon of Old Testament scripture of all the books not included in the Hebrew Bible. The Reformers, therefore, put what they regarded as the non-canonical books into a separate section called The Apocrypha, whilst the Roman Catholic Church at the Council of Trent (1545–63) officially adopted the larger canon on the grounds that these books had been used in the liturgy of the Christian church from its foundation.

The doctrine of the divine inspiration of scripture was one that was destined to have a long history in the Christian church. When that church came to formulate its own canon of scripture – The New Testament – the belief was that the writers of the texts which eventually came to form the Christian canon were, like those who composed the books that went to make up the canon which the Christian Church called The Old Testament (i.e. The Hebrew Bible), directly inspired by the Holy Spirit.

The necessity for the Christian church to formulate an authoritative canon of New Testament scripture arose from the fact that by the middle of the second century a large number of (often conflicting) writings purporting to report the teaching of Jesus were in circulation.[32] The problem for the early Christian church, faced as it was with a number of conflicting accounts of the teaching of its founder, was ultimately one of authority. Who, it was forced to ask, could be said to have relayed the authentic tradition of the teaching of Jesus? This problem was met by what in the course of time became the orthodox Christian church by emphasising the authority of the duly ordained bishops of that church, and by establishing, once and for all, an authoritative canon of Christian scripture.

In the first century the Christian scriptures had simply been The Hebrew Bible, read in the Septuagint version, and the oral tradition of the sayings and doings of Jesus. It was the controversy with Marcion in the first half of the second century that brought matters to a head. Marcion, a teacher from Asia Minor who came to Rome towards the end of the first century, not only rejected the authority of the Jewish scriptures within the Christian church, but also claimed that the Christian tradition had been corrupted by those within the church whom he called 'Judaisers'. The church thus found it necessary to define the authoritative sources of its teaching for the situation regarding even its own scriptures was not at all clear. It would appear that whilst the Church, by and large, accepted the first three

Gospels (Matthew, Mark and Luke), there were those who had grave reservations about accepting the Gospel attributed to John as well as some of the other texts which it was claimed had been written by one or other of Jesus' apostles. The principle which guided the church in what writings were to be accepted as scripture was apostolicity, which meant that to be included in its own growing canon of scripture a text had either to have been written by an apostle, or have the patronage of an apostle – as was claimed was the case with the Gospels of Mark (Peter) and Luke (Paul). It was on this criterion that the Western church initially rejected the Letter to the Hebrews which was, it knew, not written, as many of the Eastern churches supposed, by the apostle Paul, accepting it finally only under pressure from the Eastern church. The criterion of apostolicity also led to the exclusion of other writings highly valued in the early Christian church, such as The Didache, The Shepherd of Hermas, and The Epistle of Clement to the Corinthians. Other disputed documents which, however, made it into the canon, although on grounds of apostolic authorship that biblical scholars are today almost unanimous in rejecting – which lead some sceptics to query the claimed ongoing guidance of the Holy Spirit in this process – were the Revelation of John, the Epistles of James and Jude, and the second and third Epistles of John. The so-called Acts of Paul and the Apocalypse of Peter were among texts which did not make it into the canon.

It is interesting to note that at no point in the discussions surrounding what texts should be in the canon of sacred scripture was there any attempt to evoke the kind of internal witness of the texts themselves to their revealed or inspired origin such as emerged in the Protestant tradition in the sixteenth century and which was vigorously proclaimed in the twentieth century by Karl Barth who claimed that the 'Word of God' which spoke to men and women through the scriptures was 'self-authenticating'. The church prior to the Reformation of the sixteenth century rested its case for the canon, and for the revelation which it believed that it enshrined, not on any internal criterion, but on what it believed to be the provenance of the texts, and on their conformity with established doctrine handed down from the time of the Apostles in the great centres of Apostolic foundation, of which Rome was *primus inter pares*. It also believed that the Holy Spirit would not allow the Christian church to err in matters appertaining to correct belief. What is important to note is that it was the church which decided what constituted the authentic canon of holy scripture, something which those who reject the authority of the church and evoke against it the authority of scripture itself have difficulty in explaining away.

Another question which arises at this point is where, in the complicated process of the formation of the canon, inspiration is to be located, for in the light of the critical work that has been done on the formation of the individual books that make up the canon it is difficult today to maintain that it was the original 'author' who was inspired, for almost all the books in the canon of both the Hebrew and the Christian scriptures do not have an 'author', having undergone a complex process of recension before coming into being as we have them today. Is it that every step in this process was inspired or is inspiration, as some biblical scholars maintain, operative only at the point of the final recension?[33] A positive answer to this latter question allows those who accept it to accept the results of the critical study of the biblical texts. It must be noted, however, that, once the canon had been established, it tended to be accorded a status of its own within the Christian church so that, for the Reformers of the sixteenth century, scripture became the *sole* vehicle of divine revelation.

The Protestant Reformers rejected the claim of the Roman Catholic Church to be the sole authoritative interpreter of the scriptural revelation and allowed each and every individual believer, under what was believed to be the guidance of the Holy Spirit, to be the authoritative interpreter of scripture – a concession which led to a multitude of often conflicting interpretations and to a process of fragmentation within Protestant Christianity which has continued to the present day.

The problem of the place of scriptural revelation within Protestant Christianity is illustrated in the 1923 correspondence between Adolf von Harnack and Karl Barth. This correspondence came about as the result of 'Fifteen Questions' which Harnack, who represented the liberal wing of Protestant Christianity, challenged the conservative, bible-based Lutheran theologians in Germany, led by Barth, to answer.[34]

Harnack's first question went straight to the point. 'Is the religion of the Bible', he asked, 'or are its revelations, so completely a unity that in relation to faith, worship and life one may simply speak of "the Bible"? If this is not so, then is not the consequence that the determination of the content of the gospel is left solely to the individual's heuristic knowledge (*Erfahrung*) and subjective experience (*Erlebnis*).' 'Is the experience of God (*Gotteserlebnis*),' he further enquired, 'different from the awakening of faith or identical with it?' Further, can experience of, and faith in, the risen Christ be separated, as Harnack was aware that they were in Barth's theology, from 'knowledge' of the historic Jesus and, if so, how can one be sure that one is not putting an imaginary Christ in the place of the real one? And, with reference to Barth's now well-known assertion that there is no point of contact between human culture and human striving after God (religion) and the revealed 'Word', Harnack asked: 'If God is simply unlike anything said about him on the basis of the development of culture … and on the basis of ethics, how can this culture and in the long run one's own existence be protected against atheism?'

In his response Barth restated his now well-known position that historical knowledge and critical reflection are simply irrelevant to that 'World of God' to which the scriptures bear witness and which believers 'hear' through the miracle of the God-given gift of faith – a position very similar, as we shall see, to that taken by the Roman Catholic Church. Barth wrote:

> The Scriptures, then, witness to revelation. One does not have to believe it, nor *can* one do it. But one should not deny that it witnesses to revelation, *genuine* revelation that is, and not to a more or less concealed religious possibility of man but rather to the possibility of God, namely that *he* has acted under the form of a human possibility – and this as *reality*.[35]

And later in the same letter he wrote:

> The *acceptance* of this unbelievable testimony of the Scriptures I call faith. Again I do not claim that this is a discovery of *my* theology. I do ask, however, what else faith could be – disregarding sentimentalities – but the obedience I give to a human word which testifies to the Word of God as addressed to me, as if it were God's Word? Let no one have any delusions here about the fact that this is an unprecedented event, that here one must speak of the *Holy Spirit*.

And of 'faith' he wrote:

> I distinguish faith as *God's working* on us … from all known and unknown human organs and functions, even or so-called 'experiences of God'. … God who, according to the witness of the Scriptures has spoken 'the Word of Christ', speaks that Word also *to me through* the witness of the Scriptures empowered through the *testimonium Spiritus Sactus internum*, so that I *hear* it and by hearing it *believe*.[36]

·Harnack's reply to Barth was to point out that 'revelation' is not a scientific concept and that science can neither draw together under one generic concept, nor explain in terms of 'revelation' either the experience of the founders of religions or of those who claim religious experience in the more general sense of that term. There is no future, he maintained, 'in the attempt to grasp a "Word" of this kind as something "objective" so that human speaking, hearing, grasping and understanding can be eliminated from its operation'.[37] At which point he called a halt to the exchange, for there was nothing more that could be said. Barth's closed circle of those who 'hear' is as immune to criticism as is that of those such as Dewi Philips and Norman Malcolm who, following Wittgenstein, maintain that religion is a closed 'form of life' and that religious language has an internal logic of its own.[38] Indeed, as a contemporary commentator on Barth's theology has written: 'The assertions of faith [Barth argued] have their own internal coherence with one another, and demonstration of theology's rationality consists in tracing the spider's web of their connections.'[39] However, the price of taking this position in the modern world is the ghetto, for taking this position cuts the person taking it off from the accepted standards of rationality that alone make the serious discussion of religious belief possible. Barth's subjectivism has recently been criticised for just this reason by the contemporary German theologian Wolfgang Pannenberg.[40]

The tendency to see scripture as the *locus classicus* of revelation was not, however, confined to the Reformers. In the Roman Catholic Church the Council of Trent (1545–63) also claimed that the scriptures had been given *Spiritu santo dictante*, at the dictation of the Holy Spirit, a phrase that was repeated at the Vatican Council of 1869–70 and repeated yet again in 1893 by Pope Leo XIII in his encyclical *Providentisimus Deus* where he wrote:

> All the books and the whole of each book which the Church receives as sacred and canonical were written at the dictation of the Holy Spirit; and so far is it from being possible that any error can co-exist with divine inspiration that not only does the latter in itself exclude all error, but excludes and rejects it with the same necessity as attaches to the impossibility that God Himself, who is the supreme Truth, should be the author of any error anywhere.[41]

The second Vatican council moderated this position but slightly when it declared that 'The books of Scripture teach firmly, faithfully and without error that truth which God willed to be put in the sacred writings for the sake of our salvation' and it went on to declare that 'everything asserted by the inspired authors or sacred writers must be held to be asserted by the Holy Spirit'.[42]

Revelation is held by the Roman Catholic Church to be the imparting to men and women, via the inspired scriptures, of a body of divinely authenticated propositions, and this, with the proviso that only the Church can, through its authorised representatives, interpret the scriptures aright, has continued to be the official view within the Roman Catholic Church to the present day. Thus the *Catholic Encyclopaedia* defines 'revelation' as 'the communication of some truth by God to a rational creature through means which are beyond the course of ordinary nature'.[43]

The correct response to revelation is faith, which in the Roman Catholic Church is defined, as is consistent with the way in which it has defined 'revelation', as divinely given intellectual assent to divinely revealed truths – a position not too far removed from Barth's definition referred to above.

'Faith', declared the Vatican Council of 1870, 'is a supernatural virtue whereby, inspired by and assisted by the grace of God, we believe that the things which He has revealed are true.'

The view that the *locus* of divine revelation is enshrined in the inerrant text of scripture had, however, been under attack from about the end of the nineteenth century, as John Baillie demonstrated in a book which he published in 1956 entitled *The Idea of Revelation in Recent Thought*. In that book Baillie attempted to show that the view of revelation that was, at the time he was writing, becoming increasingly current in Protestant circles was one that saw the biblical understanding of revelation not as something which involved the communication of supernaturally revealed truths via an inerrant text, but as one in which God gradually revealed himself to his people through history – a position developed with great skill by Keith Ward in *Religion and Revelation*.[44] In support of this contention Baillie quoted from the article on 'revelation' by Professor Albrecht Oepke of Leipzig University in Kittel's *Theological Dictionary of the New Testament* where Oepke had written that in the Old Testament:

> Revelation is not the communication of supernatural knowledge ... The revelation can indeed give rise to knowledge ... yet it does not itself consist in [this] but is quite essentially the action of Yahweh, an unveiling of His essential hiddenness, His offering of Himself in fellowship.

Whilst in the New Testament, Oepke maintained that: 'revelation is likewise understood, not in the sense of a communication of supernatural knowledge, but in the sense of a self-disclosure of God'.[45]

Baillie himself held that 'the recovery of this fundamental insight is the first thing we notice as running broadly through all recent discussions, marking them off from the formulations of earlier periods'.[46] On this understanding of revelation scripture ceases to be in and of itself the *locus* of revelation and becomes rather the human witness to the divine self-disclosure in history, something which allows it to be regarded as fallible and open, therefore, to revision. Christian thinking had come a long way from the view of the thirteenth-century Christian theologian St Thomas Aquinas who, in the first section of his *Summa Theologica*, took the inerrancy of Christian scripture for granted and used this as the basis for the rational explication of revelation which was the task, as he saw it, of Christian theology.

This new understanding of revelation has commended itself to many theologians in that it has allowed the more ecumenically aware of them to develop theologies of revelation which can incorporate the very real insights which such theologians see in religious traditions other than their own and we shall return to this point at the close of this chapter.

The third great religion of the Semitic religious tradition, Islam, was brought into being by the prophet Muhammad who was born in Mecca about 570 CE. At the age of forty he began to hear voices or, to be more precise, a voice, which he, and later his followers, believed to be that of the archangel Gabriel dictating to him what eventually became the Qur'an, a term which literally means 'the recitation' and which became the sacred scripture of Islam. Muslims draw a distinction between *ilham* (inspiration), *wahy* (prophetic rapture or trance), and *tanzil* (sending down). *Ilham* can come to any holy person and is not confined to those within the Islamic tradition. It is essentially the gift of insight into matters appertaining to religion. *Wahy*, on the other hand, comes only in states of rapture. According to the Muslim understanding of *wahy*, revelation occurs in three modes: the coming into the mind of an inspiring idea which is not yet formulated in precise words; 'revelation from behind the veil', that is revelation that comes to the inspired person in dreams and trances; and revelation which comes to prophets alone and which is recited to them in words. Muslims believe that whilst Muhammad was the supreme vehicle for all modes of revelation, revelation in these senses was also granted to prophets within other religious traditions and especially to Moses and Jesus. The supreme form of revelation, however, and this Muslims believe was vouchsafed to Muhammad alone, is *tanzil*, that is the 'sending down' of the eternal and uncreated Qur'an. Muslims believe that the Qur'an came into the mind of Muhammad in a single night – the Night of Destiny – to be gradually revealed piecemeal (and memorised and written down by his followers) as and when occasion demanded. For Muslims the Qur'an, therefore, is the very speech of God (*Allah*). As the Islamic Council of Europe put it in a statement issued in 1976:

> The Qur'an contains the Word of God and nothing but the Word of God. In it is preserved the divine revelation, unalloyed by human interpolation of any kind, unaffected by any change or loss to the original. In it is distilled the essence of all the messages sent down in the past. In it is embodied a framework for the conduct of the whole of a man's life.[47]

The Qur'an, as the above statement makes plain, is regarded by Muslims not only as the vehicle whereby God communicates his will to human beings, but as containing the very words in which this will is expressed. Inseparable, for Muslims, from Muhammad having received the truth is his having also received the verbal text of that truth. Muslims believe that earlier prophets, such as Moses and Jesus, had also received something of that truth, but that as their followers had corrupted the message that they had received, God, in his mercy, therefore, had finally revealed the eternal, heavenly, uncorrupted scripture definitively and for all time through the prophet Muhammad, 'the seal of the prophets'.[48] Echoing, perhaps, Christian language with regard to Jesus, Muslims came to believe that the Qur'an was the uncreated Word of God, so that the revelation of this Word to Muhammad was not the Word made flesh, as Christians believe Jesus to have been, but the Word made book. The Qur'an, they came to believe, was a copy of an archetypal Book which has always existed in Heaven, inscribed there, as the Qur'an itself proclaims, in Arabic on a 'well-guarded tablet'.[49] A consequence of this belief is that Muslims hold that the Qur'an cannot be translated – only interpreted.

Apart from the Qur'an, Muslims believe that the divine will can also be found in the traditions (ahadith) of the sayings and doings of Muhammad (sunna) as recorded by his immediate Companions. Whilst Muslims do not believe that Muhammad was anything other than human, there developed early in Islam the view that he was the perfect man and that at all times he was under divine guidance, so that whilst his utterances and his actions do not have the status of the suras in the Qur'an, they constitute an additional source of guidance for those endeavouring to live according to the divine will. It therefore became important to collect as many of these reported sayings and records of his actions as possible and this was done in the second Muslim century (ninth century CE). Two collections of ahadith – those compiled by al-Bukhari (810–70 CE) and al-Muslim (817–75 CE) – rapidly came to be well nigh universally accepted throughout the Muslim world and to enjoy an authority second only to the Qur'an itself. The sifting, from the many thousands of traditions claiming to record the sayings and actions of Muhammad, of 'sound' from 'unsound' traditions has, from the ninth century, become one of the main branches of Muslim religious science.

Muhammad died in 632 CE and whilst it is the view of Muslims today that his prophetic role died with him, and that the Caliphs who succeeded him inherited his secular authority only, there is some evidence that, for a time at least, the early Caliphs saw themselves as inheriting not only the military and political leadership of the Muslim community ('umma), but also the prophetic mantle of Muhammad. As God's vice-regents on earth, they had the power to continue to reveal his will – a sort of Muslim papacy, although the model was more than likely to have been derived not from Rome, but from the role that the emperor played in the Byzantine Christianity of Constantinople.[50] This dual role, however, even if it existed, was soon made redundant as those who had made the study of the Qur'an and the ahadith a professional occupation – and who became known as the 'ulama, or the learned – gradually established themselves as the authoritative interpreters of the will of God as disclosed in the Qur'an, in the sunna or practice of the Prophet, and in the growing corpus of *Shari'a* (law). By the eleventh century, however, interpretation (*ijtihad*) of the Qur'an was severely limited and the 'gates of *ijtihad*' were declared closed. From that time the *'ulama* have, for the most part, concerned themselves with what is known as *taqlid* – the preservation and imitation of the theological and legal judgements of scholars of what is believed to have been the golden age of Islam. However, from about the middle of the nineteenth century a number of Muslim reformers, particularly in India, have sought to reopen the gates of *ijtihad*.

Shi'a Islam has a rather different view of the continuance of divine inspiration within Islam than have the Sunni, for the Shi'ites believe that *ilham* (inspiration) and to a certain extent a lesser form of *wahy* continued for a considerable period of time after the death of the Prophet through a line of infallible Imams descended from Muhammad's cousin and son-in-law 'Ali. Moojan Momen, a leading authority on Shi'a Islam, has this to say of the status accorded to the Imams in Shi'ite tradition:

> Although the consensus of the Shi'is is that the full prophetic revelation (*wahy*) that came to Muhammad and other apostles of God (such as Moses and Jesus) did not come to the Imams, nevertheless some of the Shi'i scholars have allowed that a lesser form of *wahy* did come to the Imams ... [but] in any case, if there is disagreement among the Shi'i scholars on the question of *wahy*, there is no disagreement on the fact that the Imam received inspiration (*ilham*) from God. The following is attributed to Muhammad al-Baqir, the fifth Imam: ''Ali used to act in accordance with the Book of God, i.e. the Qur'an, and the Sunna [example and tradition] of His Apostle [i.e. Muhammad] and if something came to him and it was new and without precedent in the book of the Sunna, God would inspire him.' [51]

The function of the Imams was to guide their followers by explaining and clarifying the *Shari'a* and to direct true believers along the inner spiritual and intellectual path of Islam. Today the Shi'ites are divided into a number of groups distinguished by the answers they give to the question who actually constituted, and for how, the line of infallible Imams. Of the two major Shi'ite groupings which have survived to the present day the *Ithna-'ashariyya* (Twelvers), who are to be found mainly in Iran and southern Iraq, believe that the infallible Imamate only came to an end when the twelfth Imam, Muhammad al-Mahdi (born 868 CE) was taken by God out of human sight, an event known as 'occultation' (*ghayba*), and who, it is believed, will return at the end of time to establish true religion and herald in the Last Judgement. Before that time the *Ithna-'ashariyya* believe that the hidden Imam continues to guide his community through his representatives, the leaders of the *Ithna-'ashariyya* community.

The other major group of Shi'ite Muslims are the Isma'ilis, known also as the Seveners, who believe that the infallible Imamate came to an end with Isma'il, the eldest son of the sixth Imam of the Twelvers, Ja'far al-Sadiq who died in 765 CE. However, the Ismailis believe that they are still guided by the descendants of Isma'il, who have a religious authority possessed by no single person in Sunni Islam. The present leader of the Isma'ilis is the Aga Khan.

This belief in the continuance of inspiration within the Shi'ite communities of faith has allowed the various Shi'ite groups a wider and often a more progressive range of interpretation of the Qur'an than that of the more conservative Sunni Muslims. They can also address more creatively than can Sunni Muslims the pressing problems of the times in which they find themselves and can the more easily, with the memory of the military and political defeat of the house of 'Ali and the martyrdom of their Imam Husain at the battle of Karbala in 680 CE ever in mind, accept a less triumphal political role in the world community than can Sunni Muslims.

Muslims then, with the exception of the Shi'ites who, under the guidance of their Imams, often engaged in the esoteric interpretation of scripture, are, where Qur'an is concerned, 'fundamentalists' in something approaching the Christian sense of that term, and there has thus been no attempt within Sunni Islam to use the kind of critical approach to the Qur'an that has characterised the liberal Jewish and Christian approaches to the Hebrew Bible and to the Christian scriptures over the past century or so.[52] As one Western commentator on Islam, Martin Forward, has said: 'To be sure, some modern Muslims acknowledge a human element in scripture, but only at the level of agreeing that it contains historical references to events in the life of the Prophet. The vast majority, however, hold that an investigation into the sources of the Qur'an is simply unbelief.'[53] Investigating the composition of the Qur'an falls into what the liberal Muslim thinker Muhammed Arkoun, who teaches at the Sorbonne, has called the realm of the unthought (because unthinkable) within Islam.[54]

The Qur'an, however, did not immediately come into being in the form in which we have it today. From traditions collected by al-Bukhari in the ninth century it would appear that *ayas* (verses) were written down when uttered by Muhammad on anything that lay to hand – palm leaves, flat stones, the bones of animals – and then committed to memory. Whilst there are traditions which claim that Muhammad himself supervised the collection that makes up the text, Muslim tradition has, on the whole, excluded him from having anything at all to do with its compilation. The standard Muslim account – as given, for example, in al-Bukhari's *Sahih* – credits Zayid ibn Thabit, who had acted as an amanuensis to Muhammad, with the compilation of the text. He did this, it is said, despite initial reservations about doing something which the Prophet himself had not done, on the orders of the third Caliph, Uthman (d. 656 CE) who, after Zayid had finished this task, ordered all previous collections of Quranic material to be destroyed.[55] This skeleton text, which consisted of the constants alone in a rudimentary form, formed the basis on which, over the next two centuries, the final text was established.[56] Recent research, however, has shown that the Qur'an's status and authority was much debated during the early centuries of Islam, both within the Muslim community as well as among the numerous religious groupings within the Islamic world.[57] The Christian thinker al-Kindi, for example, who wrote a defence of Christianity against Islam at the court of the Caliph al-Mamun about 830 CE, mentioned, among other charges, that in the Qur'an 'histories are all jumbled together and intermingled', an indication, he argued, that 'many different hands have been at work therein, and caused discrepancies, adding or cutting whatever they liked or disliked'.[58] The charge of getting history wrong has been repeated in our day, but without the added charge of multiple authorship, by the Edinburgh Arabist and student of Islam, Professor William Montgomery Watt.[59] It is not, however, a charge that Muslims have taken very seriously: on the contrary, like the tenth-century thinker al-Rummani, they have turned the difficulties inherent in the text of the Qur'an into an argument for what Rummani termed its i'jaz or 'inimitability' – proof, he argued, of its divine origin.[60] On the whole a critical approach to the formation of the Qur'an has been more a feature of Western study of the origins of Islam than of Muslim scholarship. Certainly, where the notion of 'revelation' is concerned, Muslims have more in common with the conservative Christian understanding of scripture than they have with the views of those who see the *locus* of revelation in a divine self-disclosure within history witnessed to and recorded in the writings of fallible and historically conditioned human beings. The problem for those seeking to legitimate their tradition on the basis of a claim to divine revelation is that we have here a very good example of two well-established religious traditions each maintaining that it and it alone has been the recipient of revealed scriptures enshrined in an inerrant text and yet maintaining very different things about the content of what each claims to have been revealed to its own prophetic founders. Towards the end of this chapter we shall be looking at some of the ways in which theologians have sought to resolve this dilemma. The situation is further complicated, however, by claims to revelation made by the Indian religious tradition.

– THE INDIAN RELIGIOUS TRADITION –

Although the predominant religion within the Indian religious tradition is what Western scholars from the end of the nineteenth century have called 'Hinduism', the Indian religious tradition has given rise to a number of breakaway movements of which Buddhism and Sikhism are the most important.

If we turn, first, to the Hindu religious tradition we see that that tradition also has a body of sacred writings which are held to enshrine the content of a primal revelation. However, unlike the Semitic scriptural tradition, Hindu sacred scriptures were handed down orally for the greater part of their long history. In the Hindu tradition, as Gavin Flood has reminded us, the revealed world is the 'heard' word 'received through the tradition in an unbroken succession from teacher (*guru*) to disciple.'[61]

Yet the 'heard' word is a revealed word and the belief in the Hindu tradition is that the sacred texts which make up the Veda record what was 'heard' by the ancient sages (*rishis*) over a period of time ranging from the very outset of the tradition, probably before the entry of the Aryan Indians into the Indian subcontinent sometime in the second millennium BCE, to the composition of the principal Upanishads which close the sacred canon sometime before the second century BCE. There are in fact four major strata in the canon of sacred texts: (1) the hymns (*samhita*) to the gods which are found in four collections known as the Rig, Sama, Yajur and Atharva Samhita respectively; (2) the Brahmanas which tell how the sacrifices to the gods and goddesses of the Hindu pantheon are to be performed and offer an interpretation of the sacrificial ritual; (3) the Aranyakas (forest treatises) which develop the hermeneutic material found in the Brahmanas in a more philosophical direction; and, finally, (4) the Upanishads where the religio-philosophical teaching found in embryo form in the Aranyakas comes to fruition. The post-*Samhita* collections of texts (Brahmanas, Aranyakas and Upanishads) are somewhat artificially divided and attached to one or other of the original four-fold collection of hymns. It is the whole of this body of sacred literature that is called the Veda.

This 'heard' word, the Veda, is also known as *shruti* and is distinguished from that other category of religious literature in the Hindu tradition known as *smriti*, which means 'that which was remembered', and which contains among other material the Puranas (stories about the gods and goddesses), as well as the popular epics the Mahabharata and the Ramayana. The most well-known text in the whole of the Hindu religious tradition, the Bhagavadgita (The Song of the Lord), which is included in the Mahabharata, is thus part of the *smriti* literature and not, as many have assumed, part of the more authoritative *shruti* literature.

Shruti, the revealed word, is the eternal word which Hindus believe was not, as was *smriti*, composed by human beings (nor, in some traditions, even by the gods), but which, being eternal, is thought of as having in some sense existed even before it was 'heard' in the heart by the sages. It should also be noted that the context of the earliest portions of the Hindu sacred scriptures found in the Vedic Samhita was the sacrificial ritual performed by the Brahmins (the priestly caste) who were also the guardians of the sacred text. However, the later texts, and particularly the Upanishads, became the basis for intense religio-philosophical speculation out of which emerged the distinctive Indian view of the world.

By about 800 BCE, when the first Upanishads came into being, certain groups in Indian society were beginning to move away from the religious beliefs and practices of the early Vedic period and to develop a form of religion in which knowledge (*jnana*) took precedence over ritual action (*karman*). It was during this period that the doctrine which was to play so large a part in the subsequent articulation not only of all forms of Hinduism, but also of Buddhism, Jainism and Sikhism, came into being. This was the doctrine of the eternal round of birth and rebirth (*samsara*) according to the law of *karma* and of the desirability of finding the way to liberation (*moksha*) from this. This was the salvic knowledge, which, together with knowledge of the relationship of the soul (*atman*) to Ultimate Reality (*Brahman*), constituted the core doctrines of the revelation which later thinkers in India believed to have been revealed to the sages of old.

The role that the revealed texts have played and continue to play in the refinement and development of the Indian tradition can be seen from the fact that almost all later developments in religion and philosophy in the Hindu tradition began with commentary on one or other of the sacred texts, more often than not the Upanishads, but also of texts from the *smriti* corpus such as the Bhagavadgita and the Brahma-sutra. It is in fact the Bhagavadgita that most closely resembles the scriptures of the religions of the Semitic tradition, for the teachings which it enshrines are held to have been revealed by Lord Krishna, an *avatar*, or manifestation, of the great God Vishnu.

In ancient India revelation came to be seen as serving two, often interrelated, purposes: that of providing the Brahmins with the knowledge of the ritual actions which were necessary for the upholding and sustaining of the cosmos; and that of providing individuals with the knowledge necessary for obtaining release from the round of birth and rebirth.

The most thorough exposition of the Hindu notion of revelation as a guide to ritual action is found in the Purva Mimansa (Primary Investigation) School which came into being in the second century BCE after the composition of the Mimamsa-sutra by Jaimini. For this school *sruti*, the revealed word heard by the *rishis*, is held to be eternal and the relationship between words and meanings constant. Thus meaning is not something which is acquired by convention, as are personal names, for example, but is held to be an inherent power residing in the words of the sacred texts themselves. As Gavin Flood has put it:

> The Veda is inherently meaningful; it is self-revealed and self-illumined, though its meanings may be obscured by human consciousness. The inherent meaning of the sacred texts transcends the human condition in so far as it predates and will post-date human reality. In itself the Veda is the primary source of all knowledge (*pramana*), which shines independently of finite, human error which obscures its pristine validity. The task of philosophical enquiry is the retrieval of this original meaning (though there was, of course, wide disagreement as to what this was).[62]

This view of the significance of sacred texts is not without parallels to that found in the Semitic tradition although no religion within that tradition drew the conclusion that the Purva Mimansa drew, for as Flood says:

> There is no need in this system, therefore, for a God who sustains the cosmos and who is the author of revelation. Although the Mimansa school accepted the plurality of deities, it comes to regard them only as names which serve in the process of the sacrifice; their ontology is simply unimportant. The more impersonal the Veda is, the clearer the message and the more powerful its message and the more forceful its injunctions when stripped of any personal, limited will. Indeed the Veda is the prime source of knowledge because a human, personal source, which is subject to error and deceit, cannot be the source of a cognition of that which is eternal and transpersonal.[63]

The second view of revelation referred to above, that of providing the knowledge (*jnana*) necessary to achieve release from the samsaric round, was developed by the Uttara Mimansa, better known as the Vedanta school of religio-philosophy. This meant that the Vedanta school was more concerned to interpret such texts as the Upanishads, rather than those which were primarily concerned with ritual action. The Vedantins also had a high regard for the Bhagavadgita and the Brahma-sutra, even though these, being *smriti* and not *sruti*, were not strictly speaking revealed texts.

Although the various schools of Vedanta that developed within the Indian tradition were divided over the exact nature of the relationship of the *atman* or soul to *Brahman* or Ultimate Reality, they were all agreed that the Veda was not authorless or eternal. Even Shankara, the great exponent of the advaita, or non-dualistic Vedanta, taught that the Veda was revealed by Brahman. As he wrote in his commentary on the Brahma-sutra:

> Brahman is the *yoni* (i.e., the material and efficient cause) of great scriptures like the Rg-veda etc. which are supplemented by other scriptures are themselves sources (of various kinds) of knowledge, which reveal all things like a lamp, and which are almost omniscient. For scriptures like the Rg-veda, possessed of all good qualities as they are, cannot possibly emerge from any source other than the all-knowing One.[64]

Thus, for Shankara, the Veda, rather than being an end in itself, mediates that (saving) knowledge about Brahman, or to be more precise about the soul's relationship to *Brahman* – the existential and experiential realisation of which constitutes liberation from *samsara*.

As the Indian tradition developed various schools arose which, whilst not denying the authority of the Veda, based themselves on groups of texts which fell well outside even the loose Vedic canon. Two such groups were the Tantrikas, who based their beliefs and practice on a group of texts known as the Tantras, and the Agamikas, who based their belief and practice on a cognate group of texts known as the Agamas. Both these groups came into being in the period from the seventh to the eleventh centuries of the common era and both came to believe that their sacred texts had also been revealed – a claim not accepted, of course, by the followers of Brahmanical orthodoxy. As the Indian tradition developed further groups of writings, in particular those representing the vernacular tradition of devotional poetry to the god Shiva, came to hold, *de facto*, a place in the lives of their adherents – who were often from the lower castes – equivalent to that held by the Veda in the lives of the higher castes. There is thus justification for Flood's judgement that 'in India revelation is not static, and whilst there is certainly a central corpus of unchanging texts, there is also fluidity and acceptance of new texts', so that revelation is not 'something in the far distant past, but is a constant and present possibility'.[65]

If we turn to what is held to have been revealed in the religions of the Indian tradition there are three topics on which the Indian tradition appears, *prima facie*, to have a different understanding of the nature of reality from that found in the Semitic tradition. These are the nature of God and God's relationship to the world, the nature of time and history, and the nature of the human soul.

The classic contrast in the history of religion has often been seen as a contrast being between the different conceptions of the nature of ultimate reality found in the Semitic and Hindu religious traditions. Whereas in Judaism, Christianity and Islam Ultimate Reality (God) is conceived as personal, in the Hindu tradition, so it has been maintained, Ultimate Reality (*Brahman*) is held to be impersonal. Alternatively the contrast has been presented as being between theism, in which God is seen as transcending the world he is held to have created, and monism where, in a sense difficult to define, God, the world and the human soul are held to be identical. However, with the increasing knowledge of the Hindu tradition which we now possess, these supposed contrasts between the Semitic and the Indian traditions need severe qualification and, as we shall see shortly, the real difference between the Semitic and the Indian religious traditions lies elsewhere.

It is in the Indian Advaita Vedanta tradition, whose major exponent was the eighth-century religious thinker Shankara, that the view that *Brahman* (Ultimate Reality) is impersonal and that, when seen from the proper perspective, the human soul (*atman*) and Ultimate Reality (*Brahman*) are seen to be identical, is classically expressed. Yet the Advaita Vedanta represents only one strand within a more complex Vedanta tradition and the Vedanta tradition itself is but one small part of the total Hindu religious tradition. In fact it was over the nature of *Brahman* and its relationship to *atman* that the Vedanta tradition became divided, with Ramanuja (c. 1077–1157) and Madhva (c. 1197–1276) – the founders respectively of the Vishishtadvaita (qualified non-dualistic) and Dvaita (dualistic) schools of Vedanta – maintaining positions which can only be described as theistic, and with both maintaining, unlike Shankara, that the destiny of the human soul was to seek union with rather than absorption into *Brahman*. Both Ramanuja and Madhva were practising Vaisnavas (that is, devotees of the god Vishnu) and it was through their experience of practising *bhakti* – loving devotion to a personal *Isvara* (Lord) – that they became dissatisfied with the monistic teachings of Shankara.

The greatest exponent of the superiority of the way of *bhakti* over all other ways of achieving release from the eternal round of birth and rebirth is the author of the *Bhagavadgita* who, as the closing speech which he puts into the mouth of Krishna, the *avatar* of Vishnu, makes clear, asserted not only that loving devotion to a personal *Ishvara* was the best way to attain liberation, but that liberation consisted in union with God and not simply in achieving that state of bliss that he called the 'nirvana of Brahman'.[66] Theism is as common – if, indeed, not more common – in the Hindu tradition than the monism that is so often, though erroneously, claimed to be the distinguishing characteristic of that tradition. The *bhakti* tradition is far more widespread, and has far more adherents both in India and in Hinduism outwith India, than has Vedanta. The majority of Hindus, in fact, know little of Vedanta and the religion which they practise is more accurately described as polytheism, although among the more sophisticated it is a polytheism that more often than not moves over into monotheism. As the Rig Veda itself says:

> They call him Indra, Mitra, Varuna,
> Agni, and he is heavenly noble-winged
> Garutman [the sun],
> To what is one, sages give many a title.[67]

Further, the widespread, almost primal recognition, of a god above the gods, whom Hindus across the subcontinent refer to simply as *Bhagvan* (The Lord), is testimony to the implicit monotheism found within the Hindu tradition.

We thus see that the Hindu and the Semitic traditions are not as far apart as many have claimed on the question of the existence of God. The fundamental difference between the religions of the Semitic or Abrahamic tradition and the religions of India lies elsewhere. It lies, in fact, in the belief which is fundamental to the entire Indian religious tradition – Hindu, Buddhist, Jain and Sikh – in the eternal round of birth and rebirth (*samsara*) of the soul (*atman*) operating according to the law of *karma*, and of the desirability of achieving release (*moksha*) from this. Almost all the differences which scholars have seen between the Semitic and Indian religious traditions – the devaluation of life in this world, the down-playing of evil, the search for illumination and for fulfilment of the self, and an apparent indifference to history in the Indian tradition – flow from this belief. This belief also underlies Buddhist and Sikh understanding of the nature and destiny of human beings.

Buddhism, which came into being towards the end of the sixth century and the beginning of the fifth century BCE as a breakaway movement from the predominant Hindu tradition in India, was founded by Siddharta Gautama, known after his enlightenment as 'the Buddha' or Enlightened One. Buddha totally rejected the notion of God and Buddhism is one of the few examples in the history of religion of a wholly atheistic religion. On this count there are those who have doubted whether it should be called a religion at all.[68] Yet Buddhism, with its monastic orders, its techniques of meditation, its magico-religious rituals, its claim to lead its adepts to 'enlightenment' and, in popular practice, its worship of Buddha (and, in the Mahayana tradition, of those known as Bodhisattvas), has so many 'family resemblances' to the religions of the world that, mindful of what was said in the introduction to this present work about 'concepts with blurred edges', it would be hard not to regard it as a religion. It does not, however, claim to have been revealed in any sense other than that in which all knowledge can be said to be revealed. Much as his ontological stature changed as Buddhism grew and developed – particularly in the Mahayana, or Great Vehicle, tradition – Buddha has remained essentially a human being who *discovered* the path to release from the suffering endemic in the human condition and to release from the eternal round of birth and rebirth (samsara) into that blessed state that the Buddhist calls *nirvana* and who, out of compassion, sought to pass on this knowledge to suffering humanity. However, it must be noted that, from its earliest days, there developed in Buddhism an ever-growing canon of sacred scripture which claims to record the teachings (overt or esoteric) of the historic Buddha and in no other tradition has the magical use of scripture been developed and formalised as it has in Buddhism.[69] Buddhism, however, is not a religion of revelation in the accepted sense of that term and therefore falls outwith the remit of this chapter, but this must not be taken to imply that it offers no insights into the nature of religion. In fact of all the religions of the East, it is from Buddhism that many contemporary Christian theologians claim that they have the most to learn.[70] Buddhism is also the most often quoted counter-example to the understanding of religion that we shall meet with when we come to look at the theories of religion put forward by Marx, Freud and Durkheim.

Sikhism was founded in the early years of the sixteenth century CE by Guru Nanak, an itinerant preacher from the Punjab. Although Sikhism is basically a Hindu movement, with roots in Vaishnavite devotion (*bhakti*) to Vishnu, and a religion, therefore, which accepts the basic Hindu doctrine of *samsara*, Nanak was also influenced by Islam and upheld a doctrine of the transcendence of God such as had not before been seen in the Indian tradition. Sikhism is a good example, in fact, of the symbiosis that can take place when two traditions meet, although in this case the repercussions on the parent traditions have been minimal. However, Nanak sought to transcend both Hinduism and Islam and to found a new universal religion and he claimed that the beliefs and practices of this new religion had been revealed to him by God.

As recorded in the scriptures which he bequeathed to his small group of followers and which today form the nucleus of the Sikh sacred book, the Adi Granth, he taught that God is one, the creator of all, and that he is immune from birth and rebirth. He is transcendent, yet union with him can be achieved through loving devotion (*bhakti*) and, above all by mediating on the divine name. By so doing the believer will be released from the karmic round of *samsara*, from egoism, and from the five evil passions.

Nanak despised outward, and as he believed, empty rituals and he utterly rejected the Indian caste system. Inner purity was for him the essence of true religion.

The ten gurus (teachers) who followed Nanak and under whose guidance Sikhism grew and developed, and whose writings were added to the growing body of sacred scripture, also believed that they were divinely inspired in what they taught and did. The last guru, Gobind Singh, who died in 1708, announced on his deathbed that the line of inspired gurus had come to an end and that, henceforth, the now completed scripture, designated Guru Granth Sahib, would take the place of the inspired guru and this, today, is the case. Sikhism, therefore, is yet another example of a religion claiming to have come into being through an act of divine revelation recorded in inspired scripture.

There are a number of ways in which those who claim that their tradition is the outcome of revelation have responded to the claims of others that their tradition is also derived from revelation. One, of course, is simply to deny that any other claim to revelation but that made by one's own tradition is true – a position that in today's world of inter-religious inter-action is becoming increasingly difficult to maintain. The more common way today is to see one's own tradition as fulfilling what are regarded as the imperfect revelations contained in other traditions. This is a position taken by a number of Hindu and an increasing number of Christian theologians. It was also the way in which Islam originally saw Judaism and Christianity. A third way, taken by some Christian theologians, is to see all religious traditions as more or less true with none, including one's own, as possessing truth absolutely – a position which involves, of course, giving up traditional Christian claims to exclusivity and its attendant belief in the absolute centrality for salvation of accepting the atoning death of Jesus of Nazareth which has characterised Christian faith from its inception.

A useful review of the various ways in which Christian theologians have sought to come to terms with the claims to revelation made by the adherents of religions other than their own can be found in an anthology edited by John Hick and Brian Hebblethwaite entitled *Christianity and Other Religions*. It is an anthology which covers almost the whole spectrum of Christian response to other religions ranging from outright rejection of the claims of other religions (Barth and Kraemer), to a recognition of the fact that all religious traditions possess some degree of truth (Troeltsch and Hick).[71] Hick's later position that all religions possess a great deal of truth but that none possesses it absolutely is not, however, represented in this anthology as it was a position which Hick espoused only after its publication.

The view that religions other than the Christian are simply untrue is, as we have said, not one that commands much adherence among Christian theologians today. Most seem to have taken to heart remarks such as that made by Cantwell Smith that today 'the data for theology is the data of the history of religions',[72] although a leading contemporary theologian, Colin Gunton, giving the Warfield Lectures in 1993 on 'the theology of revelation' managed to do so without any reference to religions other than the Christian, in sharp contrast to Keith Ward who, in Gifford Lectures on the same topic delivered at Edinburgh University in the same year, sought to discuss the Christian claim to revelation within the context of the claims made by other traditions.[73] The more common approach today, and this is the stance taken by Ward, is to hold that religious traditions other than the adherent's own are not so much false as only partially true and that they come to fruition only in Christianity, and such theologians often also maintain that Christians have much to learn from the insights and emphases found in other traditions.[74]

The idea that Christianity fulfils other religions is, of course, found in the approach taken by Christianity to both Judaism and Greek philosophy, and the notion of a universal 'progressive revelation' which culminates in the Christian religion begins to re-emerge in Christian thinking – particularly missionary thinking – from about the middle of the nineteenth century. It can be found, for example, in the thought of the missionary scholar J. N. Farquhar who, in his book *The Crown of Hinduism*, argues, as the title implies, that Christianity brings to fruition the partial insights into the truth of the Christian religion which Farquhar saw in the religions of India. An earlier missionary scholar, James Legge, had taken a similar position with regard to the religious truth that he saw in the Confucian tradition in China and had, indeed, drawn an explicit parallel between the Chinese and the Jews, holding that both were 'prepared' by God for the preaching of the Christian Gospel.[75]

This approach, as we have said, goes back to the earliest period of the Christian religion. It was in this way that the Greek Fathers in the Christian church – Irenaeus, Clement of Alexandria and Origen – came to terms with the truth which they saw in the teachings of Plato and in other Greek philosophers. It was only a short step for Christian thinkers in the nineteenth and twentieth centuries to adapt this approach to the new situation that Christianity found itself in *vis-à-vis* the great world religions with which it was now increasingly coming into contact. A Christian apologist of an earlier generation, Alan Richardson, put it as follows: 'We must try', he wrote, to reach an understanding of the nature of man's knowledge of God which will take due account of the genuinely religious features of the non-Christian faiths, some of which they share with Christianity, and which will yet at the same time adequately comprehend those distinctive elements of the Christian religion which are not found in any other religious system or philosophy ... The only kind of theory of the knowledge of God which will adequately embrace all the facts of man's experience will be one which recognises that there are two kinds of revelation or divine disclosure of truth. There is first *general* revelation, which pertains to the universal religious consciousness of mankind; and there is also *special* revelation, which is mediated through particular episodes at definite times and places in history.[76]

Today, however, Christian theologians, such as Hick and Ward, are disinclined to accept the rigid qualitative distinction between claims to revelation that this distinction implies. The tendency today is rather to see religions other than the Christian as possessing rather more of the truth than the bare revelation of monotheism and natural law contained in the traditional notion of 'general revelation' allows. There is also growing recognition that the notion of 'special revelation' raises, as we have seen, so many difficult questions that it is better to abandon the claim to exclusivity that it implies.

For those who still wish to base religious knowledge on revelation, but who are aware of the differences which exist in terms of what has been claimed to have been revealed, a way out of the impasse, as was mentioned earlier, has been to reformulate the problem, so that it is no longer a question of which tradition is true, but of what truth there is in each tradition when seen from either the perspective of Christian faith or, for some, from a perspective in which no tradition – even the theologian's own – is held to be in sole possession of the truth. The former position, as we have seen, is that taken by Keith Ward in *Religion and Revelation*; the latter by John Hick in *An Interpretation of Religion*. In this book Hick sought to reconcile the views of those who see truth in religious traditions other than their own and those who see no way of reconciling the profound differences that exist between religions. Thus, whilst emphasising that religions have more in common than they are often seen to have – the endeavour to move human beings away from self-centredness to Reality-centredness is, for Hick, the central theme in all religions – Hick recognises that there are profound differences between religions although these, he contends, in that they are not soteriologically significant, can be 'lived with' by those espousing the pluralistic hypothesis – a view which many of his critics felt ignored the centrality that the traditional Christian doctrine of the atoning death of Jesus of Nazareth has for Christians.[77] Believers are encouraged, on

Hick's understanding of pluralism, to remain within the particular traditions in which they find themselves, for all traditions lead to salvation – a view that some historians of religion might claim ignores the profoundly different ways of living that adherents of differing religious traditions derive from their understanding of what they believe to have been revealed in those traditions.

One popular way of seeking to come to terms with the problem posed by the plurality of claims to revelation is to look for what is common in religious traditions and to elevate this to the level of a universal religion – a tendency that began in India in the last century and has since spread to the Western world. Many of the reform movements within Hinduism sought to reconcile adherents of all the major religions with which their founders were familiar. Thus, for example, Keshab Sen (1838–84), the founder of the Brahmo Samaj, wrote:

> I believe in the Universal Church which is the deposit of all ancient wisdom and the receptacle of all modern science, which recognises all prophets and saints in harmony, in all scriptures a unity, and through all dispensations a continuity, which abjures all that separates and divides, always magnifies unity and peace, which harmonises faith and reason, yoga and bhakti, asceticism and social duty in their highest forms and which shall make of all nations one kingdom and one family in the fullness of time.[78]

However, laudable as these sentiments no doubt are, to speak of a 'harmony' in all prophets and saints and of a 'unity' in all scriptures is, quite simply, to fly in the face of the evidence. This, however, has not stopped a number of Western thinkers, often under the influence of the Indian tradition, from continuing to search for the common kernel of truth which they believe is contained in all religions. We shall be considering their views in the next chapter.

The time has come to take leave of those who base their claim to religious truth on revelation and to turn to look at those who have explained religion on a wider and rather more democratic understanding of religious experience than that enshrined in claims to revelation. There is, of course, a certain continuity between these two ways of seeking to justify religious knowledge, for that which a tradition claims as a revelation was, at some point in time, some particular persons' (or a number of such persons') religious experience.

– NOTES –

1. E. R. Dodds, *Pagan and Christian in an Age of Anxiety*, Cambridge: CUP, 1965, p. 54.
2. Athanasius, *De Incarnatione*, 12.

3. A. F. Walls, 'Primal Religious Traditions in Today's World', in F. Whaling (ed.), *Religion in Today's World*, Edinburgh: T. & T. Clark, 1987, p. 252. The same point is made by S. A. Thorpe, *Primal Religions Worldwide*, Pretoria: University of South Africa Press, 1992, pp. 3–6.
4. C.f. Wilfred Cantwell Smith, *The Meaning and End of Religion*, New York: Mentor Books, 1962. For the origins of the modern usage of the term 'religion' c.f. Peter Harrison, *'Religion' and the Religions in the English Enlightenment*, Cambridge: CUP, 1989.
5. C.f. Thorpe, *Primal Religions*, pp. 9, 112–13, 118–23.
6. Henri Frankfort (ed.), *Before Philosophy: The Intellectual Adventure of Ancient Man*, Harmondsworth: Penguin Books, 1949, p. 14.
7. Ibid., p. 14.
8. Mary Douglas, *Purity and Danger*, Harmondsworth: Penguin Books, 1970, p. 107. For Douglas's justification of her use of the term 'primitive' c.f. p. 91f.
9. Keith Ward, *Religion and Revelation*, Oxford: Clarendon Press, 1994, p. 68.
10. Bronislaw Malinowski, *Magic, Science and Religion*, New York: Doubleday Anchor Books, 1954, pp. 28–9.
11. Plato, *Phaedo*, 96–100.
12. Robert Segal, *Religion and the Social Sciences*, Atlanta: Scholars Press, 1989, pp. 109–35.
13. Keith Thomas, *Religion and the Decline of Magic*, Harmondsworth: Penguin Books, 1970, pp. 3–57.
14. For a detailed study of these techniques c.f. Mircea Eliade, *Shamanism: Ancient Techniques of Ecstasy*, New York: Pantheon, 1965. For a discussion of the social function of shamanism c.f. I. M. Lewis, *Ecstatic Religion*, Harmondsworth: Penguin Books, 1971.
15. For a fuller discussion of the origins of prophecy in ancient Israel c.f. A. R. Johnston, *The Cultic Prophet in Ancient Israel*, Cardiff: University of Wales Press, 1962; R. E. Clements, *Prophecy and Covenant*, London: SCM Press, 1965, pp. 11–34; J. Lindblom, *Prophecy in Ancient Israel*, Oxford: Blackwell, 1962, chap. 2.
16. E.g. c.f. Michael Stephen, 'Dream, Trance and Spirit Possession: Traditional Religious Experience in Melanesia', in Victor C. Hayes (ed.), *Religious Experience in World Religions*, Bedford Park, South Australia: Australian Association for the Study of Religions Publications, 1980, pp. 25–49.
17. C.f. also Peter L. Berger, 'Charisma and Religious Innovation: The Social Location of Israelite Prophecy', *American Sociological Review*, vol. 28 (1963), pp. 940–50. There is evidence that this is still the case in contemporary primal societies. C.f. A. F. C. Wallace, 'Revitalisation Movements', *American Anthropologist*, vol. 58, no. 2 (1956), pp. 264–81.
18. 1 Samuel, 10:5–6.
19. 1 Samuel, 19:9–24.
20. Bernard Anderson, *The Living World of the Old Testament*, London: Longmans, 1967, p. 193.
21. Gore, *Belief in God*, London: John Murray, 1921, p. 75.
22. Ibid., p. 78.
23. C.f. Albert Hourani, *Islam in European Thought*, Cambridge: CUP, 1991, pp. 36–41.
24. *Tagebuch*, Leiden, 1978, p. 71; quoted Hourani, *Islam in European Thought*, p. 38.
25. I. Goldziher, *Introduction to Islamic Theology and Law*, trans. A. and R. Hamori, Princeton: PUP, 1981.
26. Hourani, *Islam in European Thought*, p. 40.
27. Ward, *Religion and Revelation*, p. 130.

28. C.f. Anderson, *Living World of the Old Testament*, pp. 169–87.
29. C.f. Peter L. Berger and Thomas Luckmann, *The Social Construction of Reality: A Treatise on the Sociology of Knowledge*, Harmondsworth: Allen Lane, 1967; and Peter L. Berger, *The Social Reality of Religion*, London: Faber & Faber, 1969.
30. Samuel Sandmel, *The Hebrew Scriptures*, New York: OUP, 1978, p. 14.
31. Matt. 22:40.
32. The texts of many of these writings – some previously known only in part, some only by name, and some not at all – were recovered only in 1945 at Nag Hammadi in Egypt where, in their Coptic versions, they had been buried sometime probably in the fourth century. For a stimulating, if controversial, account of these texts c.f. Elaine Pagels, *The Gnostic Gospels*, Harmondsworth: Penguin Books, 1982. For the texts themselves c.f. James M. Robinson, *The Nag Hammadi Library*, Leiden: Brill, 1977.
33. This is the position taken by Brevard Childs. C.f. Brevard S. Childs, *Introduction to the Old Testament as Scripture*, London: SCM, 1979; and *The New Testament as Canon: An Introduction*, London: SCM, 1984.
34. The German text was published by Barth as *Theologische Fragen und Antworten* in 1957. It can be found in English in Martin Rumscheidt, *Adolf von Harnack*, Minneapolis: Fortress Press, 1991, pp. 85–106.
35. Rumscheidt, *Harnack*, pp. 98–9.
36. Ibid., *Harnack*, pp. 100–1.
37. Ibid., p. 106.
38. Those who take this position have been designated by Kai Neilson as 'Wittgensteinian fideists'. C.f. Neilson, 'Wittgensteinian Fideism', *Philosophy*, vol. 42 (1967), pp. 191–209.
39. Robert W. Jenson in David Ford (ed.), *The Modern Theologians*, Oxford: Blackwells, 2nd edn, 1997, pp. 27–8.
40. W. Pannenberg, *Systematic Theology*, Edinburgh: T. & T. Clark, 1991, vol. 1, pp. 45–8.
41. H. Denzinger and A. Schönmetzer, *Enchirdion Symbolorum*, Freiburg: Herder, 1963, p. 544.
42. *Dei Verbum* 11 in W. M. Abbott, *The documents of Vatican II*, London: Geoffrey Chapman, 1966.
43. *Catholic Encyclopedia*, ed. Charles G. Herbermann, New York: Robert Appleton Co., 1907–22, Vol. XIII, p. 1.
44. Ward, *Religion and Revelation*, pp. 221–35.
45. Kittel, *Dictionary of the New Testament*, Grand Rapids: Eerdmans, 1976, pp. 575 and 586.
46. Baillie, *The Idea of Revelation in Recent Thought*, Oxford: OUP, 1956, p. 29. For a contemporary discussion of the propositional view of revelation c.f. Colin Gunton, *A Brief Theology of Revelation*, Edinburgh: T. & T. Clark, 1996, pp. 1–19.
47. *Islam: A Contemporary Statement*, issued by the Islamic Council of Europe and published by The Islamic Foundation, Leicester, 1976. C.f. Whitfield Foy (ed.), *Man's Religious Quest: A Reader*, London: Croom Helm (for the Open University), 1978, p. 532.
48. The Qur'an states that all these earlier messages emanated from a single source variously referred to as 'the Mother of the Book' (43.4; 13.39) and 'the Hidden Book' (56.78). The Qur'an also states that God guidance is universal and not restricted to any single nation. For example, 13:7 reads 'For every people a guide has been provided', and 35:24 states that 'There is no nation wherein a warner has not come.'
49. Qur'an, Sura 85.22.
50. Those who wish to pursue this question should read Patricia Crone and Martin Hinds,

God's Caliph: Religious Authority in the First Centuries of Islam, Cambridge: CUP, 1986.

51. Moojan Momen, *An Introduction to Shi'i Islam*, New Haven: Yale University Press, 1985, p. 149.

52. For a study of 'Fundamentalism' c.f. James Barr, *Fundamentalism*, London: SCM Press, 1977.

53. Martin Forward, 'Islam', in Jean Holm and John Bowker (eds), *Sacred Writings*, London: Pinter, 1994, p. 111.

54. Muhammed Arkoun, *Pour une critique de la raison islamique*, Paris: Maisonneuve, 1984, p. 58f.

55. Bernard Lewis gives the standard account as found in al-Bukhari in his anthology of Muslim texts, *Islam: From the Prophet Muhammad to the Capture of Constantinople*, New York: OUP, 1987, Vol. II, pp. 1–2.

56. C.f. Andrew Rippin, *Muslims: Their Religious Beliefs and Practices*, London: Routledge, 1990, Vol. 1, p. 24.

57. C.f. John Wansbrough, *Quranic Studies: Sources and Methods of Scriptural Interpretation*, Oxford: OUP, 1977, sect. 4.

58. C.f. William Muir, *The Apology of al-Kindy, written at the Court of al-Mamun in Defence of Christianity against Islam*, pp. 18–19 and 28; quoted Rippin, *Muslims*, p. 26.

59. C.f. Montgomery Watt, *Islamic Fundamentalism and Modernity*, London: Routledge, 1988, pp. 82–4.

60. For an exposition of this argument c.f. Rippin, *Muslims*, pp. 26–7; and for a translation of Rummani's argument c.f. A. Rippin and J. Knappert, *Textual Sources for the Study of Islam*, Manchester: MUP, 1986, sect. 2.3.

61. Gavin Flood in Holm and Bowker (eds), *Sacred Writings*, p. 72.

62. Ibid., p. 81.

63. Ibid., pp. 81–2.

64. Sankara, *Brahmasuttrabhasa* 1.1.3, trans. Swami Gambhirananda; quoted Flood, ibid., p. 84.

65. Flood, ibid., p. 97. This point is also made by Vasuda Narayanan in her book *The Vernacular Veda: Revelation, Recitation, and Ritual*, Columbia, SC: University of South Carolina Press, 1994 in which the notion of a fifth Veda, open to all castes, is explored with reference to the Srivaisnava tradition in south India.

66. For a detailed exposition of the argument summarised here c.f. R. C. Zaehner, *The Bhagavadgita*, Oxford: Clarendon Press, 1969.

67. Rig Veda, 1.164 verse 4.

68. So W. D. Hudson, *A Philosophical Approach to Religion*, London: Macmillan, 1974, p. 16.

69. C.f. Ulrich Pagel, 'Buddhism', in Holm and Bowker (eds), *Sacred Writings*, pp. 40–2.

70. So Keith Ward, *Religion and Revelation*, p. 173.

71. John Hick and Brian Hebblethwaite (eds), *Christianity and Other Religions*, London: Collins, 1980.

72. W. C. Smith, *Towards a World Theology*, Philadelphia: Westminster Press, 1981, p. 126.

73. Colin Gunton, *A Brief Theology of Revelation*, Edinburgh: T. & T. Clark, 1996; K. Ward, *Religion and Revelation*.

74. So Harvey Cox in *Turning East: The Promise and Peril of the New Orientalism*, London: Allen Lane, Penguin Books, 1977; and Ward, *Religion and Revelation*, pp. 191–2.

75. C.f. J. N. Farquhar, *The Crown of Hinduism*, London: Milford, 1920; James Legge, *Christianity in Relation to Confucianism*, London: Trübner, 1887.

76. Alan Richardson, *Christian Apologetics*, London: SCM Press, 1947, pp. 116–17.
77. Hick, *An Interpretation of Religion*, pp. 365–70. Hick's position is even more forcefully expressed in a more recent book, *The Rainbow of Faiths*, London: SCM Press, 1995, a book in which Hick seeks to come to terms with his critics. C.f. especially chapter 4, 'Incarnation and Uniqueness', and chapter 6, 'A Christianity that Sees Itself as One True Religion among Others', pp. 125–47.
78. Quoted Wilhelm Halbfass, *India and Europe: An Essay in Understanding*, Albany, NY: State University of New York Press, 1988, p. 225.

CHAPTER 3

Religion as Experience

The explanation for the existence of religion considered in the last chapter claimed that religion was the outcome of the experience of certain chosen or religiously gifted individuals. A variation on this way of explaining religion is the claim that religion arises out of, or is confirmed by, not just the experience of religiously outstanding individuals, but by experiences which are potentially within the reach of each and every one of us. It is a view associated in the Western tradition with the names of Friedrich Schleiermacher, Rudolf Otto and William James. It is also associated with the views of those, such as Aldous Huxley, who have maintained that the essence and unity of all religions is to be found in a set of uniform mystical experiences which they hold to constitute the truth at the heart of all religions. It is also a claim made by advocates of the Advaita Vedanta school of religious philosophy within the Indian religious tradition.

– FRIEDRICH SCHLEIERMACHER –

In his book *Types of Modern Theology* H. R. Mackintosh, writing in the early years of the twentieth century, claimed that Schleiermacher 'opened up a new era not only in theology as a whole but still more definitively in the scientific interpretation of religion'.[1] And a contemporary sociologist, Peter Berger, commending what he calls Schleiermacher's 'inductive method', argues that anyone seeking to rehabilitate religion in the contemporary world should follow Schleiermacher in turning from authority to experience.[2] Clearly Schleiermacher is a theologian whom the student of religion must take seriously.

Schleiermacher was born in Breslau in 1768. His father, an army chaplain, had leanings towards Count Zinzendorf's *Brüdergemeine*, a Pietistic sequel to the Bohemian or Moravian Brethren, and Schleiermacher was educated at the Moravian school at Niesky and at the Moravian theological college at Barby. However, whilst at Barby, he revolted against the narrow sectarianism and religious dogmatism of the religion of his childhood and in 1787 enrolled as a theological student at the University of Halle where he was introduced to the philosophy of Kant, and against whose rational redefinition of the Christian religion he was to react so strongly. After graduating from Halle, he seems to have overcome his doubts about the divinity of Christ, and the necessity for his atoning death, as well as doubts about the immortality of the soul, to proceed to the ordained ministry of the Reformed Church and, after ordination and a probationary pastorate, to accept appointment as chaplain to the Charité Hospital in Berlin. It was in Berlin, at the house of Frau Henrietta Hertz, that he became friendly with a group of early 'Romantics' which included the poet Friedrich Schlegel, and whose influence, reinforcing that of his pietistic upbringing, led him to question the excessive rationalism of the European Enlightenment and to re-evaluate the place of feeling and more particularly the feelings associated with religion in human life.

Schleiermacher's thinking revolved around two questions, 'what is religion?', and 'what is Christianity?', and his answers to both were highly original, if somewhat unorthodox. It was in the famous *Speeches* – or to give them their full title, *Speeches on Religion to Its Cultured Despisers* – which he published anonymously in 1799, that he addressed the question 'what is religion?', and whilst the answer which he gave shows the influence of both Pietism and of early Romanticism, it also shows Schleiermacher's own unique insight into the nature of religion. Religion, said Schleiermacher, must not be confused with either metaphysics or morality, for living religion is not a matter of metaphysics or morality, but of feeling and relationship. What, for Schleiermacher, lies at the heart of all living religion is a feeling or sentiment (*Gefühl*) which he termed 'piety' (*Frömmigkeit*). As H. G. Schenk put it in his classic study of European Romanticism, *The Mind of the European Romantics*: 'For Schleiermacher religious sentiment is the master-key and indeed the only key to religion. Theology is for him nothing but religious feeling which has become articulate.'[3] Schleiermacher's ascription of religion to the realm of feeling marked the start of modern Protestant Christianity's emphasis on 'subjectivity' and its insistence that knowledge of God is inward and experiential and open to all.

Like his friends who frequented Frau Hertz's salon, Schleiermacher was impressed by the significance of human feelings and intuitions in human life – elements in the human make-up which, he believed, the rationalism of the eighteenth century gravely undervalued. Yet Schleiermacher's ascription of religion to the realm of feeling was more than an attempt to find a safe sanctuary for religion in the inner life of human beings. It was rather an attempt to see religion as an indelible aspect of human existence and one without which no human life can be considered complete. What, in the opinion of a recent student of Schleiermacher, Keith Clements, Schleiermacher offers is a 'whole new anthropology of human existence'.[4]

How exactly Schleiermacher understood the feeling that lay at the heart of true religion and of the fully human life is, however, difficult to determine, but it was a feeling, he believed, which was *sui generis*. It is, in his own words:

> the immediate consciousness of the universal existence of all finite things in and through the Infinite, and of all temporal things in and through the Eternal. Religion is to seek this and find it in all that lives and moves, in all growth and change, in all doing and suffering. It is to have life and to know life in immediate feeling, only as such an existence in the Infinite and the Eternal. Where this is found religion is satisfied, where it hides itself there is for her unrest and anguish, extremity and death. Wherefore it is a life in the infinite nature of the Whole, in the One and in the All, in God, having and possessing all things in God, and God in all.[5]

In a later work, *The Christian Faith*, this feeling, which is the essence of what Schleiermacher calls 'the pious consciousness', is more precisely defined as 'a feeling of absolute dependence' (*schlechtin abhängig*).

Eschewing both the traditional metaphysical arguments for the existence of God and Kant's attempt to confine religion within the limits of reason alone, as well as Christian claims to special revelation, Schleiermacher sought to return to what he regarded as the mainsprings of religion by examining what he took to be the basic human experience and the basic human need out of which religion arose. This was the sense which he believed all men and women have that the world constitutes a unity, a harmonious whole and which was also, for Schleiermacher, an awareness of God. The self-consciousness of which Schleiermacher speaks is, he says, in reality, a consciousness of the self in relation to that which is the object of that consciousness – whether that object be nature, other people or society. However, the 'Other', for Schleiermacher, is more than the sum of the 'others' constituted by nature, people or society, for it is a consciousness of the self in relationship to what he calls 'the whole'. The ambiguity in what he is saying lies in the fact that he does not make it at all clear in the *Speeches* whether this is a consciousness of 'the Other' as wholly immanent in the world , as pantheism suggests, or whether it is a consciousness of 'the Other' as ultimately transcending the world, as traditional Abrahamic theism has maintained. He thus lays himself open to the charge brought, for example, by Keith Ward, that if the history of religion from the seventeenth century to the present day is seen as the driving back of faith from history, from the physical world and from the realm of morals, then religion becomes, as Ward thinks it does in Schleiermacher, simply a matter of internal feeling. Ward writes:

> So religion, withdrawing from its claim to give objective truth about the nature of reality in all its aspects, ends by seeking to stimulate certain sorts of inner feeling in those who care for that sort of thing. It becomes an option for Romantic sentimentalists, an aesthetic exercise which has surrendered all claims to objective truth, but which, when tastefully expressed helps to engender a 'basic feeling for the infinite' in sensitive souls.[6]

Keith Clements, however, disagrees. He writes:

> His [Schleiermacher's] emphasis upon the 'emotions' or 'consciousness' was not an attempt to find a safe sanctuary for religion in the inner life, beyond the reach of rationalism and scientific materialism. ... the 'feeling' or 'sense' of God as the Infinite in which all finite things exist, does not subsist in isolation as some self-contained element in human consciousness. It does not live *apart from* artistic or ethical activity, or from scientific or speculative knowledge. In turn none of these activities can flourish without the 'pious consciousness'.[7]

The obvious and, perhaps, deliberate ambiguity in Schleiermacher's position was partly cleared up in *Christian Faith*, published in 1821, in which Schleiermacher adopted a more overtly theistic position. In this work Schleiermacher stated quite unambiguously that not only are the 'feelings' out of which religious faith arises cognitive, in the sense that they tell us something about the nature of the world, but also that the Infinite – his preferred term for 'the Other' – which is perceived in and through the finite, is also perceived as the ground of the world – something which looks suspiciously like the cosmological argument for the existence of God, which Schleiermacher, following Kant, had rejected as an argument, now intuited, as it were, from the inside. We thus see that feelings, for Schleiermacher, are not significant in themselves, but significant because they are a valid response to realities which lie outwith the self. The world is the medium through which the Infinite (God) acts upon us and through which it is apprehended. Unlike his disciple Rudolf Otto, whose own view of what is distinctive in religious experience we shall consider shortly, Schleiermacher maintained that it is the world of normal experience that mediates the Object of the religious consciousness. The problem for Schleiermacher's interpreters has been to ascertain just what that Object is. Is it simply the world considered as a totality or is it an Object which ultimately transcends the world, but which is also active in and through the world and in the souls of men and women? Clements's interpretation of what Schleiermacher says does little to resolve this ambiguity. He writes:

The sense of being utterly dependent is given in and with this experienced world of relatedness. It is a world in which we feel partly, but never wholly, free as personal agents. It is a world in which we feel partly dependent in relation to many objects (other persons, family, nation, and so on). But further, in and with all this, in our openness to what is other than us, we have a sense of ourselves and all else being *utterly* dependent on – what? There is no item in the finite world to which such a feeling is appropriate. It can only refer to the Infinite. God is the correlate of this religious consciousness. This of course is in a way parallel to Kant's argument for God as the inferred lawgiver behind the moral imperative.[8]

This comment fails to resolve the ambiguity in Schleiermacher's position because Clements's claim that the feeling of absolute dependence of which Schleiermacher writes can refer only to the Infinite or God bypasses the question whether the sense of absolute dependence might, in fact, relate not to a transcendent God, but simply to the world considered as an ordered whole. In the *Speeches* Schleiermacher says little about the nature of the Infinite Object perceived in and through the finite, although in his later writings, and particularly in *Christian Faith*, he leaves no doubt that the Spirit – a term which by the time he wrote *Christian Faith* began to replace the impersonal 'Infinite' – which he believed was operative in nature, society and history is personal, although he continued to remain suspicious of an over-rationalised theology, seeking wherever he could to ground theological discourse within the ongoing experience of the life of the Christian church. Theology, as we have said, is, for Schleiermacher, religious experience which has become articulate. It is not, therefore, a description of God as he is in himself, for God is not an Object to be differentiated from other objects, but an articulation of the feelings men and women have of their relationship with the divine apprehended as the ground of both their own being and that of the world. Theology, therefore, at least initially, can speak of God only as he is intuited as the ground of being – an understanding of theology that was developed in the work of Schleiermacher's greatest twentieth-century disciple, the theologian Paul Tillich.

It was in this way that Schleiermacher met the criticism of those Enlightenment thinkers who sought to banish God from their accounts of the workings of the world. Not for him the solutions to the post-Newtonian mechanical account of the workings of the world available in the theology of his day, for neither the Deist solution of making God simply the Cause of the world and the author of the Natural Law, nor Spinoza's equating of God and the world, nor the position of those who allowed that overall the world works according to its own inexorable laws, but who allowed for special, if only very occasional, acts of direct divine intervention, were sufficient. What was needed, Schleiermacher believed, was an entirely new view of the world – human and non-human – as 'grounded' in, but in no way thought of as being identical with, God (or the Infinite). This is not pantheism, but what is today called 'panentheism', a term which we shall meet with again when we come to look at the way a number of contemporary commentators interpret Hegel's view of the relationship between Absolute and finite spirit. It is this primal apprehension of the unity of the world, without which science and, perhaps, even human life itself would be impossible, that, for Schleiermacher, is of the essence of the religious understanding of the world.

Yet Schleiermacher was also a Christian and, as a Christian, he realised that this primal religious understanding was, of itself, an insufficient account of what it is to be religious, and as a Christian he felt bound also to maintain that it was in the historical figure of Jesus that the Infinite was manifested in ways to be found nowhere else. Schleiermacher was no proponent of the Enlightenment notion of 'natural religion', a form of religion which he believed, despite the attempts of many of the thinkers of the Enlightenment to find it in the Confucian tradition in China, has never existed at any time or in any place.[9] For him there exist only the positive historical religions, and it is with these that the Christian theologian must come to terms. His own view is that no religion is wholly in error and, whilst he recognises, as a Christian, the unique redemptive message taught, as he believes, by Jesus of Nazareth, he did not see religions other than the Christian as being totally discontinuous with that religion. For him the Christian religion is the highest form of religion and religions other than the Christian are to be judged by how closely they approximate to the redemptive faith taught by that religion. The adherents of religions other than the Christian might, of course, as indeed have Muslims and Hindus, take up a not dissimilar position with regard to the Christian religion.

Schleiermacher's position has not only been criticised by theologians from within his own religious tradition, it has also been criticised by philosophers suspicious of claims to 'intuition' unsupported by incontrovertible and universally acknowledged evidence. One might also doubt whether the response to the world identified by Schleiermacher as lying at the heart of religion, even if it can be intelligently articulated, which might be doubted, is as natural or as universal a response as Schleiermacher assumes, for not everyone experiences that sense of the unity of the world which, for Schleiermacher, is of the essence of the religion. Indeed many of the Romantics themselves, poets such as Leopadi, Senancour and Lenau, philosophers such as Schopenhauer, and painters such as Hogarth and Goya, for example, felt, and expressed in their art, not a sense of harmony with the world, but a sense of alienation from it. As the eighteenth-century Scottish philosopher David Hume suggested in his *Natural History of*

Religion, when we contemplate the disharmony that exists in the world, polytheism might appear a more natural and rational response than theism, for the world, more often than not, as Hume noted, is experienced not as a unified, harmonious whole, but as an infuriating diversity. He wrote:

> If, leaving the works of nature, we trace the footsteps of invisible power in the various and contrary events of human life, we are necessarily led to polytheism and to the acknowledgement of several limited and imperfect deities. Storms and tempests ruin what is nourished by the sun. The sun destroys what is fostered by the moisture of dews and rains ... sickness and pestilence may depopulate a kingdom in the most profuse plenty ... In short, conduct of events, or what we may call the plan of a particular providence, is so full of variety and uncertainty that, if we suppose it immediately ordered by any intelligent beings, we must acknowledge a contrariety in their designs and intentions, a constant combat of opposite powers, and a repentance or change of intention in the same power from impotence or levity.[10]

A further criticism that has been brought against Schleiermacher is that the near monism implicit in his sense of the oneness and wholeness of the world fails to take into account the reality of evil in the world.

This said, it must be recognised that many theologians at the end of the twentieth century would accept that Schleiermacher's dissatisfaction with the language of traditional theism, and in particular the use in traditional Christian theology of spatio-temporal language to talk about the being of God, is justified, for such language involves the theologian (whether Jewish, Christian or Muslim) in speaking of a God who is 'out there' – a kind of super-object in his own universe. Such talk leads, as Kant argued, to 'the antinomies of pure reason' where language, forged to talk about objects and relationships within the world, becomes meaningless when used to talk about that which is other than or lies beyond the world. Yet Schleiermacher, many theologians would accept, forces them to reconsider the models used to describe the relationship of the Infinite (God) to the finite although they have rarely, for a variety of reasons, accepted his own panentheistic model.

However, the enduring influence of Schleiermacher lies in his attempt to ground theology in religious experience and to identify the specific feeling or sentiment out of which religion arises, and whilst many have criticised the particular range of feelings on which Schleiermacher himself laid emphasis, his work has proved something of a challenge to others to better articulate this feeling and no one took up this challenge more readily than Rudolf Otto, the author of the highly influential *Das Heilige*, translated into English as *The Idea of the Holy*.[11]

– RUDOLF OTTO –

Otto, who was born near Hanover in 1869 and educated first at the conservative evangelical University of Erlangen and then at the more liberal University of Göttingen, was, by the time he came to write *Das Heilige* in 1916, a much travelled historian of religions, well acquainted at first hand with the major religious traditions of the world and, more particularly, with their liturgical practices.[12] On the basis of his wide acquaintance with worship in the world's religions Otto was led to reject Schleiermacher's identification of the essential element in the religious response to the world as 'a feeling of absolute dependence'. Giving Schleiermacher credit for his insight into the *sui generis* nature of the religious response to the world, Otto's criticism was that, whilst the 'feeling' which lay at the heart of the religious response to the world had certain elements in common with feelings of dependence, that is, with feelings of personal insufficiency and impotence, of being determined by circumstance and environment beyond our conscious control, these were analogies rather than descriptions of the essential religious experience. Nor, for Otto, was identifying the essential religious experience simply a matter of distinguishing between relative and absolute feelings of dependence, for the feeling which Otto identified as of the essence of the religious response to the world was not one of dependence, but of 'creature-consciousness'. The paradigm of religious experience, for Otto, was the passage in Genesis XVIII:27 which tells of Abraham's self-deprecation before his God: 'Behold, now I have taken upon me to speak to the Lord, which am but dust and ashes.' Otto's comment on this is that there is more in Abraham's response to the divine presence than 'a *mere* feeling of dependence'. Abraham's response, says Otto, is 'the emotion of a creature, abased and overwhelmed by its own nothingness in contrast to that which is supreme above all creatures'.[13] It is this sense of 'creature-consciousness' that Otto believes lies at the heart of the religious response to the world and it is also, for Otto, a direct cognitive apprehension of the Other. Thus does Otto get round the inherent subjectivism which he saw in Schleiermacher's description of religious experience. As Otto reads Schleiermacher, Schleiermacher can only extricate himself from the subjective nature of his position by postulating a cause of such feelings. Otto on the other hand claims that the sense of 'creature-consciousness' that is the religious experience *per se* 'indubitably has immediate and primary reference to an object outside itself'.[14] We shall be returning to the problems inherent in this claim at the close of this chapter. For the moment we must simply note that it is at this point that Otto's understanding of religious experience begins to merge with that understanding of revelation which, as we noted in the last chapter, surfaced in Protestantism in the nineteenth century, although it has its roots in the claim made by the Reformers that the 'inward testimony' of the Holy Spirit gave to all believers the assurance that they were themselves directly and immediately in contact with the God who revealed himself through the scriptures. Thus the theologian H. H. Farmer, wrote:

> If ... we ask how we would expect such a reality as God to reveal itself to us, the answer can only be that we can have no expectancy of the matter at all: for in the nature of the case there can be no parallels, no analogies on which expectancy might be based. The divine reality is, by definition, unique. Or, in other words, we would expect that if we know the reality of God in respect of this fundamental aspect of His being, at all, we shall just know it, we shall just know that we are dealing with God, the ultimate source and disposer of all things, including ourselves, and there will be nothing more to be said. It will not be possible to describe the compelling touch of God. To anyone who has no such awareness of God, leading as it does to the typically religious attitudes of obeisance and worship, it will be quite impossible to indicate what is meant; one can only hope to evoke it, on the assumption that the capacity to become aware of God is part of normal human nature like the capacity to see light or hear sound.[15]

And the Scottish theologian John Baillie made a similar point in his book *Our Knowledge of God* where he wrote:

> It is not as the result of an inference of any kind, whether explicit or implicit, whether laboriously excogitated or swiftly intuited, that the knowledge of God's reality comes to us. It comes rather through our direct personal encounter with him.[16]

In one of his early works John Hick also claimed that Hebraic faith in God was a far cry from the rationalist proofs of either medieval scholastic philosophy or post-Cartesian rationalism. He wrote:

> Empiricist reasoning is in agreement with the epistemological assumptions of the Bible. Philosophers of the rationalist tradition, holding that to know means to be able to prove, have been shocked to find that in the Bible, which is the basis of Western religion, there is no attempt whatever to demonstrate the existence of God. Instead of professing to establish the reality of God by philosophical reasoning, the Bible takes his reality for granted ... for they [the Biblical writers] were already having to do with him, and he with them, in all the affairs of their lives. God was known to them as a dynamic will interacting with their wills, a sheer given reality, as inescapably to be reckoned with as destructive storm and life-giving sunshine ...They thought of God as an experienced reality rather than an inferred entity ... God was not a proposition completing a syllogism, or an abstract idea accepted by the mind, but a reality which gave meaning to their lives.[17]

Otto would have agreed, although in the early part of *Das Heilige* he is concerned to describe only the most primitive form of the divine – human encounter. Only later in the book does he consider the way in which the primal encounter develops into the full theistic faith of the Abrahamic and other religious traditions.

The primal form of the divine–human encounter, Otto contends, is neither rational nor moral. It is for this reason that he felt it necessary to coin the neologism 'numinous', from the Latin *numen* (sacred), to describe what he took to be the primal religious experience. He wrote: 'accordingly in our enquiry into that element which is separate and peculiar to the idea of the holy it will be useful, at least for the temporary purpose of the investigation, to invent a special term to stand for "the holy" *minus* its moral factor or "moment" and … minus its "rational" aspect altogether.'[18] Otto was not, of course, countenancing irrationality or immorality in religion – a charge that some theologians did indeed bring against him: in fact so frequently was this charge made that Otto felt it necessary to rebut it in a special foreword which he wrote to the second edition of his book. What he sought to make plain in that foreword was that, whilst the rational and the moral are indeed part of what we, today, mean by the 'holy' or the 'sacred', they are only a part, for there is, Otto claimed, in addition, an over-plus of meaning which is non-rational and non-moral and it was this element or 'moment ' in the experience of 'the numinous' with which he was concerned in his book. However, being non-rational this element was ultimately beyond conceptualisation, and 'the experience of the numinous' can, therefore, Otto claimed, only be evoked and not described. He wrote: 'It will be our endeavour to suggest this unnamed Something to the reader as far as we may, so that he may himself feel it', and he adds, 'There is no religion in which it does not live as the real innermost core, and without it no religion would be worthy of the name'.[19] No statement could more clearly proclaim that what Otto was offering was nothing less than a general theory of religion. However, 'creature-consciousness' is only one element of the primal religious experience which it is the purpose of the early chapters of *Das Heilige* to describe and to evoke. Otto describes the complete experience as an experience of a *mysterium tremendum et fascinans* and for a fuller understanding of how Otto interprets the origin and nature of religion it will be necessary to look at what he has to say about this in some detail.

To begin with the *mysterium tremendum*. Otto used the Latin phrase to try to convey a sense of strangeness that would be lost, he claimed, in a literal translation into German. He begins his description of the primal religious experience, however, not with the noun but with the adjective, and by *tremendum* he intends to convey the fact that when we experience the *numen*, we are aware first of its 'awfulness': the object arouses in us feelings of dread akin to, but not to be identified with, natural fear. The feeling Otto is seeking to convey is, he says, analogous to the 'fear' or 'dread' that many experience when they believe that they are in the presence of the supernatural. It is characterised by 'shudders' and by a 'creeping of the flesh' before that which is felt to be 'weird' or 'uncanny'. Had Otto lived in the era of horror films, he might well have used the reaction that many experience when watching these as an analogy to convey the 'dread' (and, as we shall see, also the fascination) that the numinous object arouses in us. In experiencing the *tremendum* aspect of the numinous Otto claims that we are also aware of a sense of 'majesty', of power and might. It is before this majesty that we are conscious of being but dust and ashes – conscious, that is, of the ontological nothingness of the self before the transcendent, over-powering nature of the numinous object. A further 'moment' in the experi-ence of the *tremendum* element in the experience of the numinous is a sense of 'urgency' or 'energy' in the numinous object so that it is dangerous for human beings to approach it.

If we now turn to the *mysterium*, what Otto intends to convey by the use of this term is the fact that the numinous object is ultimately beyond our comprehension. Perhaps the distinction drawn between puzzles, problems and mysteries by the French philosopher Gabriel Marcel might help to elucidate what Otto means here. Puzzles, according to Marcel, are solved by rearranging what we already know; problems by evidence and logical reasoning; mysteries, however, can never be solved, only penetrated: the deeper we penetrate the more we realise that there is more to be known. Mysteries are inexhaustible.[20] With these distinctions in mind, the *numen* can be said, for Otto, to be a mystery which progressively discloses more and more of itself to us, but whose richness can never be exhausted. We see, for example, that the *mysterium* might also be called *mysterium stupendum*, for it is a mystery which arouses stupor and amazement and which strikes us dumb. We are also aware of the fact that it also attracts and fascinates us. This fascination Otto sees in the intoxication, the transport, the ravish-ment induced by religious rituals, as well as in the solemnity and calm of public worship and private devotion and in the sense of peace which this gives. The *numen* also attracts us because it contains what we lack and what we sorely need. Here we see the beginnings of what, refined and developed, will, in the great religious traditions, lead to those experiences associated with mysticism and with the feelings associated with having been 'saved'.

Such, briefly, is Otto's account of the numinous experience which he takes to lie at the heart of all religions. No summary, however, can do justice to Otto's own rich and evocative account of this experience. That it corresponds to feelings or affective states, to use another of Otto's expressions, that many people appear to experience is shown by the immense popularity Otto's work has enjoyed.

That Otto has isolated elements within the religious response to the world that are often neglected by theologians cannot be denied, but it is a big step from recognising a range of feelings associated with religion to postulating, as Otto does in *Das Heilige*, that human beings possess a special faculty, which he terms a 'faculty of divination', by means of which they become aware of both an objective transcendent reality and of its objective value. Otto claims that this 'faculty' is present in all men and women, albeit in differing degrees, and that it is at work throughout the historical development of religion. Although this 'faculty' is manifested at first in feelings which are barely articulated – in shuddering and in creeping of the flesh – it is this 'faculty' which drives human beings to articulate a 'good' known only to religion and which is not to be identified with the moral conscience. This, says Otto, is because 'above and beyond our rational being lies hidden the ultimate part of our nature'. The mystics, he says – and apart from the work under consideration it must also be remembered that Otto also wrote a classic study on *Mysticism: East and West* – referred to it as the deep places of the soul, the *fundus animae*.

We shall be returning to mysticism later in this chapter. For the moment we must note that Otto, drawing on Kant's epistemology, further claims that this 'faculty' has the status of an '*a priori* category' by which the human mind knows God. This is the most contentious part of Otto's entire theory of religion. The 'categories' of the understanding were Kant's answer to the question, posed by David Hume, of how the ways in which we order our understanding of the world – the 'laws' of cause and effect, for example – come to have the *a priori* certainty attached properly only to tautologies and logical arguments. How, Kant asked, was the 'synthetic *a priori*' possible? And his answer was that our experience of the world is filtered through the 'categories of the understanding' which constitute the mental structure by which we order our experience of the world. Whilst there has been much discussion about the actual list of such categories postulated by Kant, such categories as are used in ordering our experience of the world do not have the problematical status possessed by Otto's proposed additional category of 'the divine'. The theistic understanding of the world, as a matter of empirical act, has never had the same kind of certainty attached to it that appertains to Kant's *a priori* categories of the human understanding. However, if we discard Otto's use of the term 'a priori', what he appears to be saying is that the religious response to the world and its elaboration in theology is an activity which depends for its character on an original disposition of the soul – a much more plausible claim and one that places Otto firmly within the mystical tradition – both East and West – which he did so much to elaborate. However, as the Kantian scholar H. J. Paton pointed out, such a predisposition of the soul also requires a Reality other than the soul which the soul apprehends, for without this human beings would simply spin the web of religion, spider-like, out of themselves.[21] There are, of course, as we shall see when we come to consider Feuerbach, those who believe that human beings do just that, but Otto is not one of them. However, if we abandon Otto's attempt to express his theory of religion in terms of Kant's epistemology, the gist of what he claims becomes clearer and it is that there is a primal, *sui generis* apprehension of the super-natural and that this is gradually elaborated in the light of the ongoing and progressive experience of the numinous Object in the religions of the world. This brings Otto back into the mainstream of explanations of religion in terms of experience and revelation. Such explanations are not without problems, but they are problems of a more general kind than the problems generated by Otto's attempt to articulate the experience of the numinous in terms of Kant's categories of the human understanding.

– WILLIAM JAMES –

The next thinker to claim our attention is the American psychologist and philosopher William James, who in the Gifford Lectures delivered before the University of Edinburgh in 1901–2, and published under the title *The Variety of Religious Experience*, offered a much more wide-ranging and a much more complex account of religious experience than was offered by Otto. James's account can now be supplemented by the volumes currently in the process of being published by the Religious Experience Research Unit (RERU) at Manchester College, Oxford.[22]

James was concerned, as Otto was not, to stress the continuity that exists between feelings evoked by non-religious objects and feelings evoked by religion. He wrote:

Consider also the religious sentiment which we see referred to in many books as it were a single sort of mental entity … The moment we are willing to treat the term 'religious sentiment' as a collective name for the many sentiments which religious objects may arouse in alternation, we see that it probably contains nothing of a psychologically specific nature.

There is religious fear, religious love, religious joy and so forth. But religious love is only man's natural emotion of love directed to a religious object; religious fear is only the ordinary fear of commerce, so to speak, the common quaking of the human breast in so far as the notion of divine retribution may arouse it;

religious awe is the same organic thrill which we feel in a forest at twilight or in a mountain gorge, only this time it comes over us at the thought of our supernatural relations; and similarly all the various sentiments that may be called into play in the lives of religious persons ...

As there seems to be no one elementary religious emotion, but only a common store house of emotions on which religious objects may draw, so there might conceivably also prove to be no one specific and essential kind of religious object and no one specific and essential kind of religious act.[23]

James was born in New York in 1842. His father, who had felt deeply the religious and moral problems of his time, had finally found satisfaction in Swedenborgianism, although not, as A. D. Nock wryly remarked, in other Swedenborgians.[24] He would appear to have passed to his son his own rugged individualism to such an extent that, as Willard Perry has remarked in his book *Religion in America*, James was all his life 'attracted to cranks and geniuses and unclassified waifs, none of whom were impounded with the conventional ninety and nine, safely walled in by historic creeds and codes'.[25] Like Schleiermacher and Otto, James was suspicious of religions which overemphasised the rational at the expense of the emotional, affective side of human nature. As he himself said in his final lecture in Edinburgh, religion was, in the last resort, a matter for individuals, rather than for institutions, and that was why he had been 'so bent on rehabilitating the element of feeling in religion and subordinating its intellectual part'.[26]

James, however, was a philosopher as well as a medical practitioner and psychologist, and he tried, therefore, to draw rational conclusions from his exploration of religious experience. But it was the vast number of case studies – many of them drawn from the fieldwork of his younger colleague Starbuck – and the delightful and entertaining way that James recounted these that have impressed his readers. James was also the first thinker of note to attempt to categorise and classify religious experiences and to offer a vocabulary in terms of which these experiences and claims made on the basis of them could be seriously discussed, and it is the terms which he invented to describe the variety of religious experience – the religion of healthy-mindedness, the sick soul, the divided self – which remain with the readers long after they have put down James's book. Yet, as Eric Sharpe has noted, the very titles of James's lectures betray an over-riding concern with the problems of American Protestantism in which a pessimistic Calvinism vied with the more positive religious outlook of the American Transcedentalists led by Ralph Waldo Emerson.[27] However, whilst James's acquaintance with religion was predominantly Christian and Protestant, he does, throughout the *Varieties*, not only make reference to Roman Catholicism, but also shows some knowledge of the Advaita Vedanta religious philosophy being promulgated in the West at the time that he was writing by the Indian guru Vivekananda. His knowledge of religions other than the Christian is, however, limited and this allows him to discern resemblances, but largely to ignore differences.

Unlike James H. Leuba, his younger contemporary in American psychological study of religion, James was not a materialistically minded Positivist seeking to explain away religious experiences as a physiological aberration: indeed, part of the appeal of the *Varieties* lies in the open approach which James adopts to experiences which are claimed to be religious. Yet whilst not doubting the significance of many of the experiences which he describes – including one which he later confessed to be his own – James remains agnostic with regard to the claims that religious experience justifies belief in what he calls the Transcendent. As the last lecture of the *Varieties* makes plain, James is first and foremost a scientist fully aware of the impersonal nature of the scientific explanation of the workings of the world and of incongruity of seeking, at the same time, to interpret the world in terms of personal 'presences' and personal providence. He was also aware of the explanation of religion as a 'survival' of primitive ways of thinking being put forward by many of the leading anthropologists of the day – explanations which we shall be considering in due course. Yet James saw that these two seemingly opposed interpretations of our experience of the world are not necessarily incongruous. He wrote:

> In spite of the appeal which this impersonality of the scientific attitude makes to a certain magnanimity of temper, I believe it to be shallow, and I can now state my reason ... that reason is that, so long as we deal with the cosmic and the general, we deal only with the symbols of reality, but *as soon as we deal with private and personal phenomena as such, we deal with realities in the completest sense of the term.*[28]

Feelings, for James, are no more and no less important than facts – indeed, for him, they are facts in that they record our living experience of the world and without them the vitality, the colour, the richness, the meaning and the 'glory', to use a word James is not ashamed to use, would go out of life. It is for this reason that, for James, faith, and especially religious faith, is a biological necessity, and he believes that the core feeling is the same in all religions. He is, therefore, not much concerned with the particular form that that faith takes, for religious feeling is fundamentally the same no matter where it occurs. For James it is belief that divides the adherents of the world's religions not feeling. He wrote:

> When we survey the whole field of religion, we find a great variety in the thoughts that have prevailed there; but the feelings on the one hand and the conduct on

the other are almost always the same, for Stoic, Christian, and Buddhist saints are particularly indistinguishable in their lives.[29]

This, of course, is not wholly true, for Christian saints, with one or two exceptions, have related to the world in ways in which Buddhists and Stoics, practising non-attachment, have not. Certainly, as James recognises, where belief is concerned religions differ widely, but so do the ways of life associated with those beliefs.

It is when James comes to discuss the 'objective truth' of the claims made by the various religions that his fundamental agnosticism with regard to such claims and, indeed, his antagonism to theological discourse (which, as we have seen, he believes to be divisive) becomes clear. James believes that all religions offer a not similar diagnosis to the ills that they all hold to be endemic to the human condition and he also contends that the solutions religions offer to this diagnosis also have a great deal in common for all believe that this consists in men and women making contact with some higher power or process, with 'the more', as he terms it, which religious people perceive in their experience of the world. It is over the ontological status to be accorded to this 'higher power' that James is agnostic, for he finds himself unable to decide whether theism or pantheism offers the truest account of the operations of such power or powers, that is whether the power active for good in the world is to be thought of in terms of a personal God or gods, or whether, as he puts it, it is to be thought of rather as 'a stream of ideal tendency embedded in the eternal structure of the world'.[30] He also recognises, as he believes that he has demonstrated in the body of his lectures, that religions are most at odds with each other when they speak of the experience of 'union' with this higher power.

James, like Max Müller, the founding father of the newly emerging 'science of religion', looked to this newly emerging 'science' for a solution to the difficulties that he saw in the conflicting theologies of the various religions, for it is the duty of this 'science', he believed, to extrapolate from the body of knowledge which it is acquiring about the religions of the world that 'common body of doctrine' which religions hold in common. James also drew on the knowledge of what he terms 'the subconscious self' (as postulated by Frederic Myers) and hoped that the solution which he had to offer would be in accord not only with the 'science of religions' but also with the newly developing science of psychology. James framed his hypothesis as follows:

> Let me then propose, as a hypothesis, that whatever it may be on its *farther* side, the 'more' with which in religious experience we feel ourselves connected is on its *hither* side the subconscious continuation of our conscious life. Starting thus

with a recognised psychological fact as our basis, we seem to preserve a contact with 'science' which the ordinary theologian lacks. At the same time the theologian's contention that the religious man is moved by an external power is vindicated, for it is one of the peculiarities of invasions from the subconscious region to take on objective appearance, and to suggest to the Subject an external control. In the religious life the control is felt as 'higher'; but since on our hypothesis it is primarily the higher faculties of our own hidden mind which are controlling, the sense of union with the power beyond us is a sense of something, not merely apparently, but literally true.[31]

This, for James, is the core belief at the heart of all religions. The particular, diverse, and often discordant beliefs found in the various religions, he calls 'over-beliefs' and with these he is at a loss. 'Those of us', he says, 'who are not personally favoured with such specific revelations must stand outside of them altogether and, for the present at least, decide that, since they corroborate incompatible theological doctrines, they neutralise one another and leave no fixed results.'[32] Here individuals are free to choose what seems to them the intellectually most satisfying account, provided that they respect the right of others to choose differently – a choice, of course, only open to those who live in the increasingly tolerant and pluralistic West.

James concludes his final lecture by stating his own 'over-beliefs' – beliefs which he recognises will appear to the stauncher adherents of the established faiths as 'sorry under-beliefs'. However, these are not uninteresting, and, with hindsight, can be seen to presage one of the major topics in contemporary theological and religious debate, namely, how best to 'picture' or 'image' God. He also, in a quite remarkable way, presages the views of the psychologist Jung, whose explanation of religion will be considered in Chapter 7. Here is how James summarises his own view of the matter. He writes:

> The further limits of our being plunge, it seems to me, into an altogether different dimension of existence from the sensible and merely 'understandable' world. Name it mystical religion, or the supernatural region, whichever you choose. So far as our ideal impulses originate in this region ... we belong to it in a more intimate sense than that in which we belong to the visible world ... Yet the unseen region in question is not merely ideal, for it produces effects in this world. When we commune with it, work is actually done upon our finite personality, for we are turned into new men, and the consequences in the way of conduct follow in the natural world upon our regenerative change. But that which produces effects within another reality must be termed a reality itself, so I feel as if we had no philosophic excuse for calling the unseen or mystical world real.[33]

This, as we would expect from one of the founders (together with Charles Pierce) of the American school of philosophy known as Pragmatism, is a very pragmatic explanation of religion: religion is what religion does. The problem, however, is that James concentrates on the positive, beneficial, 'regenerative' aspects of religious belief and ignores the downside. Not everyone would agree that the belief that one is in contact with the supernatural has at all times and places been conducive to human welfare in the way that James appears to suggest. Many Humanists would certainly contest the clean bill of health that James gives to the effects of religious experience, pointing to the intolerant and often lethal fanaticism that this has all too often engendered.

It is, however, James's interpretation of the theism in which he himself professed to believe that has caused the most problems, with many Christian theologians doubting whether James can be considered a theist at all. James certainly rejected much in the traditional theism of his day. Yet what he says presages what is rapidly becoming commonplace in contemporary Christian discourse which is today inclined to question the notion of 'objectivity' when used of God and which is, at the same time, as it begins to explore new models to express the relationship between God and human beings, beginning to explore the deep places in the soul and the mystery of human subjectivity in ways previously found rather more in the Eastern than in the Abrahamic religious tradition.

But this aside, it is James's claim that there is an underlying core of religious experience which all religions have in common that has caused the greatest problems for philosophers and theologians. It is, however, a view today more associated with the name of Aldous Huxley than with William James.

– THE MYSTICAL TRADITION –

At the outset of *The Perennial Philosophy*, published in 1946 – the book in which he first put forward the thesis that behind the diversity of religious beliefs found in the world there is a single experience which the mystics of all religions have in common – Aldous Huxley wrote:

PHILOSOPHIA PERENNIS – the phrase was coined by Leibnitz; but the thing – the metaphysics that recognises a divine Reality substantial to the world of things and lives and minds; the psychology that finds in the soul something similar to, or even identical with, divine Reality; the ethic that places man's final end in the knowledge of the immanent and transcendent ground of all being – the thing is immemorial and universal. Rudiments of the Perennial Philosophy may be found among the traditionary lore of primitive peoples in every region of the world, and in its fully developed forms it has a place in every one of the higher religions. A version of this Highest Common Factor in all preceding and subsequent theologies was first committed to writing more than twenty-five centuries ago, and since that time the inexhaustible theme has been treated again and again, from the standpoint of every religious tradition and in all the principal languages of Asia and Europe.[34]

Huxley's book is essentially a thematic anthology of selections from the mystical writings from almost all of the world's religious traditions and what he sought to demonstrate by presenting his argument in this way was the striking similarity, as he saw it, in the accounts of mystical experience the world over. Here, he claimed, was the essence of all religion.

Huxley was by no means alone in his belief that there was a core religious experience underlying the diversity of religious expression found in the world and that this was to be found in mysticism. Rudolf Otto in a seminal study of *Mysticism East and West*, written a decade after *The Idea of the Holy*, wrote, after comparing the thought of the Indian mystic Śankara and the Christian mystic Eckhart – two thinkers whose description of the mystical experience is remarkably similar despite the difference in time and culture that separated them – that 'a deep-rooted kinship ... unquestionably exists between the souls of the Oriental and the Occidental'.[35]

The most thoroughgoing philosophical attempt to show that mystical experience at all times and places has a common core was, however, made by W. T. Stace in his book *Mysticism and Philosophy* published in 1961. The core mystical experience Stace described as a direct apprehension of the unity and ultimately the identity of all things. He wrote:

> The whole multiplicity of things which comprise the universe are identical with one another and therefore constitute only one thing, a pure unity. The Unity, the One, we shall find, is the central experience and central concept of all mysticism, of whatever type, although it may be more emphasised or less in different particular cases, and sometimes not even mentioned explicitly.[36]

It is difficult to know what this means, for to assert that the multiplicity of the things we observe in the world are 'identical' is to use language in a way that goes so far beyond the everyday meaning of the term 'identical' as to descend into nonsense – as Professor A. J. Ayer had no difficulty in demonstrating in the famous passage on mystical language in his book *Language, Truth and Logic*.[37] The most, perhaps, that can be said for this statement is that it is a rather odd way of stating the belief that all things are ultimately aspects of a single reality – a position, as we have seen, that was espoused by Schleiermacher. Stace, however, prefers the formulation of this view as it is found in the opening verse of the Mandukya Upanishad which reads:

> OM. This eternal Word is all: what was, what is and what shall be and what beyond is in eternity. All is OM. Brahman is all and Atman is Brahman.[38]

But not all mystics stress the identity of the self and whatever it is that constitutes Ultimate Reality and thinkers other than Huxley and Stace have stressed not the unity but rather the variety of mystical experience – and none more so than the late Spalding Professor of Eastern Religions and Ethics at Oxford, Robert Zaehner.

In his book *Mysticism, Sacred and Profane*,[39] Zaehner recognises that basic to all forms of mystical experience is an experience of union – though not necessarily of identity – but he recognises, as Huxley and Stace do not, that within the various mystical traditions there are a number of different ways in which union has been understood and a number of different understandings of the Object with which (or with whom) the mystic feels united. The feeling that 'all is one' is only one of a variety of mystical experiences and, for Zaehner, it is one that need not necessarily be religious in the common understanding of that term. The heightened sense that some people have of being 'at one' with nature – as described for example in Richard Jeffreys' *The Story of My Heart* to which Zaehner makes reference – is one such profane form of mystical experience. However, only where the Object of the mystical experience is felt to be Spirit manifesting itself through nature, as in Wordsworth's well-known *Lines Composed a Few Miles above Tintern Abbey*, can we speak, according to Zaehner, of the mystical experience as 'religious'. For this form of mystical experience Zaehner reserves the term 'pantheism', the view that all is God and God is all, expressed in Spinoza's phrase *Deus sive natura* as well as in the claim that 'all is Brahman' which was the claim made in the Upanishad quoted by Stace. Not all Upanishads, however, assert the identity of the self and Brahman.

For the profane experience of unity with the world Zaehner uses the term 'pan-en-hen-ism' which literally means 'all-is-one-ism'. However, if this experience is regarded as an experience of the fundamental unity and coherence of the all, then it is always possible that, whilst not in and of itself a religious experience, it might well lead, as it did in Schleiermacher's own developed theology, to a recognition of God as the author and guarantor of that unity.

Theistic mystical experience, as found, overall, in the Jewish, Christian, Muslim and in the Indian tradition outwith the Advaita Vedanta, is, argues Zaehner, of an entirely different order. In such experience the ontological distinction between the human soul and God is rarely breached. In mystical discourse in these religious traditions the experience is spoken of as an experience of union with an Object who is regarded as other than the person having the experience. Rarely does the mystic claim to be God, although such claims are not unknown. The great Muslim mystic al-Hallaj came very near to making this claim, as did the Christian mystic Meister

Eckhart. Both, needless to say, ran foul of the religious orthodoxy of their day.

The questions posed by the claim that mystical experience gives us knowledge of reality are legion, but two are of over-riding importance. The first is whether there is a single mystical experience which is interpreted differently within different religious traditions or whether there are different types of mystical experience and, if so, whether they are all equally valid? The second question is whether mystical experience, in whatever form it is found, is what William James called 'noetic', in the sense that it gives us direct knowledge of realities which cannot be had in any other way? This is an important question. Unfortunately it is not one that can be discussed here, for that would take us far beyond the limited parameters of this book. Those interested in the philosophical questions involved in evaluating and interpreting religious experience can find a perceptive and readable introduction in Peter Donovan's book *Interpreting Religious Experience*, where the important point is made that there are no non-interpreted experiences, that it is what we bring to an experience in terms of our wider intellectual and moral commitments that determines, overall, how we interpret a particular experience. This is not to say, of course, that certain experiences might not force us to re-evaluate or change those commitments, but to assess their true significance they must be set within the wider context of a belief system that has been espoused on other grounds. In other words, there is no way we can by-pass the need for a sound natural theology or philosophical world-view.[40]

This position is particularly relevant to the question whether the experiences that mystics have sought through prayer and fasting might not be more easily acquired by the taking of drugs or indulging in practices such as rhythmic dancing and chanting, designed to produce 'exhalted' states of mind – practices found in all of the world's religions – a position eventually espoused by Aldous Huxley. In *The Perennial Philosophy*, as we have seen, Huxley had claimed that the religious or mystical experience, described in the extracts given from the writings of the mystics themselves, could only be had by 'those who have chosen to fulfil certain conditions, making themselves pure in heart and poor in spirit'.[41] Nine years later, when he came to write *The Doors of Perception*, no such conditions were deemed necessary, for by then Huxley had himself had experiences which he identified with those described in *The Perennial Philosophy*, but he had come to these not by practising the austere moral code described in that earlier book, but by taking mescalin, a form of LSD. In the latter work he now claimed that the fundamental religious experience, previously known only to those who fulfilled certain moral and spiritual conditions, could be had by anyone able to acquire a few grains of LSD. It was a gospel that was picked up and preached in the 1960s and 1970s by psychologists such as Timothy Leary and Ronald Laing. For Huxley, Leary and Laing, having a religious experience was simply a matter of inducing the requisite changes in bodily chemistry. No distinction was made between experiences brought about by more traditional means – meditation, prayer and fasting – and those induced by drugs, and perhaps no hard and fast distinction can be made, for drug-induced experiences and physical techniques for producing ecstasy are also widely practised in certain religious cultures. Whether such states gave us knowledge of a reality outwith the mind of those experiencing them is, of course, another problem. This latter claim can and has, of course, been disputed. What has also been disputed, by Zaehner and by others, is that experiences induced by drugs are of the same order as the experiences described in the mystical literature of the world's religions – a major point in the case presented by Zaehner being that drug-induced experiences, unlike what he would regard as genuine mystical or religious experiences, have little or no spiritual or moral content or consequence. This, however, is not a question that can be discussed in this present book and readers must turn to the relevant literature. The problem for those looking at the various explanations which have been offered of religion has to do rather with the place that mystical experience occupies in religion considered as a whole, and more particularly with the claim made by Huxley and others that mysticism is of the essence and the heart of religion. It is a problem that with the renewed interest in mysticism and mystical experiences in the Western world today has become one of the central questions in contemporary study of religions.

What impressed Huxley, as it has impressed others students of religion, is the fact that that mysticism, in some form or other, is found in almost all of the world's religions. It appears, in fact, to be the one feature that all the world's religions have in common, and it is this that led Huxley to argue that it is, therefore, what religions are ultimately about. Yet this claim needs severe qualification, for mysticism is only one aspect of the complex phenomenon that is religion and hardly touches the lives of the vast majority of religious believers who keep religion in being. It is the experience of ordinary believers which is the more likely to take us to the heart of religion rather than the experiences of the few. This is not to say that mysticism is an unimportant element in the complex phenomenon that is religion, only that it is not the archetypal religious phenomenon that many have claimed. Religion serves many ends and fulfils many functions and to try to isolate any one of these and to term it the 'essence' of religion is something which most students of religion have now abandoned. Mystical experience is important – certainly to those who have experienced it – but equally important are the moral demands of religion, the sense of social identity which it engenders, and the hope of better things that it promises both in this world and in the world to come, the meaning and sense of purpose that it gives to life. To isolate one aspect of the multifaceted phenomenon that is religion and to say that this is what religion is about is to show oneself insensitive to what is a complex historical, social, intellectual phenomenon. Like all theories of religion which seek to isolate one element within the phenomenon of religion and raise it to the status of what religion is really about, this theory fails to do justice to the complexity of religion and as such is as reductive as the naturalistic theories which we shall be considering shortly.

I shall bring this survey of religious experience to a close by briefly mentioning the problem that, for many, vitiates the claim that the truth of religious claims can be established on the basis of such experience – whether that of the great prophets, the mystic, or the ordinary believer. I shall do this by reference to a paper by the Australian philosopher C. B. Martin, entitled significantly 'A Religious Way of Knowing'.[42]

This paper offers a critique of the claim put forward by the Protestant theologians H. H. Farmer and John Baillie, referred to earlier in this chapter, who asserted that knowledge of God is mediated not by logical argument, but by direct personal encounter. Martin's point is that claims to religious experience have rather more in common with psychological claims which describe feelings than they have with statements purporting to give us knowledge of the external world. How, Martin asks, can we get beyond statements about our feelings to existential statements about the supposed Object or cause of these feelings when the only thing that I can establish beyond correction on the basis of having certain feelings and sensations is that I have these feelings and sensations? The problem, as Martin sees it, is that, unlike statements about the existence or non-existence of physical objects, statements which purport to record an encounter with a non-natural object, such as a god or a spirit, do not admit of the checks and counter-checks which come into play to resolve disputes about whether or not the physical object that a person claims to perceive actually exists or not. This, of course, might simply show that gods and spirits are not physical objects, and Martin appears at one point in his argument to grant this. But even though gods and spirits are not physical objects, the claims to have encountered them, and the variety of what they have supposedly communicated to those who have encountered them, are so various and contradictory that such claims cannot be accepted without question. Conviction is no guarantee of truth. It needs the support of sound argument. The only way out of this impasse – although Martin himself does not suggest this – is to see religious experience within the wider context of natural theology, that is within the context of an integral intellectual and moral vision of the nature of ultimate reality, and of the meaning and purpose of human life – which is to say that it is possible to interpret an experience, including a claimed religious experience, only within the conceptual apparatus that is brought to it and which must be justified on grounds other than the experience which it interprets.[43]

– NOTES –

1. H. R. Mackintosh, *Types of Modern Theology*, London: Collins, 1937, Fontana edn 1964, p. 36.
2. Peter L. Berger, *The Heretical Imperative: Contemporary Possibilities of Religious Affirmation*, London: Collins, 1979, pp. 64–5.
3. H. G. Schenk, *The Mind of the European Romantics*, Oxford: OUP, 1959, p. 112.
4. Keith Clements, *Schleiermacher: Pioneer of Modern Theology*, London: Collins, 1987, p. 37.
5. Schleiermacher, *Speeches on Religion*, trans. John Oman, New York: Harper Torch Books, 1958, p. 36.
6. Keith Ward, *Religion and Revelation*, Oxford: Clarendon Press, 1994, p. 284.
7. Clements, *Schleiermacher*, p. 36.
8. Ibid., p. 38.
9. For attempts on the part of a number of eighteenth-century thinkers to find Deism and natural religion within the Confucian tradition in China c.f. J. J. Clarke, *Oriental Enlightenment: The Encounter between Asian and Western Thought*, London: Routledge, 1997, pp. 43–52.
10. Hume, *The Natural History of Religion*, sect. II, in Charles W. Hendel Jr (ed.), *Hume: Selections*, New York: Charles Scribner, 1927, pp. 259–60.
11. Rudolf Otto, *The Idea of he Holy*, trans. John W. Harvey, Oxford: OUP, 1924.
12. No biography of Otto has, as yet, been published, but a brief account of his life by Peter McKenzie can be found in Harold Turner's *Rudolf Otto: The Idea of the Holy*, Aberdeen: Centre for the Study of Religion, 1980, pp. 3–7.
13. Otto, *The Idea of the Holy*, pp. 10–11.
14. Ibid., p. 10.
15. H. H. Farmer, *Towards Belief in God*, London: SCM Press, 1942, p. 40.
16. John Baillie, *Our Knowledge of God*, Oxford: OUP, 1939, p. 143.
17. John Hick, *Philosophy of Religion*, New York: Prentice Hall, 1963, pp. 60–1.
18. Otto, *The Idea of the Holy*, p. 6.
19. Ibid.
20. Marcel, *The Mystery of Being*, Vol. 1, trans. G. S. Fraser, and Vol. 2, trans. R. Hague, London: Harvill Press, 1950 and 1951 respectively. The distinctions referred to can be found at the outset of Vol. 1.
21. C.f. H. J. Paton, *The Modern Predicament*, London: Allen & Unwin, 1955, p. 137.
22. C.f. *The Original Vision* (1977) and *This Time-Bound Ladder* (1980), edited by Edward

Robinson, and *A Sense of Presence* (1977), edited by Timothy Beardsworth. All published by the RERU, Manchester College, Oxford.

23. William James, *The Varieties of Religious Experience*, London: Collins/Fontana, 1960, pp. 46–7. All references to the *Varieties* are to this edition.

24. A. D. Nock in his introduction to the Fontana edition of James's *The Varieties of Religious Experience*, p. 17.

25. Willard L. Sperry, *Religion in America*, p. 41; quoted Nock, introduction to Fontana edition of James, *Varieties*, p. 16.

26. James, *Varieties*, p. 478.

27. Eric Sharpe, *Comparative Religion: A History*, London: Duckworth, 1975, pp. 108–12.

28. James, *Varieties*, pp. 475–6.

29. Ibid., p. 481.

30. Ibid., p. 485.

31. Ibid., pp. 487–8.

32. Ibid., p. 489.

33. Ibid., pp. 490–1.

34. Aldous Huxley, *The Perennial Philosophy*, London: Chatto & Windus, 1946; Collins/Fontana, 1958, p. 9.

35. Rudolf Otto, *Mysticism East and West: A Comparative Analysis of the Nature of Mysticism*, New York: Meridian Press, 1957, pp. xvi–xvii.

36. W. T. Stace, *Mysticism and Philosophy*, London, Macmillan, 1961, p. 66.

37. A. J. Ayer, *Language, Truth and Logic*, London: Gollanz, 1936, pp. 118–20.

38. Stace, *Mysticism and Philosophy*, pp. 100, 88, 94. The quotation is from Juan Mascaro's translation of the Madukya Upanishad in *The Upanishads*, Harmondsworth: Penguin Classics edn, 1965, p. 83.

39. R. C. Zaehner, *Mysticism, Sacred and Profane*, Oxford: OUP, 1961.

40. Peter Donovan, *Interpreting Religious Experience*, London: Sheldon Press, 1979, pp. 71–2.

41. Aldous Huxley, *The Perennial Philosophy*, London: Collins/Fontana, 1958, p. 10.

42. C. B. Martin, 'A Religious Way of Knowing', in A. G. N. Flew and Alisdair MacIntyre (eds), *New Essays in Philosophical Theology*, London: SCM Press, 1957, pp. 76–95.

43. This argument is used to great effect by John Bowker in his discussion of the claim that hallucinogenic drugs can induce religious experience. C.f. John Bowker, *The Sense of God*, Oxford: The Clarendon Press, 1973, pp. 133–57.

CHAPTER 4

Religion as Philosophy

The view that the religious beliefs and practices of ordinary believers are inferior to or a less than adequate expression of what religion is truly about is one that has been widespread in the history of religions. Intellectuals, even where they have sympathised with and participated in the rites and rituals of the common people, have often felt uncomfortable, if not downright embarrassed, in so doing. The three thinkers whom I shall now consider – Plato, Kant and Hegel – each in his own way sought to transpose the discourse of religion into what he regarded as the intellectually more acceptable discourse of philosophy. Religion, for these thinkers, whilst not false, was a less than adequate attempt to express what could better and more truly be expressed by philosophy, yet each allowed that the beliefs, rites and rituals of traditional faith were necessary for those who were not as sophisticated as themselves.

– PLATO –

What Plato (c. 439–347 BCE) thought about the religion of his day is difficult to determine. Whilst the religious philosophy which he developed towards the end of his life was far removed from popular religion, even in the *Laws*, his last work, he continued to express the view, which he had put forward earlier in the *Republic*, that it was the duty of the state to promote the cults of the gods as conducive to both private and public morality. However, at other places in his writings, he appears to have had little sympathy with traditional Greek mythology, preferring, as he did in the *Timaeus*, to put forward an alternative mythology of his own.[1] Perhaps, as Harry Lesser has surmised, Plato 'regarded all mythologies and cults as metaphorical expressions of religious truth, necessary for the non-philosophical majority to make contact with the divine, so that it does not matter which one a particular society adopts'.[2] In Plato's own alternative mythology, whilst the world is conceived as having been brought into being out of pre-existing matter by a Divine Craftsman or Demiurge, the model from which the Craftsman worked was that of the pre-existent world of the Forms of which the Craftsman was aware, but which he himself had not created. Plato's 'Divine Craftsman' is thus far removed from the God of the Abrahamic tradition. The world was thus an imperfect copy of a more perfect world, the world of the Forms. Further, since Plato assumed that order is good in and of itself, he also held that the Form of the Good is the supreme Form and the Form in which all other Forms participate. Whether Plato thought of the Form of the Good as being in any sense God is, however, difficult to determine, although his remarks at 508 of the *Republic* lends support to the view that he did. What we do know, however, is that the tradition which took its inspiration from his philosophy, and in particular the neo-Platonic tradition founded by Plotinus in the third century CE, as well as the many attempts within the Christian tradition to develop a Christian Platonism, certainly drew this conclusion. The Form of the Good, however, is not the God who rules and orders the world, for this, for Plato, was not a Form but a Soul, what in the *Timaeus* he called the 'World Soul', and which is best thought of as that intelligence or rationality which is diffused throughout the world and present supremely in God or the gods, as well as to a lesser degree in men and women – a view we shall meet with again when we come to consider Hegel's philosophy of Spirit and which also has parallels to the Advaita Vedanta to which it might, indeed, owe its origin.[3] How Plato understood the relationship between the 'World Soul', the 'Form of the Good', the gods, and the individual souls of men and women is one of the most difficult things to establish in his entire philosophy. What, however, is certain is that Plato thought of the World of the Forms as the true home of human beings, or at least of that element in human beings that constitutes their true being, namely 'the soul', for Plato thought of human beings as being essentially rational souls imprisoned in human bodies in a world from which they craved release.

The soul, according to Plato, contained three elements: the intellect, the conscience or a person's sense of honour and duty, and the passions. Only the first element, the rational intellect, was immortal, driven by a 'desire' (*eros*) for 'the good' and destined to achieve final bliss only when this desire has been realised. Like his master, Socrates, and the Pythagorean philosophers by whom he was also influenced, Plato believed that this element in the soul was divine, in the sense that it was immortal, having existed before its 'imprisonment' in the body and continuing to exist after the death of the body. The soul's true home is the world of the Forms, not this present world in which it is imprisoned and in which it must, before it returns to its true home, undergo a series of rebirths. The link with the Indian doctrine of *samsara* is undeniable, although how Plato got this world-view is a matter of ongoing debate among historians of ancient philosophy. It does, however, provide an early link between the Western and Eastern religious and philosophical traditions and one that some religious thinkers in the West are, today, seeking to develop.

As this world is not the soul's true home, the soul must not only make itself at home in the world, but must, through intellectual and moral endeavour, seek for that knowledge of the Forms and, more particularly, of the Form of the Good, which constitutes its true destiny and by knowledge of which it achieves release from imprisonment in this world. This knowledge, for Plato, comes through anamnesis or recollection, which demonstrates that the soul has known the Forms in a previous existence and is 'reminded' of them by perceiving the Forms as these are reflected in the things of this world. Philosophy, for Plato, is, therefore, a religious and, indeed, a mystical quest, in which the soul ascends from the world of the senses to what is both an intellectual intuition and a mystical vision of the world of the Forms.[4] It is a vision which has haunted religious thinkers in both the Christian and the Islamic traditions to the present day.

Consequent upon the criticism levelled against the anthropomorphism, the supernaturalism, and the exclusivity of the Christian religion by the thinkers of the European Enlightenment, the feeling that the Christian religion needed to be recast in order to bring it into accord with both reason and with natural religion was widespread towards the end of the eighteenth century and nowhere more so than in Germany.[5] Two thinkers in particular sought to recast the Christian religion by transposing its basic message, the one into the universal discourse of morality and the other into the universal discourse of rational philosophy. They were Immanuel Kant and George Friedrich Hegel.

– IMMANUEL KANT –

Kant was born in Königsberg in Prussia in 1724 and spent his entire life in that city. His parents, who were of modest means, were members of the well-known Pietist pastor Johann Schultz's congregation, and Kant was subjected during his formative years to Pietistic influence. Pietists emphasised the necessity of 'rebirth' as an experience of personal conversion and salvation which issues in the doing of good works and, whilst Kant reacted strongly against the Pietistic emphasis on feeling, the Pietistic spirit of quiet, earnest moral endeavour remained with him until the end of his life. Kant was educated first at the local grammar school, the *Collegium*

Fridericianum, where Schultz was also the principal, and then at the university where, after a spell as a private tutor, he was appointed to a chair in logic and metaphysics in 1770, a chair which he held until his death in 1804. Woken, as he himself tells us, from his dogmatic slumbers by reading the works of the sceptical Scottish philosopher David Hume,[6] Kant spent the greater part of his life exploring both the scope and the limits of human reason and laying the foundations for a set of moral absolutes which would – at least as formal principles – be independent of all religion, even though, as we shall see, Kant believed that religion was the only context in which these principles ultimately made sense.

Kant offers no explanation for the existence of religion as such. What he offers is an account of what he calls 'true religion', by which he means a religion which will be acceptable to all rational men and women. The religious understanding of the world is, or ought to be, for Kant, an understanding of the world as a moral economy – a far cry, however, from Matthew Arnold's claim that religion was simply 'morality touched with emotion'. There is, in fact, very little, if any, emotion in Kant's understanding of religion, despite his Pietistic background. 'True religion', for Kant, is an attitude of mind in which, as he put it, 'in all our duties we regard God as the universal legislator who is to be reverenced'.[7] By 'reverencing' God Kant meant no more, and no less, than obeying the moral law and acting only from a sense of duty. This, for him, is what 'true religion' is about and he attached little value to expressions of adoration, to prayer, either public or private, or to credal confessions.[8] Why people had come to hold the particular religious beliefs that they did was of no concern to him, although in writings composed towards the end of his life he did allow that the Christian religion, and to a lesser extent other religions also, could be regarded as symbolical and practical ways for the unsophisticated to conceive of the dictates of the practical reason. Thus in Book Two of *Religion within the Limits of Reason Alone* and in an essay written a year later, in 1782, *On the End of All Things*, he suggested that the beliefs and practices of the Christian religion can have useful symbolical and practical value as aids to living the moral life – a view that was re-expressed by the Cambridge philosopher Richard Braithwaite in his 1955 Eddington Memorial Lecture 'An Empiricist's View of the Nature of Religious Belief'.[9]

The Devil, Kant says, symbolises the power of one's own evil choice, Heaven and Hell the radical gulf between the pure and the impure will, and Christ symbolises the moral perfection for which we should all strive. Yet such ideas, for Kant, 'reside only in our morally-legislative reason' and their empirical instantiation, if any, is worthless.[10] The historical Jesus was, therefore, of no interest to Kant, for Jesus is, in his philosophical restatement of Christian Faith, simply 'the archetype of the pure moral disposition' which all men must seek to imitate in themselves. The historicity of Jesus, he writes, 'in no way benefits us practically'. There is thus no place in Kant's philosophy for the central Christian doctrine of the atoning death of the historic Jesus of Nazareth. This too must be reinterpreted to make it fit into Kant's view that whilst the doctrines of religion can be of use to practical reason, they remain incomprehensible to pure reason. Similarly, in *On the End of All Things*, Kant sees the Christian doctrine of the Last Judgement as expressive of the awareness that men and women should have that they ought to act as if, in another life, the judgements of their conscience will be made absolute and unalterable. The doctrine of universal salvation, however, he rejected completely on the grounds that it lessened a person's sense of the ultimate significance of his or her moral actions, although he did recognise that it might also be regarded as expressive of the ultimate triumph of God's love for human beings. Here, as with so many of the doctrines of traditional Christian faith, Kant recognised the limits of speculative reason to think rationally about them and took refuge by referring to them as the 'holy mysteries' of religion, mysteries which may be of practical use to those seeking to live a moral life, but which cannot be understood by speculative reason. The ultimate mystery, for Kant, is the way in which God will bring about the *summum bonum* in which our moral endeavours will reach their final fulfilment. Kant also finds a place for prayer and public worship in his moral reinterpretation of Christian religion, for private prayer can be a way in which one establishes goodness within oneself and public worship a way of making known within the community the seriousness of one's moral endeavour. Similarly, the rite of Baptism can be regarded as the acceptance of the individual into the moral community and Holy Communion as a means of maintaining fellowship within it. But Kant rejected any notion of divine grace and of the power of petitionary prayer, for such notions would, he believed, undermine moral endeavour. It is here that Kant parts company with Christianity (and, indeed, we may add, with most of the world's religions) for he cannot accept that 'God' can in any sense interact with men and women, or be an object of experience or an agent able to influence states and human dispositions.

In the first of his three famous critiques, the *Critique of Pure Reason*, Kant offers a devastating critique of the traditional arguments for the existence of God. However, in his second critique, the *Critique of Practical Reason*, he reinstates 'God, Freedom and Immortality' as postulates of the practical reason on the grounds that whilst morality does not presuppose religion, in the sense that men and women need the idea of God to be able to recognise their duty, it does lead to religion – in Kant's limited understanding of religion – and it does so because he believes that it is only within the context of a world-view which postulates 'God, Freedom and Immortality' that moral endeavour makes sense. He wrote:

> Through the idea of the supreme good as an object and final end of the pure practical reason the moral law leads to religion, that is to the recognition of all duties as divine commands, *not as sanctions, that is, as arbitrary commands of an alien will which are contingent in themselves*, but as essential *laws* of every free will in itself, which, however, must be looked on as commands of the supreme Being, because it is only from a morally perfect (holy and good) and at the same time all-powerful will, and consequently only through harmony with this will, that we can hope to attain the highest good, which the moral law makes it our duty to take as the object of our endeavour.[11]

Morality requires freedom, because human beings can only be said to have acted morally if their actions are freely chosen. It requires belief in God and in immortality because, although it is possible to adduce the claims that morality lays upon us from the *a priori* principles of the practical reason, without these being related to what, in the passage quoted above, Kant describes as 'the highest good', they would make little sense, for Kant did not believe, as he is often credited with believing, that virtue is its own reward. A comment he made in his *Critique of Practical Reason* on the Stoic ethic of duty is very much to the point in this respect. 'The Stoics,' he wrote, 'left out the highest good and the second element [personal happiness], since they placed the highest good only in acting and in contentment with one's own personal worth ... But the voice of their own nature could have sufficiently refuted this.'[12] Ethics, for Kant, only makes sense when it is seen within the wider context of a developmental view of human nature. The moral endeavour, that is the human striving after virtue, only makes sense, for Kant, if there is a life beyond death in which what Kant calls the 'coincidence of virtue and happiness', so patently not the case in this life, comes to fruition. Kant's ethics are thus what are called teleological – that is to say that, for him, moral action is ultimately directed towards an end in which whilst perfectly consistent with his view that whilst we must perform an action because of its intrinsic worth, we must also see moral activity within the wider and more meaningful context of the end to which the striving after virtue is directed. The argument for this reading of Kant has been forcefully put by Keith Ward in his book *The Development of Kant's View of Ethics*. In a section of that book, significantly entitled 'The Teleological Nature of Kantian Ethics', Ward writes:

One aim of sketching the development of the widely-known ethical views of the *Groundwork* has been to counter the idea that Kant is purely a Stoic philosopher of stern duty by placing his ethical doctrines in their wider context of a spiritual and purposive view of reality. Indeed, if religion is understood to consist in metaphysical beliefs about God, the soul and immortality, rather than in specific cults or practices, Kant's ethics is essentially religious.

And after castigating those who have read Kant only in terms of what he says in his three *Critiques* he continues:

> Such interpretations can only arise through ignorance. While Kant held that moral effort is of supreme worth, and while he believed that particular duties were somehow derivable from a purely formal principle, he always held that the pursuit of morality would be senseless if it was not aimed at the realisation of one's natural perfections in a harmonious community. His main ethical concern was with human fulfilment and the conditions of its attainment.[13]

Kant's attempt to isolate the central core of what he considered the essential meaning of religion is, from the point of view of the history of religions, limited, parochial and culture-bound. The slightest acquaintance with the history of religions will show that religion has been concerned with more than moral endeavour – with prediction and control of events in the world, with the search for communion with the divine, with the assuaging of grief, with thankful and joyful celebration, with the quest for holiness, to name but a few. These Kant ignores as either unimportant or, where prediction and control of events in the world and in human affairs are concerned, as superseded by science. Yet it must be borne in mind that Kant does not seek to offer a theory of religion as such, only to reinterpret religion so as to make it acceptable in the post-Enlightenment world. The same can be said of the next thinker whom we shall consider and who also offers a normative, interpretative theory of religion which will, so he believed, make it acceptable to modern men and women – George Friedrich Hegel.

– GEORGE FRIEDRICH HEGEL –

Hegel was born in Stuttgart in 1770, the son of a minor civil servant in the administration of the Duchy of Würtemberg. He was educated at the local *Gymnasium* and then at the famous Lutheran theological seminary, the Stift, in Tübingen, where he read philosophy and theology and, along with his friends Friedrich Hölderlin and Friedrich Schelling, immersed himself in the writings of the European Enlightenment and of the German and Swabian mystics. He began his academic career as a private tutor first in Berne and then in Frankfurt, before, in 1801, joining his friend Schelling at the University of Jena where he taught as a *Privatdozent* (freelance lecturer). It was at Jena that he became acquainted with Friedrich Schleiermacher, who was also teaching at the university, and with whose emphasis on the role of feeling in religion he had little sympathy. He is reputed to have told Schleiermacher that if religion is essentially a feeling of dependence then his dog was the most religious of creatures.[14] When Napoleon captured Jena in 1806 the university was closed and Hegel's academic career appeared to have come to a premature end. Growing financial difficulties forced him to become first the editor of a literary journal and then Rector of the Nüremberg *Gymnasium*. It was, however, during these years that he published two of the four books which would eventually make him the leading German philosopher of his day – the *Phenomenology of Spirit* and the *Science of Logic*. As a consequence of his growing reputation he was appointed in 1816 to the chair of philosophy at Heidelberg and then, in 1818, to the chair of philosophy at Berlin, where he again became a colleague of Schleiermacher, and where he taught until his death in 1830.

Hegel published four major works during his lifetime: *The Phenomenology of Spirit* (1807), *The Science of Logic* (1812–16), *The Encyclopaedia of the Philosophical Sciences* (first published in 1817, but reissued in a revised form in 1827) and *Elements of the Philosophy of Right* (1821). His lectures on the philosophy of history, the philosophy of art and the philosophy of religion, together with his lectures on the history of philosophy, were all published after his death from notes taken by his pupils. Whilst all these works are relevant to understanding Hegel's fundamentally religious conception of reality, it is the *Lectures on the Philosophy of Religion*, which contain the substance of the lectures Hegel gave on this topic at Berlin in 1821, 1824, 1827 and 1831, that give the fullest exposition of Hegel's proposed transformation of religion into philosophy.[15]

At the outset of the 1824 lectures Hegel makes the important observation that a philosophy of religion cannot limit itself simply to the phenomenon of religion for religion is concerned with the relationship of human beings to God and the ultimate referent of a genuine philosophy of religion must, therefore, be God. Having recognised the transcendental reference in religion, Hegel also shows that he is aware of the way in which this referent had been rendered problematical by the philosophers of the Enlightenment and by the critical philosophy of Immanuel Kant in particular. His task, therefore, as he sees it, is to re-establishing religion on a more acceptable philosophical footing by creating a new post-critical philosophy of religion. Hegel came onto the philosophical scene at that critical juncture in European thinking where the philosophy of religion had the choice of either continuing to attempt to re-establish itself on its traditional foundations in the face of the critique which Hume and Kant had brought against it, or to reduce itself to seeking to present religion as nothing more than a mistaken expression of human needs. The former was not without its supporters, particularly within the Roman Catholic Church, whilst the latter would become the assumption of those seeking to understand religion from within the newly emerging 'empirical' disciplines of anthropology, sociology and psychology. Hegel himself, however, sought to offer an entirely new way of overcoming the problems bequeathed to German and European philosophy by the critical philosophy of Kant.

Hegel's earliest thoughts about religion can be found in essays which he wrote, but did not publish, whilst still an undergraduate.[16] In these essays in which he was severely critical of all forms of Christian theology, Catholic and Protestant, he contrasted what he called 'objective religion' and 'subjective religion' to the detriment of the former, a somewhat surprising position for someone who would become a severe critic of both Schleiermacher and the Romantic Movement to take. In one of the earliest of these essays he wrote:

> Objective religion is *fides quae creditur* [the faith that is believed] ... [it] can be systematised, presented in a book or a lecture; subjective religion expresses itself only in feelings and acts ... Subjective religion is all that matters ... Let the theologians quarrel about dogmas, about that which belongs to objective religion ... Subjective religion is pretty much the same in all good human beings, while objective religion can have almost any colour whatever.[17]

In support of his contention that subjective religion, unlike theology, is essentially the same no matter where it is found, Hegel referred to Lessing's drama *Nathan*, in which the protagonists – a Christian, a Jew and a Muslim – are shown to be at one in their view of what constitutes true religion, and the lesson Hegel draws from this is that, whilst we should respect all religions, we should not respect the theologies to which they have given rise and which are parochial and divisive. (Had, one may wonder, William James read his Hegel?) 'The worthiest people,' he wrote, 'are not always those who have done the most speculating about religion, who are given to transforming their religion into theology' and he unequivocally condemned the self-important conceit that characterises the sectarian spirit 'which deems itself wiser than all persons of other parties'.[18] As a substitute for Christian theology Hegel toyed with the possibility of creating a new folk religion which would help human beings to attain an integrated moral personality and resolve the tension between reason and passion which Kant and the Christian tradition had accepted as integral to human nature, but which Hegel, like his friend Schelling, utterly rejected. However, as his thinking matured, he came to see that what was needed was not so much a new religion, as a transformation of the essential truths of religion into the language and concepts of a new philosophy of religion. 'Religion,' he claimed, 'anticipates philosophy; philosophy is nothing but conscious religion.' The question that must be borne in mind is whether, in this transmutation, it is religion that determines philosophy or whether it is not rather Hegel's understanding of philosophy that determines his understanding of religion – a question which was raised by Feuerbach who quipped that in Hegel's philosophy of religion 'speculation only lets religion say what speculation itself has thought and said much better; it determines religion without itself being determined by religion'.[19]

Hegel's philosophy of religion first makes its appearance in *The Phenomenology of Spirit*, published in 1807, which, as the title indicates, focuses on the notion of *Geist* (Spirit). The German term *Geist* can be translated both as Spirit and Mind, but the unmistakable religious and theological overtones in Hegel's use of *Geist* makes 'Spirit' the more appropriate translation. 'Spirit', for Hegel, as is made clear in a number of points in his writings, is the distinctive ontological quality of God. It is also the distinctive ontological quality of human beings – something which allows Hegel to explore the possibility of a non-extrinsic relationship between the divine and the human which will emphasise the essential unity between them without obliterating the differences which undoubtedly exist – the perennial problem, as we have seen, in the writings of the mystics. As Hegel wrote in one of the more interesting of his early essays, 'The Divine in a Particular Shape': 'Faith in the divine is only possible if in believers themselves there is a divine element which rediscovers itself.'[20] And in another early essay, 'The Spirit of Christianity and Its Fate', written in 1799, he wrote: 'The hill and the eye which sees it are the object and subject, but between humanity and God, between Spirit and spirit, there is no such cleft of objectivity and subjectivity; one is to the other only in that one recognises the other.' This is elaborated in the 'The Divine in a Particular Shape' where he wrote: 'How could anything but a spirit know a spirit?' Believers are not illuminated by an external light, but 'on the contrary, their own inflammability takes fire and burns with a flame that is their own'.[21] These early thoughts regarding the relationship between the human and the divine presage the development of Hegel's mature philosophy and they are still, for many contemporary theologians, relevant to reformulating religion in the modern world.

The great central idea of *The Phenomenology of Spirit* is that the different philosophical outlooks which have characterised the history of philosophy, as well as the variety of religions to be found in the world, are but stages in the evolution of Spirit. They are not, therefore, to be regarded in any absolute sense as true or false, but only as immature formulations of a truth not yet fully comprehended and articulated. Religion, for Hegel, is the creation of the imagination, and its natural mode of discourse, therefore, is not rational thought but mythology. *The Phenomenology of Spirit* is the story of the gradual realisation by the human, finite mind of what Hegel calls the 'Absolute Idea' or 'Absolute Knowledge' when the Infinite Spirit comes to full self-knowledge in and through finite human spirits. Hegel's system is, therefore, a form of monism in which finite spirits (men and women) come to realise that they are manifestations of Infinite Spirit – a view which brings Hegel close to ideas enunciated in Indian religious philosophy.[22] There is also rather more than an echo of what Aristotle had said about *Nus* or pure rationality in the *Protrepticus* where he had written that 'Man has nothing divine … except whatever there is in us of *Nus* and reason'.[23] However, where Hegel differs from Shankara and Aristotle, is that, for him, both Infinite Spirit and finite spirit (human beings) evolve together in time. Infinite Spirit only comes to knowledge of Itself through the progressive development of finite spirit. 'God,' he wrote, 'is God only in so far as He knows Himself; His self-knowledge is His self-consciousness in man.'[24]

Hegel's thought, unlike the religious philosophies of India, is grounded in history, and it is in history, and more particularly in the historical evolution of human self-consciousness, that God comes to the realisation of Himself. History, for Hegel, evolves through the gradual unfolding of a single principle (the Infinite Spirit) which manifests itself in a succession of various and contrasted forms, each organic with its predecessor, and all contributing to the final expression of that principle which gives unity to the historical process as a whole. For Hegel, history is also a process which operates dialectically through affirmation, denial and the reconciliation of opposites. It is a process in which both thought and being alike make their way tortuously forward to the goal of the total self-realisation of Spirit, to that state of Being where finite and Infinite become One. Spirit, for Hegel, is pure potentiality (*An-sich-sein*) which, through its self-alienation and self-objectification in nature (*Dasein*) and then through its progressive self-reconciliation in the history of human self-consciousness – that is, in the interlocking histories of art, morality, religion, science and philosophy – finally comes to the full awareness of itself as Absolute Spirit (*Für-sich-sein*).

In the lectures on the philosophy of religion which he gave in 1824 Hegel entered a caveat into what he had to say about God that many of his commentators have overlooked. In these 1824 lectures he stated that what he had to say about God relates not to God as he is in himself, but only to God as he is apprehended by the finite, human mind. His concern, he stated, was not with 'God as such or as object, but with God *as [present] in his community'*, and he continued

> It will be evident that God can only be genuinely understood in the mode of his being as *spirit*, by means of which he makes himself into the counterpart of a community and brings about the activity of a community in relation to himself; thus it will be evident that the doctrine of God is to be grasped and taught only as the doctrine of *religion*.[25]

As this quotation makes clear, Hegel does not presume to lecture on the nature and being of God as God is in himself, but only as God is apprehended by the finite human mind – that is, on God as he has chosen to reveal himself by an act of self-alienation (*selbstentaüsserung*) which is also the supreme and, for Hegel, it would appear, the only act, of self-revelation. It is because Hegel believes history is the working out of consequences of this self-alienation of the Infinite Spirit that he believes history is meaningful. What happens in history, therefore, happens necessarily in the sense that 'the world historical process' could not be other than it is. Yet history, as is made clear in the *Phenomenology*, is fundamentally a history of consciousness, a history in which consciousness becomes gradually more aware of itself until it reaches that stage that Hegel calls 'absolute knowledge' in which it becomes fully aware of itself and of its relationship to God. By 'absolute knowledge' Hegel does not, of course, mean a knowledge of everything. 'Absolute knowledge' is rather knowledge of reality as it really is. The point of the *Phenomenology*, therefore, is that although ostensibly it sets out to trace the path which Mind or Spirit travels on its way to knowledge of the really real, what, Hegel tells us, the human race has really been doing is to watch Mind or Spirit itself as it constructs reality. Absolute knowledge is reached when the mind realises that what it has been seeking to know is itself, that there is no 'beyond' for it to seek to know, nothing, that is, that is beyond its grasp. This is the way in which Hegel resolves the dichotomy in Kant's philosophy between reality as known to the mind and reality as it is in itself. Yet the Spirit that is known is more than the sum total of human or finite minds, for it is Spirit itself that is the true subject and the ultimate object of the historical process.

It is admitted by all commentators on Hegel that his view of the nature of ultimate reality is hard to understand. However, if we take Hegel at his word, what he is saying is that there is nothing outside of Spirit so that individual minds are, in the last resort, but partial manifestations of Spirit. That is why Hegel calls his philosophy *absolute* and not subjective idealism. Ultimately, for Hegel, there is only one Spirit and this, for him, as the *Lectures on the Philosophy of Religion* make clear, is what the religions of the world have called 'God'. This is also made clear in the definitions which Hegel gives of 'spirit' in the *Phenomenology* and in the *Encyclopaedia*. In the *Phenomenology* he wrote: 'that substance is essentially subject is expressed in the notion that represents the absolute as *spirit* – the most sublime concept, one appertaining to the modern age and its religion.'[26] And in the *Encyclopaedia* he claimed that 'Absolute Spirit, while an identity that is eternally self-contained, is likewise an identity that is returning and has returned into itself [from difference].' It is this return that evokes religion which is, says Hegel, 'to be seen as proceeding from and located in the subject no less than proceeding from absolute spirit'.[27] In the *Lectures on the Philosophy of Religion* he wrote that 'Spirit is an eternal process of self-cognition in self-consciousness, streaming out to the finite focus of finite consciousness, and then returning to what spirit actually is, a return in which the divine self-consciousness breaks forth'.[28]

This view of the relationship between finite and Infinite Spirit brings Hegel close, as we have noted, to views found in the Indian tradition and more particularly to views expressed in the Advaita Vedanta philosophy of Shankara. For Hegel, as for Shankara, God is not 'outwith' or 'beyond', but 'within' the universe, and men and women are but moments in the self-realisation of the Absolute which the religions of the world have symbolised by the term 'God'. Yet, as we have said, Hegel parts company with Shankara in that he sees the Absolute's coming to knowledge of itself through finite spirit as a historical process.

In accordance with this view of the nature of reality Hegel stated at the outset of the *Lectures on the Philosophy of Religion* which he gave in 1821 that:

> God is the beginning of all things and the end of all things; [everything] starts from God and returns to God. God is the one and only object of philosophy. [Its concern is] to occupy itself with God, to lead everything back to God, as well as to derive everything particular from God and to justify everything only insofar as it stems from God, is sustained through its relationship with God, lives by God's radiance and has [within itself] the mind of God. Thus philosophy *is* theology, and [one's] occupation with philosophy – or rather *in* philosophy – is of itself the service of God.[29]

The 'absolute idea', says Hegel, 'contains every determinateness', which is to say that it includes in itself every determinate or distinct thing to be found in the world. Nature and Mind are simply different ways in which the 'absolute idea' is manifested. Art, and above all religion, are simply immature ways in which human beings comprehend the 'absolute idea'. When compared with philosophy – or at least with idealist philosophy – they are seen as lower forms of comprehension, necessary, perhaps, for the vast majority of men and women, but less true than the formulations of philosophy in that they belong to the realm of the imagination rather than to the realm of conceptual thought.

The ongoing, developing, self-comprehension of the Absolute Idea is the *leitmotif* of Hegel's entire philosophy. This, of course, is not theism as it has been understood in the Abrahamic tradition. However Hegel might think of God, God is never, for him, conceived as a Being apart from, or beyond, the world. If God exists, he is in the world and human beings partake of his nature. Hegel is thus faithful to one aspect of the Christian thought about the *Logos*, but to one aspect only. In no sense could Hegel have countenanced a theology, such as that of Karl Barth, in which God is thought of as the 'Wholly Other'. To regard God as a Being apart from the world is, for Hegel, to alienate the soul of man. Yet Hegel is not a pantheist – a position he criticises in no uncertain manner in his *Lectures on the Philosophy of Religion*. Perhaps the best term to describe his position is that coined, as we saw in the previous chapter, by Robert Zaehner to describe the position of those mystics who whilst not pantheists – in that they did not maintain that 'all was God' – saw everything as existing 'in God', namely, panentheism – a term which can also be applied to the religious philosophy of Schleiermacher.[30]

Hegel's understanding of the role of religion was, therefore, essentially historical. Religions prepared the way for that philosophical understanding of the relationship of finite and Infinite Spirit which Hegel believed he had finally captured conceptually in his own philosophical system. Hegel, however, had little to say about religions other than the Christian except to chart their place in the evolutionary development of religion which in turn gave place to philosophy. It was an approach that he would bequeath to the nascent discipline of the comparative study of religions and can be found, for example, in the work of Friedrich Max Müller.

Thus what Hegel offers is a history of religions, but it is an ideological and teleological history in which the end point – Hegel's own idealist philosophy – is known from the outset. Religions are, therefore, chartered and mapped on an evolving scale beginning with natural religion and ending, as we have said, with Hegel's own reformulation of the truths contained in the Christian religion – the end point for which the Absolute Spirit has been striving throughout the course of world history.

The details of this history of religions and Hegel's reinterpretation of the doctrines of Christianity and, in particular, of the Christian doctrines of the Trinity, the Incarnation and the Atonement need not detain us – they can be got from his *Lectures on the Philosophy of Religion*. The essential point to notice is that Hegel's theory of religion is a religious theory in that his reinterpretation of the doctrines of the Christian religion and his attempt to place the Christian religion within the wider history of religion are in no sense reductive. How this reinterpretation of religion and of the Christian religion in particular relates to traditional theism has remained a moot point to this day. His followers were equally divided and his thought was sufficiently ambiguous to allow some of his younger followers to pursue a much more radical interpretation of his thought and among these none offered a more radical interpretation of Hegel's legacy than Ludwig Feuerbach to whose understanding of religion we shall turn in Chapter 7.

The theories of religion which we have considered so far are not, of course, theories of religion as that term is used in the empirical sciences, for what they offer is not a theory which seeks to account for the existence of religion at all times and all places, but an account of what those who put them forward regarded as truly religion, which is to say that what is put forward is not so much a theory of what religion is actually about, as a theory of what religion should be about. They are thus both normative and reductive – normative, because they tell us what those who put them forward considered religion should be about; reductive, because the complex phenomenon of religion is reduced to being something rather less than 'true' religion. This was particularly so, of course, in the case of those who sought to transmute language and practice of traditional religion into the more sophisticated language of philosophy. But it is also true of those who put forward a claim to special revelation to account for their own religion and who then sought to reduce religions other than their own, where these are not dismissed out of hand, to being a less than adequate expression of the truth found only in their own religion. It is only when we come to consider the theories put forward from within the disciplines of social anthropology, psychology and sociology that we will meet with theories which claim to account equally for all forms of religion and to these we now turn.

– NOTES –

1. E.g. in Book 3 of the *Republic* and at various places in the *Laws*.
2. Harry Lesser, 'Plato', in John Hinnells (ed.), *Who's Who in World Religions*, London: Macmillan, 1991, p. 328.
3. C.f. J. J. Clarke, *Oriental Enlightenment: The Encounter Between Asian and Western Thought*, London: Routledge, 1997, pp. 37–8; M. L. West, *Early Greek Philosophy and the Orient*, Oxford: Clarendon Press, 1971.
4. C.f. *Republic*, books 5, 6, 7; Plato's *Symposium* and *Phaedo* contain Plato's account of the soul's spiritual quest.

5. The term 'natural religion' was put into circulation by the seventeenth-century English philosopher Lord Herbert of Cherbury and was used to signify the religious beliefs – chiefly belief in God and his moral governance of the world – which he believed were common to all men and women.

6. Kant, *Prolegomena to Any Future Metaphysic*, trans. Lewis White Beck, Indianapolis: Bobbs-Merrill, 1950, p. 8. C.f. also p. ix.

7. Kant, *Religion within the Limits of Reason Alone*, trans. T. M. Green and H. H. Hudson, New York: Harper Torch Books, 1960, p. 1.

8. The only recorded occasions when Kant was known to have attended public worship after adolescence was when he was Rector of his university. Kant did, however, defend the moral utility of churchgoing as an expression of membership of 'the moral community'.

9. R. B. Braithwaite, *An Empiricist's View of the Nature of Religious Belief*, Cambridge: CUP, 1955. This can also be found in John Hick (ed.), *The Existence of God*, New York: Macmillan, 1964, pp. 228–52.

10. Kant, *Religion within the Limits of Reason Alone*, p. 55.

11. Kant, *Critique of Practical Reason*, trans. by T. K. Abbott, London: Longmans, 1873, p. 226.

12. Ibid., p. 132.

13. Keith Ward, *The Development of Kant's View of Ethics*, Oxford: Blackwell, 1972, p. 95.

14. An account of the Schleiermacher–Hegel dispute can be found in Richard Crouter, 'Hegel and Schleiermacher at Berlin: A Many-sided Debate', *Journal of the American Academy of Religion*, no. 48 (March 1980), pp. 19–43.

15. These lectures are now available in a new critical edition in three volumes edited an translated by Peter C. Hodgson and others, c.f. Peter Hodgson et al., *Hegel's Lectures on the Philosophy of Religion*, Berkeley and Los Angeles: University of California Press, 1984–7.

16. A selection of these writings, but with some important omissions, was published in English translation by T. M. Knox in 1948 as *Hegel's Early Theological Writings*, Chicago: University of Chicago Press, 1948. The important missing essays were translated and published by Peter Fuss and John Dobbins in *Hegel: Three Essays, 1793–1795*, Notre Dame: Notre Dame University Press, 1984. The most important of these, together with selections from Hegel's other major works on religion, are now easily accessible in Peter C. Hodgson (ed.), *Hegel: Theologian of the Spirit*, Edinburgh: T. & T. Clark, 1997.

17. Hodgson, *Hegel*, pp. 43–6.

18. Hegel, 'Religion is One of Our Greatest Concerns in Life', in Hodgson, *Hegel*, pp. 46–7.

19. Feuerbach, *The Essence of Christianity*, New York: Harper & Row, 1957, p. xxxv.

20. Hegel, 'The Divine in a Particular Shape', ibid., p. 65.

21. Ibid.

22. For a detailed discussion of Hegel's relationship and indebtedness to Indian philosophy, c.f. Ignatius Viyagappa SJ, *G. W. F. Hegel's Concept of Indian Philosophy*, Rome: Universita Gregoriana Editrice, 1980.

23. Aristotle, frag. 61, quoted Werner Jaeger, *Aristotle*, Oxford: OUP, 1948, p. 49.

24. Hegel, *Encyclopaedia of the Philosophical Sciences*, trans. William Wallace and A. V. Miller, Oxford: Clarendon Press, revised 1970–5, § 564.

25. Hegel, *Lectures on the Philosophy of Religion (1824)*, in Hodgson, *Hegel*, p. 174.

26. Hegel, *Phenomenology of Spirit*, in Hodgson, *Hegel*, p. 122.

27. Hegel, *Encyclopaedia*, § 554.

28. Hegel, *Lectures on the Philosophy of Religion*, in Hodgson, *Hegel*, p. 250.
29. Hegel, *Lectures on the Philosophy of Religion*, in Hodgson et al., *Hegel's Lectures*, Vol. 1, p. 84.
30. This interpretation follows that offered by Robert Whittmore in his article 'Hegel as Pantheist' in *Tulane Studies in Philosophy*, vol. IX (1960), pp. 134–64.

PART II

Naturalistic Theories of Religion

CHAPTER 5

Religion as Human Construct
Some Greek and Roman Theories of Religion

The attempt to get behind the overt claims of religions and to uncover the true and the, more often than not, human origins of religion began, as is the case with so many enquiries within the Western intellectual tradition, in Ancient Greece. This was made possible by the fact that, from about the beginning of the fifth century BCE, certain Greek thinkers managed to distance themselves sufficiently from the practice of religion to ask questions about this and, on the basis of the answers given, to put forward theories to account for the nature, origin, persistence and social utility of religion, theories which anticipate some of the theories which resurface in Europe in the eighteenth and nineteenth centuries and at which we shall be looking in the next chapter.

The earliest recorded suggestion that at least some aspects of traditional religion might have a human origin is the remark made by Xenophanes (c. 570–475 BCE) that men and women make the gods in their own image: 'Men', he asserted, 'believe that the gods are clothed and shaped and speak like themselves.' And he pointedly adds: 'If oxen and horses and lions could draw and paint, they would delineate the gods in their own image.'[1]

However, the most sustained accounts of the human origins of religion in Ancient Greece are those put forward by the much maligned Sophists. Whereas the early Greek natural philosophers had claimed to find the divine (to theion) in physical nature, the Sophists approached the divine through their investigations into human nature. For these philosophers religious belief was, first and foremost, a cultural fact. Contact with cultures other than their own had made the Greeks acutely aware of the diversity of religious, moral and political beliefs in the world. Reflecting on this fact the Sophists were led to ask whether religion, morality and social structures were part of the nature of things, with the consequence that there was, ideally, but one true form of them, or whether these were rather the out- come of custom – that is socially constructed – and were, therefore, relative and subject to revision and change. As they themselves put it: were religion, morality and social structure of nature or of law? Many Sophists had little hesitation in choosing the latter alternative. For them religion, morality and social structure were but human conventions. They thus felt obliged to offer a naturalistic account of their origin.

There is, however, a teasing ambiguity about the first theory of religion that we come across among the Sophists and which was put forward by Prodicus of Ceos, for from the accounts of his views that have come down to us it is impossible to say where Prodicus himself stood on the matter of the truth of traditional religious belief. Although his views can be read as expressing a certain scepticism with regard to the existence of the gods, the Stoics of the Hellenistic age certainly did not see his theory as undermining belief in the gods. Scholars today are not so sure. Prodicus according to Sextus Empiricus, our source for Prodicus' opinions on this matter, maintained that belief in the gods arose out of gratitude on man's part towards the beneficent powers of nature. The earliest gods were, therefore, Demeter (corn), Dionysus (wine), Poseidon (water) and Hephaestus (fire). He also notes that, if this is the case, it is not surprising that the Egyptians worshipped the life-giving Nile. Prodicus also claimed that the pantheon of gods expanded as new occupations, such as agriculture and metal-working, were developed – the founders of these beneficial arts being elevated, after their death, to divine status.[2]

Another thinker who was bothered about the origin of belief in the gods was Democritus. His answer was that the source of these ideas was the apparitions of the gods that men saw in their dreams, more particularly in dreams arising out of a bad conscience in which the gods appeared as those who punish evil deeds. However, Democritus did not write these apparitions off as mere hallucinations, but saw their cause as being real objects actually perceived. These 'objects' he called *eidola* (images) and thought of them as fine membranes which had freed themselves from the surfaces of 'things' and which were capable of stimulating human sense organs. This theory allowed Democritus to recognise the effectiveness of prayer, which he interpreted as a wish on the part of the believer to encounter propitious images and so aid his or her struggle to live a virtuous life.

This, however, is not the only theory that Democritus put forward to account for belief in the gods for, according to Sextus Empiricus, he also held that men and women came by the idea of the gods from contemplating, with feelings of fear and awe, the wonders of nature.

A rather more interesting theory of religion than those we have considered so far is that put forward by the Sophist Critias in his now lost drama *Sisyphus*, fragments of which are found in the works of Sextus Empiricus.

Critias puts forward what we might term a 'policeman theory' of the origin of belief in the gods, for the gods, he claimed, were invented to stop law-lessness. As laws, for the Sophists, were but human conventions, they could see no reason why men should, if they could get away with it, disobey them. Thus many Sophists held that men would act very differently in the absence of the possibility of detection, a view Plato explored in the story of Gyges' ring – which made its wearer invisible – in the second book of his *Republic*.[3] Critias' opinion is that the gods were invented to act as hidden witnesses to deeds done in private in order to provide the necessary coercion for morality. He wrote:

> A time there was when anarchy did rule
> The lives of men, which then were like the beasts,
> Enslaved to force; nor was there then reward
> for good men, nor for the wicked punishment.
> Next, as I deem, did men establish laws
> For punishment, that Justice might be lord
> Of all mankind, and Insolence enchain'd;
> And whoso'er did sin was penalised.
> Next, as the laws did hold men back from deeds
> Of open violence, but still such deeds
> Were done in secret. – Then, as I maintain,
> Some shrewed man first, a man in council wise,
> Discovered unto men the fear of gods,
> Thereby to frighten sinners should they sin
> E'en secretly in deed, or word, or thought.
> Hence was it that they brought in Deity,
> Telling how God enjoys an endless life,
> Hears with his mind, and sees, and taketh thought
> And hears things, and his nature is divine,
> So that he hearkens to men's every word
> And has the power to see men's every act.
> E'en if you plan in silence some evil deed,
> The gods will surely mark it. ...
> So speaking words like these,
> Most cunning doctrine did he introduce,
> The truth concealing under speech untrue.
> ...
> Such were the fears wherewith he hedged men round,
> And so to God he gave a fitting home,
> By this his speech, and in a fitting place,
> And thus extinguished lawlessness by laws.
> ...
> Thus first did some man, as I deem, persuade
> Men to suppose a race of gods existed.[4]

This is the first recorded account of a theory that was to be revived in France in the eighteenth century and which has dominated sociological thinking in the Western world since that time, namely the view that religion is essentially an agent of social control. It was espoused by Polybius in Rome in the third century BCE and it is one of the major justifications offered in defence of the practice of religion by Cotta in Cicero's *On the Nature of the Gods*. As formulated by Critias it has, perhaps, more in common with views current in French aristocratic free-thinking circles in the eighteenth century, where it was held that, whilst unbelief was perfectly acceptable among the upper classes, its spread among the lower classes would be morally and socially dangerous. The eighteenth-century sceptical philosopher the Baron d'Holbach is reputed to have made sure that the doors between his study and the servant's quarters were closed before he and his friends discussed matters appertaining to religion.

But to return to the Sophists. Among them, as Werner Jaeger has remarked, 'we find every shade of the philosophy of religion, from positive defence of religion as a natural endowment of mankind, essentially wise and serving to preserve the State, to the breakdown of the whole realm of ideas which it involves as mere subjective impressions or even as deceptive fictions'.[5] In focusing attention on men and women as the creators of religion, the Sophists made their contemporaries aware of the relativity and subjectivity of religious opinions and of the question mark that this puts against their claim to be anything other than human constructs. It is a question mark that will again be put against religion with the explosion of ethnographic knowledge in Europe from the sixteenth century onwards.

The last naturalist theory of the origins of religion that has come down to us from classical antiquity is the one that is perhaps the most widely known today. It is that advanced in the second century BCE by Euhemer of Messine, and which now bears his name – Euhemerism. Euhemer held that the Greek gods were simply the deified heroes of the Greek folk tradition, a view of the origin of the gods that surfaced again in nineteenth-century Europe in Thomas Carlyle's *Heroes and Hero Worship* (1841).

Not all theories of religion found in Ancient Greece, however, were naturalistic. The theory put forward by the Stoics is essentially religious and as it is a theory that will be revived in Europe during the *Auflklärung* or Enlightenment, particularly by those who are known as the Deists, it may be as well to include it here within this brief survey of (largely naturalistic) theories which have come down to us from Ancient Greece.

The Stoics, like the Sophists, were interested in the variety of religious beliefs to be found in the world, but, unlike the Sophists, they concentrated not on diversity, but on what they took to be the underlying ideas common to all religions – *omnibus innata et in animo quasi insculpta* – and which formed the basis of what they termed 'natural religion' – a term which would be revived towards the end of the seventeenth century by the English thinker Lord Herbert of Cherbury and which would form the basis of both English and French Deism in the next century.

The Stoic school of philosophy was founded by Zeno of Citium (c. 334–261 BCE). It was a philosophy for men in dark times. As the classicist T. R. Glover put it: 'Taught by the Stoic the troubled Roman looked upon himself at once as a fragment of divinity, an entity self-conscious and individual, and as a member of a divine system expressive of one divine idea, which his individuality subserved.'[6] The Stoic philosophers saw unity where others had seen only confusion and that unity was provided, for them, by what they termed the *logos spermatikos*, the generative reason, the divine Word, that is the seed and vital principle whence all things come into being. All things, they believed, came originally from fiery breath (*pneuma diapuron*) and all things will ultimately return to it. The whole universe was, therefore, one polity (*politeia tou cosmou*) by reason of the spirit that was its origin and its life and of the absolute and universal scope of the laws it obeyed: mind and matter, God and man formed one community. The souls of men and women, for the Stoics, thus partook of the very nature of God and stood nearer to the divine than did anything else in the world. Thus all men and women were, in truth, of one blood, of one family, all and each, as the Roman Stoic Seneca put it, sacred to each and all – *Unum me donavit* [sc. *Natura rerum*] *omnibus, uni mihi omnes*.[7] The Stoics were thus the first to express what was later to become a commonplace of many twentieth-century theologians, namely the universal brotherhood of men and women under the universal fatherhood of God. Holding to this belief the Stoics could not but accept that the many and varied expressions of religion found in the world were at bottom expressive of this one fundamental religious idea.

It would be many centuries before a sustained attempt to get at the origins of religion was again mounted within the Western intellectual tradition – not in fact until the eighteenth century. However, when the attempt was made, there were those who sought to revive the Stoic conception of 'natural religion'. There were also those who following the Sophists saw religion as entirely a human construct. It is to this latter understanding of religion that we now turn our attention.

– NOTES –

1. G. S. Kirk and J. S. Raven, *The Pre-Socratic Philosophers*, Cambridge: CUP, 1957, Xenophanes, frags. 14 and 15.
2. Kirk and Raven, *Pre-Socratic Philosophers*, frag. 5.
3. Plato, *Republic*, 2.359–60.
4. Sextus Empiricus, *Ad. Phys.*, 1.54.
5. Werner Jaeger, *The Theology of the Early Greek Philosophers*, London: Oxford University Press, 1967, p. 188.
6. T. R. Glover, *The Conflict of Religions in the Early Roman Empire*, London: Methuen, 1918, p. 38.
7. Seneca, *De Vita Beata*, 20.3, in L. D. Reynolds (ed.), *L. Annaei Senecae Dialogorum Libri*, Oxford: OUP, 1977, Vol. XII.

CHAPTER 6

Religion as Primitive Error

Whilst the proponents of the eighteenth-century European Enlightenment and their followers were in no doubt that the rule of reason had triumphed in themselves, they were also aware that those less enlightened than themselves were still prey to superstition and unreason. Nowhere was this more evident, they maintained, than in the continuance into their own day of the beliefs and practices associated with religion, and no-one better illustrates this attitude than those who took it upon themselves to study the beliefs and practices of so-called 'primitive societies' and among whom, towards the close of the nineteenth century, the names of Sir Edward Tylor and Sir James Frazer were rapidly establishing themselves as pre-eminent. Their attempts to understand the so-called 'primitive mind' would be criticised and developed by, among others, Bronislaw Malinowski, Lucien Lévy-Bruhl and more recently Robin Horton, and we shall be looking at these thinkers too in this chapter.

– SIR EDWARD TYLOR AND SIR JAMES FRAZER –

Tylor was born in London in 1832, the son of a wealthy Quaker industrialist. Dogged by a weak constitution, he neither went to university nor did he enter, as it was expected he would, the family brass-making business. Advised on health grounds to seek a more temperate climate he left home in 1855 and travelled extensively in Central America where his interest was aroused in the indigenous culture of Mexico. Whilst on his travels he kept extensive notes on the beliefs and practices of the people he met and on his return to England he wrote these up and, in 1861, published them as *Anahuac: Or Mexico and Mexicans, Ancient and Modern*. Whilst on his travels he had also met a fellow Quaker, the archaeologist Henry Christy, who communicated to Tylor his own enthusiasm for pre-history. Thus began Tylor's life-long interest in primitive cultures, an interest which would eventually take him, despite his not having studied at a university, first to a Readership and eventually to a Chair in Anthropology at Oxford, a chair which he held until his death in 1917.

Some years before Frazer began work on *The Golden Bough* Tylor had published both his *Researches into the Early History of Mankind* (1865) and his more well-known *Primitive Culture* (1871). Two assumptions governed Tylor's approach to primitive culture. The first was a belief that men and women at all times and places share a common rationality, an assumption that allowed Tylor to have none of our contemporary inhibitions about his ability to penetrate into the thought processes of primitive peoples. The second assumption was that cultures progressed and that later cultures, had, therefore, a truer understanding of the world than had those which preceded them. The first assumption would soon be questioned by the French anthropologist Lucien Lévy-Bruhl, the second would survive intact almost to the end of the twentieth century.

Tylor is best remembered for his theory that the earliest form of religion was what he termed 'animism', the belief that all things, even things today considered inanimate, are possessed of, or can be possessed by, 'soul' or 'spirit'. This theory was first put forward by Tylor, not in his *Researches into the Early History of Mankind* where the problem of religious origins was not raised, but in an article written the following year, in 1866, for the *Fortnightly Review*.[1] It was a theory which Tylor expanded and developed in *Primitive Culture* published in 1871. In that work Tylor advanced the view that religion arose from the speculations of our earliest ancestors on what distinguished a living body from a dead one and from their experience in dreams of the dead whom they had known when they were alive, speculation which led them to postulate the existence of a 'soul' which could exist independently of the body. The belief that people possessed a 'soul' was eventually extended, Tylor held, to cover both animals and inanimate things such as rivers and trees, storms and tempests. It was but a further extension of this belief, Tylor surmised, for primitive men and women to deduce that there were also spirits who were wholly disembodied. Thus it was that belief in gods, goddesses and other spirits came into being and a pantheon of gods, goddesses and spirits created which was modelled on the hierarchy obtaining in human society in which one being, the chief and eventually the king, reigned supreme. Hence the conception found in many primitive societies of a 'high god', a conception which eventually led the human race to monotheism.[2] Religion, therefore, for Tylor, as for many post-Enlightenment thinkers, was seen as little more than a primitive and immature attempt to explain certain facts about the world – facts which could, he believed, be better explained by science.[3] It was, to use his own term, a 'survival' into modern times of a way of explaining the world that was destined to be superseded by science. He wrote: 'But just as mechanical astronomy gradually superseded the animistic astronomy of the lower races, so biological pathology gradually superseded the animistic pathology, the immediate operation of personal spiritual beings in both cases giving place to the operation of natural processes.'[4]

Whether early men and women actually thought along the lines proposed by Tylor we cannot say for, as Sir Edward Evans-Pritchard pointed out, there is not, and probably never could be, any evidence to support Tylor's theory. Tylor's account, says Evans-Pritchard, has, therefore, the character of a 'just-so story' of the 'if I were a primitive man' type of hypothesis. All that Tylor can say is that if he [Tylor] were a primitive man then this is the way in which he would have understood events in the world.[5] It was, however, an exercise in the imaginative re-construction of primitive thought which would capture the attention of the man who, more than any other, would bring the developing anthropological interest in the origins of human thought about the world into the public domain. I refer, of course, to Sir James Frazer, author of *The Golden Bough*.

Frazer was born in Glasgow in 1854 and, after graduating from Glasgow University in 1874, went up to Trinity College, Cambridge, to read Classics and where he was eventually elected to a Fellowship. It was whilst at Trinity that, in 1883, he met and formed a lasting friendship with a fellow Scot, the erstwhile Professor of Oriental Languages and Old Testament Exegesis at the Free Church College in Aberdeen, then a Fellow of Trinity College and the Lord Almoner's Reader in Arabic, William Robertson Smith. It was under Smith's influence that Frazer was led into the uncharted waters of what was to become known as anthropology, a discipline he was to make his own so that the first university chair in the world in the subject was created especially for him.[6] It was Robertson Smith who, as editor of the famous ninth edition of the *Encyclopaedia Britannica*, invited Frazer to contribute articles to that edition on 'Totemism' and 'Taboo', thus re-enforcing an interest in primitive thought that Frazer had already acquired through his having read Tylor's *Primitive Culture* during a walking tour in Greece in the early 1880s. It would be a problem which would occupy him for the rest of his life and the results of which, continually revised and updated, would be brought before the public in successive editions of *The Golden Bough*.[7]

The Golden Bough opens with a problem suggested to Frazer by a line in Ovid, a picture by J. M. W. Turner, some lines from a poem by Lord Macaulay, and some remarks in Servius' commentary on Virgil.[8] In a sacred grove by the lake of Nemi in the Alban hills near Rome a priest, the servant of the goddess Diana and protector of 'the sacred bough' – the mistletoe –

which grew in the grove, prowls around his domain with his sword drawn to protect himself from the designs of his would-be successor who can succeed to his office only by breaking off the golden bough and then slaying him. The unravelling of the meaning of this barbaric archaic ritual was the problem that Frazer set himself in *The Golden Bough*. It turned out to be a daunting task. From the modest two-volume edition of 1890 *The Golden Bough* expanded to three volumes in the second edition of 1900 and to twelve by the time the third and final edition appeared between 1911 and 1915. *The Golden Bough* is thus more than a long, rambling, exegetical footnote to a line in Ovid, for although Frazer's purpose, as he explained it in the letter which he sent to the publisher George Macmillan in November 1889 informing him of his intention to send him the manuscript of a 'study in primitive religion' on which he was engaged, was to explain, by means of 'the comparative method', why the priest of Nemi had to die, and why his would-be successor had, before killing him, to pluck the golden bough, the answer to this question involved Frazer in nothing less than an explanation of how the primitive mind worked. By the time that he had completed the third edition of *The Golden Bough* in 1915 what Frazer, in fact, offered his readers was an evolutionary history of the growth and development of the human mind, an 'epic of humanity' as he himself called it. It was a history in which religion was put firmly in its place as little more than a temporary aberration in the development of human thought about the world.

The Golden Bough, however, opens not with a discussion of religion but of magic,[9] for Frazer believed that it was magic, rather than religion, which offered not only an explanation of why the priest, 'the king of the wood', had to die, but also illuminated the role that the 'king' played during his lifetime. This is not the place to describe in detail what Frazer had to say about magic, although this has proven the most enduring aspect of his work: all that need be noted here is that by the time he published the second edition of *The Golden Bough* Frazer rigidly separated magic from religion and held that the former preceded the latter in the development of human understanding of the world – a view for which Frazer claimed no originality, telling his readers in the preface to the second edition of *The Golden Bough* that he had arrived at this view from his reading of the works of F. R. Jevons, Sir A. C. Lyall and Professor Oldenberg, and in particular the latter scholar's book *Die Religion des Veda*. 'Religion' Frazer defined as the 'propitiation or conciliation of powers superior to man which are believed to direct and control the course of nature and of human life'.[10] Magic, and this was what, for Frazer, distinguished it from religion, did not, as did religion, involve recourse to spiritual beings, for it operated solely in terms of the manipulation of impersonal, if occult, forces and was, on that count, more akin to science than to religion. 'Are the forces which govern the world,' Frazer asked, 'conscious and personal or unconscious and impersonal?' 'Religion, as a conciliation of superhuman powers, assumes the former ... it stands in fundamental antagonism to magic as well as to science ... [which hold that] the course of nature is determined, not by passion or caprice or personal beings, but by the operation of immutable laws acting mechanically.'[11]

Frazer went on to identify two types of magic: homeopathic (or imitative) magic – which was based upon the belief that like produces like, for example copulation with the sacred prostitutes in the Temple will increase the fertility of the land – and contagious magic – which was based on the belief that the effect resembles its cause, for example that mutilating a clay figure of one's enemy will cause actual harm to that enemy. Basing his views on insights which he took from the psychology of his day, Frazer believed that both types of magic were derived from a false application of the association of ideas and both could, therefore, be described as instances of what he termed 'sympathetic magic'. Believing that magic worked mechanically according to a rigid set of procedures, Frazer claimed that magic was more like science than religion, although it was, of course, for him, a false science. Nevertheless, magic had much in common with science in that it was an attempt to establish and use the laws of cause and effect. He wrote:

> Wherever sympathetic magic occurs in its pure unadulterated form, it assumes that in nature one event follows another necessarily and invariably without the intervention of any spiritual or personal agency. Thus its fundamental conception is identical with that of modern science; underlying the whole system is a faith, implicit but real and firm, in the order and uniformity of nature.[12]

This shows considerable insight, but as fieldwork in both anthropology and in the history of religions since Frazer's time has shown, magic is, more often than not, admixed with religious beliefs and practices. Few anthropologists (and certainly no historian of religion) would at the end of the twentieth century separate magic and religion as rigidly as did Frazer. Both would be more likely to talk of 'the magico-religious' rather than of 'religion' or 'magic' alone. As Eric Sharpe has written:

> It is true that in magic man appears to influence the course of events by deliberate means; but it does not follow that there is a direct cause-and-effect relationship between the action and the desired effect, without any intervention from outside. On the contrary, magic involves the harnessing and the manipulation of powers coming from 'beyond', from the 'parallel world' of gods, ghosts and spirits. Magic

does not assume that effect follows cause 'without the intervention of any spiritual or personal agency [as Frazer had claimed]. On the contrary, it sees such agencies everywhere, and does its best to use them, either with or without acknowledgement.[13]

But Frazer's over-riding interest was not in magic as such, nor indeed in religion, but in the development of human thought about the world, and in the second edition of *The Golden Bough* he offered an evolutionary schema of the stages through which he believed human thought about the workings of the world to have passed. As reconstructed by Frazer human thinking about the world went something like this: the first response to the workings of the world and the first attempt to manipulate those workings for the good of society is found in magic; later, as human society developed, there came a time when the more intelligent members of society came to realise that magical practices did not always achieve their ends, and that there were, perhaps, spirits which could help them in their endeavours and so religion, which, for Frazer, as we have seen, was conceived as the propitiation of spirits, was born. Much later still, more intelligent minds saw that 'spirits' too were of no avail and that only by the application of what became known as 'the scientific method', and which had no place for spirits, could reliable knowledge of the working of the working of the world be gained. Religion, which in his later works Frazer barely distinguished from superstition, should, therefore, be seen as a temporary and transitory phase in the on-going evolution of the human understanding of the world. It arose from no deeper springs in human nature than errors in primitive thought. Why such an error should have endured for so long Frazer never tells us, although others, such as Marx and Freud, offered what they believed to be definitive answers to this question, as we shall see in later chapters.

The real target of Frazer's criticism of religion was, of course, the Christian religion and in the preface to the first edition of *The Golden Bough* Frazer compared Christian beliefs to venerable walls mantled over with ivy and mosses about to be destroyed by the battery of the comparative method. At the close of the twelfth volume of the third edition of *The Golden Bough* Frazer stands again in imagination, as he had stood at the outset of the first volume of the first edition, on the shore of Lake Nemi where he imagines he hears the church bells of Rome ringing the Angelus. One religion, he muses, has been replaced by another, yet there is little to choose between them for both are the result of errors in thinking about the world and both are destined to be superseded by science. However, what is not often realised is that Frazer was equally prepared to believe that the much vaunted scientific approach to the understanding of reality might prove as ephemeral as the religious understanding. In the passage which immediately precedes the passage where Frazer 'hears' the Angelus ringing from the Christian churches in Rome he wrote:

> We must remember that at bottom the generalisations of science or, in common parlance, the laws of nature are merely hypotheses devised to explain that ever shifting phantasmagoria of thought which we dignify with the high sounding names of the world and the universe. In the last analysis magic, religion, and science are nothing but theories of thought; and as science has supplanted its predecessors, so it may hereafter be itself superseded by some more perfect hypothesis, perhaps by some totally different way of looking at phenomena – of registering the shadows on the screen – of which we in this generation can form no idea.[14]

Frazer did not, of course, attack the Christian religion directly: rather, he sought to show that the beliefs and practices of the Christian religion were part of a pattern of thought and behaviour in no way different from that of the primitive peoples whose understanding of the world *The Golden Bough* sought to chart. In the preface to the first edition of that work he had stated that its central theme was the conception of the slain god and we must presume, as the anthropologist Professor Mary Douglas has argued, that he meant it. 'The full ambition of *The Golden Bough*,' she has written, 'is to place the sacrificial doctrines of Christianity, together with the doctrines of the Incarnation and of the Virgin Birth and of the Resurrection into the same perspective of totemic worship, together with the lusty antics of the Greek pantheon and with the burnt and bleeding carcasses on [the] ancient altars of the Israelites.'[15] It was this placing of Christian beliefs and practices, and in particular of the Christian doctrine of the dying and the rising god, within the context of primitive belief and practice that the educated, and particularly the educated sceptic, took from Frazer, rather than his speculative reconstruction of the evolution of the human understanding of the world.

The latter theory, in fact, was soon overtaken by new evidence which showed that the evidence that Frazer had quoted in its support was quite other than Frazer had taken it to be. Frazer had stated that 'magic is older than religion in the history of humanity' both because logic demanded it and because it did so among those whom Frazer believed to be the most primitive people known to the anthropology of his day, namely the native Australians or Aborigines. 'Among the rudest savages about whom we posses accurate information,' he wrote, 'magic is universally practised, whereas religion in the sense of the propitiation or conciliation of higher powers seems to be nearly unknown.'[16] This, however, has turned out not to be the case, for more recent research has shown that the Aborigines possess, in fact, a very sophisticated religion.[17]

This was also a criticism which had been voiced by Frazer's great antagonist, the Scottish writer Andrew Lang, who pointed out that neither Tylor's nor Frazer's accounts of what they took to be the most primitive stage in the evolution of religion took cognisance of evidence which, on their own criterion that the most primitive societies of the present provided the best evidence for the earliest history of religion, told against their theories. In his now famous paper on 'High Gods of Low Races', Lang drew attention to the fact that many of those considered among the most primitive peoples actually believed in a supreme being (or high god) who stood far above the lesser gods and spirits – something that Lang had first observed when studying reports of Australian Totemism, and which subsequent field research into almost all known 'primitive' societies has confirmed.

Lang's observation was picked up by the German scholar Fr. Wilhelm Schmidt who used it in support of his own contention that all peoples had at some point in the distant past been the recipients of an aboriginal revelation. Schmidt saw the subsequent history of religion, on that count, not, as had Tylor and Frazer, as one of progress in the refinement and finally in the abandoning of religious ideas, but as a history of degeneration from that aboriginal revelation.[18] However, few outside the Roman Catholic Church have espoused Fr. Schmidt's thesis.

It should also be noted that Lang himself, whilst he accepted that a primitive monotheism could well have been the original religion of the human race, always expressed caution with regard to such speculation. In an essay entitled 'Theories of the Origin of Religion', which he published in 1908, he wrote:

> we cannot possibly go back to the beginning of things, and see man at the stage in which the first germs of religion become apparent in him. They may have been wonder, astonishment, awe, sense of weakness, sense of ignorance, sense of power, sense of vitality, and of personality; but these emotions can scarcely have produced religion till man began to speculate on them and what awakened them; to ask himself for a reasonable account of them, and of himself; and to brood on the ideas of power and personality. He was conscious of power in himself, of animation, of personality, of using things, of making things, of love and hatred. He made experiments in 'sympathetic magic', and persuaded himself that they were successful; that some men were more successful than others; and he evolved the idea of mana, of transcendental power ... Man must have speculated thus, under the stress of a need for answers to his curiosity about himself and the world, before he could begin to be definitely religious.[19]

Others too, from outwith the discipline of social anthropology, criticised the intellectualist approach of Tylor and Frazer maintaining, as did Max

Müller and later Rudolf Otto, that religion arose not as an attempt to understand the workings of the world, but as a primal apprehension of the fundamental character of being. But criticism of this approach was also forthcoming from within the discipline of social anthropology and one such critic was Tylor's pupil and eventual successor in the chair of Social Anthropology at Oxford, R. R. Marett.

Marett did not see primitive men and women as philosophers *manqué* and he did not, therefore, see religion as originating in primitive attempts to explain the workings of the world. Rather, he maintained, primitive religion was, in his own memorable words, 'not so much thought out as danced out'.[20] What he meant by this was that it was the motor side of primitive religion, that is affective states, and not any supposed attempts at philosophical speculation, which gave rise initially to the practices and only later to the beliefs of religion. These affective states were evoked by primitive people's apprehension of an impersonal power or force which they believed to be present both in certain natural phenomena – such as a thunderstorm – and in certain people, such as chiefs, and which Marett, drawing on the accounts of the world-view of the peoples of Melanesia popularised by the Anglican missionary R. H. Codrington, chose to call by the Melanesian word for such force, *mana*. This force was both feared and envied by those who did not themselves possess it and the rites and rituals of primitive religion were seen by Marett as so many attempts to either ward off or obtain this power. Marett also noted that this force or power was recognised in a number of cultures outwith Melanesia and was called by various names such as *wakan* among the native Americans, *ngai* among the African Masai, and *baraka* among the Arabs. Marett thus came to believe that there was an even earlier stage in the primitive response to the world than 'animism' – a stage that he called 'animatism'. Only later, he maintained, did this power become personified as a ghost, a spirit or a god. Unfortunately for Marett's thesis later research confirmed what Codrington had in fact recognised, but which Marett appears to have overlooked, and that was that whilst *mana* appertains to the supernatural, it is also thought of as linked to a personal human or superhuman agent who directs and controls it. Codrington had written:

> All success and all advantage proceed from the favourable exercise of mana; whatever evil happens has been caused by the direction of this power to harmful end, whether by spirits, or ghosts, or men. In no case, however, does this power operate, except under the direction and control of a person – a living man, a ghost, or a spirit.[21]

This caveat notwithstanding, Marett's drawing of attention to the existence of a non-personalised supra-human force in the primal outlook on the world has proven his enduring contribution to the vocabulary of the history and comparative study of religions. The real problem with this thesis is the same as that which bedevilled the thesis put forward by Tylor and Frazer, namely, that there is no evidence to tell us what early human beings thought about the world. It is also difficult to believe, as Marett seems to suggest, that early men and women did things without at all asking why they were doing them – a point made, in fact, in advance of Marett's thesis, by Andrew Lang in the quotation given from his writings above.

Whilst neither Tylor nor Frazer can be regarded as having offered an adequate theory of the origin of religion, this did not stop the next generation of anthropologists and historians of religion from continuing to search for answers to this question. The most interesting answers to emerge from these deliberations were those advanced by the French thinkers Émile Durkheim and Lucien Lévy-Bruhl and by Frazer's disciple, the Polish émigré social anthropologist Bronislaw Malinowski. Durkheim's answer to the question of the origin and nature of religion will be considered in a later chapter.

– LUCIEN LÉVY-BRUHL –

Lévy-Bruhl, who was born in 1857 and died in 1939, was a thinker who, like Marett, had made the transition from philosophy to anthropology and his interest was, therefore, as we might expect, focused rather more on primitive systems of thought than on primitive institutions. His account of what he termed 'the primitive mentality' has not, however, been well received by his fellow anthropologists. This is partly due to his own temerity in not drawing out the implications of what he was saying for thought forms still prevalent over much of the Europe of his own day, something which led him to over-emphasise the differences in the understanding of the world between primitive societies and the people of his own day, and partly to the unfortunate title given to his first major work, *Les Functions mentales dans les sociétés inférieures* (1910), translated equally unhappily into English as *How Natives Think* – titles in which some scholars, wrongly, detected overtones of racial superiority.

Yet the question which Lévy-Bruhl sought to address was an important one and one which is fundamental to all theories of religion, for what troubled this thinker was the fact that those living in 'primitive societies' believed in forces, influences, spirits, and in actions imperceptible to the senses, which to the modern world appeared absurd. For Lévy-Bruhl the 'primitive mind' was obsessed with the supernatural. He wrote:

The attitude of the mind of the primitive is very different [to that of the modern, scientific, European]. The nature of the milieu in which he lives presents itself to him in a quite different way. Objects and beings are all involved in a network of mystical participations and exclusions. It is these which constitute its texture and order. It is then these which immediately impose themselves on his attention and which alone retain it. If a phenomenon interests him, if he is not content to perceive it, so to speak, passively without reaction, he will think at once, as a sort of mental reflex, of an occult and invisible power of which the phenomenon is a manifestation.[22]

Lévy-Bruhl castigated both Tylor and Frazer for explaining the difference between the way in which primitives responded to experience of the world and that prevalent in the European society of their day in terms of errors in thinking on the part of primitives. The difference, he contended, was a difference of *mentalités*, of different modes of thinking. Primitives could not properly be compared with Europeans, as Tylor and Frazer had supposed, not because they were not in the same league as Europeans, but because they were not playing the same game. In other words, primitive thought differed from modern European thought not just in degree but in quality: European thinking was rational, logical and scientific, whilst that of primitives was affective, poetic and mystical – and it was this latter mode of responding to the world that gave rise to religion. It is important to see that this is not primarily a psychological thesis, although at the time Lévy-Bruhl was widely misinterpreted as arguing that the difference between 'primitives' and his own world was due to some innate inferiority on their part and there is a certain ambiguity in his writing that partly accounts for this. However, that it is a misinterpretation two short quotations will make plain. For Lévy-Bruhl – and we must remember that he was a disciple of Durkheim – the differences were in the last resort, to be accounted for in social terms. He wrote:

As the social environment where they live is different from ours, and precisely because it is different, the external world which they perceive differs also from that which we perceive. No doubt they have the senses … and the same cerebral structure. But one must take into account what the collective representations contribute to each of their perceptions. Whatever object with which they are faced, it has mystical properties attached to it which are inseparable, and the mind of primitive man does not in fact separate when he perceives it.

In this way, the exigencies of logical thought are elicited, established and strengthened in each individual mind by the uninterrupted pressure of the social milieu, by means of language itself and through what is transmitted in the forms of language. This constitutes a heritage of which no one is deprived in our society, and which no one can ever have thought of rejecting …

Quite other are the conditions where the pre-logical mentality obtains. No doubt it is also socially transmitted, through the intermediary of language and of concepts without which it could not find expression ... but these concepts differ from ours and, consequently, the mental operations differ also.[23]

The term which Lévy-Bruhl used to describe the mode of thought of primitive peoples and which gave rise to so much confusion about his views on primitive thought was the term 'pre-logical' and, in view of the fact that much of what Lévy-Bruhl had to say about primitive thought has been revived in our own day – albeit without acknowledgement and without the air of condescension that some have detected in Lévy-Bruhl – it will be worth our while to look closely at what he actually said about this.

It will be easier to begin by stating what Lévy-Bruhl did not mean by the term 'pre-logical'. He did not mean by this term that primitive peoples were unintelligent, nor that they were incapable of thinking logically and coherently. What he was trying to say was that primitive thought began from very different premises to those which provide the foundations for modern European scientific thought, premises which Lévy-Bruhl designated by yet another unfortunate term, 'mystical'. He wrote:

> I employ this term [mysticism], for lack of a better, not with allusion to the religious mysticism of our own societies, which is something altogether different, but in the strictly defined sense where 'mystical' is used for the belief in forces, in influences, and in actions imperceptible to the senses, though none the less real.[24]

Seeking an answer to the question why primitives and, by implication, modern religious men and women regard the world in this way, Lévy-Bruhl, like R. R. Marett, claimed that belief in occult forces arises from a predominantly emotive response to events in the world, a response in which the world is not regarded as impersonal and objective, but in which such things as dreams and visions are held to have the same ontological status as the objects of sight and touch. Further, when two objects shared the same emotional and mystical associations, they become closely associated – so close in fact as to be almost identical. Hence men or women in primitive societies, for example, can regard stones and trees not simply as stones and trees, but also as gods or goddesses. This kind of relationship Lévy-Bruhl called 'participation' and it was the prevalence of such views amongst primitive peoples that created what he saw to be a degree of indifference to logical contradictions in the primitive mind – hence his designation of such a way of looking at the world as 'pre-logical' – which allowed men and women in primitive societies to assert that objects are, at one and the same time, themselves and things other than themselves.[25]

A further characteristic of primitive thought for Lévy-Bruhl was what he termed 'communion'. As he saw it, in that primitive men and women's every perception is so heavily invested with emotion, primitives do not so much perceive the world as feel it. Because of this primitives, according to Lévy-Bruhl, see themselves as involved in a continual participation in the world, and because men, women, animals, plants and inert things are equally associated with occult influences, there is a tendency to confront all such objects as if they were personal. Primitive men and women are, therefore, described by Lévy-Bruhl as not so much perceiving the world as communing with it.[26]

This view of the world Lévy-Bruhl contrasts sharply – too sharply some would say – with the predominant view in Western societies where the emphasis is on what can be directly observed, on objectivity, on induction, on logic, and on so separating the person from involvement in an impersonal and objective world as to produce mastery over, rather than commune with, it.

Part of the problem here (and this is also the case with the views of many other early anthropologists), is that Lévy-Bruhl draws too sharp a contrast between the 'primitive' and the 'modern' mentalities, forgetful of the fact that the 'modern' mentality to which he is so committed is a fairly recent phenomenon even within Western societies, an understanding of the world which only begins to predominate in western Europe from the end of the seventeenth century and then only among a cultural and intellectual élite. The description of medieval religious culture in, for example, the early chapters of Sir Keith Thomas's book *Religion and the Decline of Magic* would not be out of place (given a few changes to accommodate the change to a different cultural region) as a description of many of the so-called 'primitive' cultures studied until very recently by social anthropologists. It is for this reason that the contrast might be better described as one between, to use Max Weber's term, two 'ideal types' which can be designated by the terms 'traditional' and 'modern', with due recognition of the fact that both mentalities continue to exist to this day within European and Western cultures.

Yet there is no gainsaying the fact that the view which has come to dominate the contemporary Western world is one in which the world is seen not as a theatre for the interplay of personal forces, but as a realm where impersonal forces hold sway, for only on such a view can science proceed, for an object, unlike a person, can always be related to other objects and appear as part of a group or series. Just so is science able to see objects and events as expressions of universal laws which make their behaviour to a large extent predictable. As the historian of Greek philosophy W. K. C. Guthrie wrote: 'Philosophy began when the conviction began to take shape in men's minds that the apparent chaos of events must conceal underlying order, and that this order is the product of impersonal forces'[27] – a process which was chartered by another British classicist, F. M. Cornford, in his book *From Religion to Philosophy*.[28]

But here it is necessary to inject a note of caution. Although Frazer, Tylor and Lévy-Bruhl, none of whom had ever lived in a so-called primitive society, wrote as if the entire outlook of those living in such societies was characterised by an overwhelming obsession with the activity of spirits, Bronislaw Malinowski, on the basis of his own first-hand experience of living among the Trobriand Islanders of the Melanesian archipelago, noted that the Trobrianders had, in fact, a highly developed knowledge of agriculture in which they were guided, as he says, 'by a clear knowledge of weather, seasons, plants and pests, soil and tubers and by a conviction that this knowledge is true and reliable and that it can be counted upon and must be scrupulously obeyed'. However, he also noted that 'mixed up with all their activities is magic, a series of rites performed every year over the gardens in rigorous sequence and order'. Further, although magico-religious rituals are regarded as absolutely indispensable, and although no-one can tell what would happen without their having been performed since, as Malinowski wryly remarks, no garden has ever been made without them despite thirty years of Christian missionary activity, to suggest to the Trobrianders that the gardens should be made entirely by magic would evoke a smile on the face of the islanders at the simplicity of such a suggestion, for the Trobriander knows as well as anyone that 'there are natural causes and conditions, and by his observations he knows that he is able to control these natural forces by mental and physical effort'. With Lévy-Bruhl's theory of a primitive, non-scientific mentality no doubt in mind, Malinowski continued:

> His [the Trobriand Islander] knowledge is limited, no doubt, but as far as it goes it is sound and proof against mysticism. If the fences are broken down, if the seed is destroyed or has been dried or washed away, he will have recourse not to magic, but to work, guided by knowledge and reason. His experience has taught him also, on the other hand, that in spite of all his forethought and beyond all his efforts there are agencies and forces which one year bestow unwonted and unearned benefits of fertility, making everything run smooth and well, rain and sun appear at the right moment, noxious insects remain in abeyance, the harvest yields a superabundant crop; and another year again the same agencies bring ill luck and bad chance, pursue him from beginning till end and thwart all his most strenuous efforts and his best-founded knowledge. To control these influences and these only he employs magic.[29]

The view that magic (and religion) arises as a response to the untoward, to the inexplicable in human life was not, of course, new. David Hume a century and a half earlier had written that:

> In proportion as any man's course of life is governed by accident ... he increases in superstition; as may particularly be observed of gamesters and sailors ... every disastrous accident alarms us ... And the mind, sunk in diffidence, terror, and melancholy, has recourse to every method of appeasing those secret intelligent powers ... all popular divines ... display the advantage of affliction in bringing men to a due sense of religion.

And Hume quoted in support of what he was saying the classical historian Diodorus Siculus who had written in the first century BCE that 'Fortune has never ... bestowed unmixed blessings on mankind, but with her gifts has ever conjoined some disastrous circumstance, in order to chastise men into a reverence for the gods, whom, in prosperity, they are apt to forget'.[30]

But let us return to Malinowski who, whilst critical of others, had his own theory about the role of religion in human life.

– BRONISLAW MALINOWSKI –

Malinowski was born in Cracow in southern Poland which was then part of the Austro-Hungarian Empire. Although a mathematical physicist and in possession of a doctorate in that subject from the Jagellonian University of Cracow, he was converted – there is no other word – to the study of anthropology by reading Frazer's *The Golden Bough* whilst convalescing from a bout of sickness. He arrived in England in 1910, hopeful of studying with Frazer in Cambridge, but began work in London under Seligman and within three years had so impressed Seligman of his potential for serious work in the discipline that Seligman secured a grant for him to pursue fieldwork in Melanesia. In 1914 he departed for the South Pacific working first in Papua and then in the Trobriand Islands where he remained until May 1916, returning for a second year in 1917–18. His experiences there were a turning point, not only in his own career, but in the embryo discipline of anthropology for, as Edmund Leach wrote in an introduction to a reissue of Malinowski's book *Coral Gardens and Their Magic* in 1965:

> The most crucial innovation was that he [Malinowski] actually pitched his tent in the middle of the village, learnt the language in its colloquial form, and observed directly at first hand ... No European had ever done this before and the kind of ethnography that resulted was completely new. Where his predecessors had spent their time describing the manners and customs and artefacts of a primitive tribe, Malinowski found himself describing a way of life.[31]

Before dealing with Malinowski's understanding of the role of religion in that way of life, we must first look further at his understanding of magic. Life, Malinowski notes, is a difficult business anywhere, but nowhere more so than in a primitive society where life is one long succession of difficulties, dangers and disasters. The question Malinowski sees primitive men and women asking is, 'How one can preserve health and prolong life and avert an untimely death in a world that seem to care not one whit for humans beings?', and Malinowski found the answer, or to be more precise saw the peoples he was seeking to understand finding the answer, in magic. It was this aspect of Trobriand culture more than any other that captured his attention. One fundamental argument runs through Malinowski's *Argonauts of the Western Pacific* (1922) and *Coral Gardens and Their Magic* (1935) and the anthropologist Leonard Glick has reconstructed it as follows:

> The peoples of the Trobriands (and by extension primitive peoples everywhere) live with ordinary human needs … in the forefront of their minds. But ordinary human powers are never adequate to guarantee that these needs will be satisfied, that fears of starvation, disease and disaster will not be realised; and so people turn to magical rites and 'spells' in hope of more firmly securing that which can never be wholly secured. No less rational than we ourselves, they turn to these seemingly inadequate devices not because they are foolish and childish, but because hard empirical experience tells them that life seldom proceeds according to plan and that only by employing every available source of power and control can they anticipate success.[32]

It is in *Magic, Science and Religion* (1925) that this argument is most fully developed. Although the title of this work is Frazerian, Malinowski explicitly rejects Frazer's conception of successive ages of magic, religion and science, contending that no age and no people have ever been without science, however rudimentary that science might be, and further that no people have ever been without some form of religion. The question Malinowski asked himself was why, if all peoples have religion and all have some sort of science, do they seem to depend so heavily on magic? And his answer was that where human powers alone are insufficient to bring about the realisation of human needs, magic helps to fill this gap. It is at this point that Malinowski departs most radically from Frazer and indeed from all earlier sociologists and social anthropologists, for Malinowski does not see the 'primitive' as being in any way different from ourselves in this respect and he rejected the view of Lévy-Bruhl that in turning to magic and religion primitives were in some way possessed of a different and pre-logical attitude to the world.

But if magic, for Malinowski, was really only an adjunct to primitive science, religion played a rather different role than it had for earlier anthropologists in that, for Malinowski, it had to do, not so much with explaining and controlling the world – that for him was the job of magic – but with the important events in life – birth, puberty, marriage and, above all, death. Religion's job was to endow these *rites de passage* with value and meaning.

Religion, unlike magic, was, for Malinowski, as we shall see it was also for Durkheim, essentially a communal affair. For Malinowski religion enshrines and re-enforces social values, but, for him, religion and society are not to be considered identical, as they were in the thought of Émile Durkheim, and thus, whilst he recognised the social dimension of religion, he recognised too that religion must also satisfy something in the individual if it was to play the pre-eminent role in human affairs that it had. Whilst Malinowski certainly offered a functional understanding of religion, maintaining that religion survived because it met needs not met by any other institution in society, he saw too that religion also met individual hopes and fears in a way that magic did not. In all his writings Malinowski reiterates his conviction that, of all the sources of religion, the supreme and final crisis of life, that is death, is of the greatest significance to the individual. Yet unlike Frazer, who saw only fear in man's attitude to death, Malinowski thought fear was only one aspect of a more complex attitude to death which was 'compounded of a passionate attachment to the personality still lingering about the body and a shattering fear of the gruesome thing that had been left over'.[33] Mortuary rites, he believed, reflected this ambiguity, although, ultimately, hope triumphed over fear and the promise of enduring life for the spirit assuaged grief over the death of the body. He wrote:

> And here into this play of emotional forces, into this supreme dilemma of life and final death, religion steps in, selecting the positive creed, the comforting view, the culturally valuable belief in immortality, in the spirit independent of the body, and in the continuance of life after death. In the various ceremonies at death, in commemoration and communion with the departed, and the worship of ancestral ghosts, religion gives body and form to the saving beliefs.[34]

It was in *Baloma* that Malinowski first stated his theory that at the heart of religious belief and practice there lies an inability on the part of men and women to accept the prospect of their own individual extinction. Belief in spirits, therefore, is a perfectly understandable expression of the human need to believe that the essential person, 'the spirit', lives on after bodily death and that such disembodied spirits continue to participate in the ongoing life of the tribe. In a much later essay, 'The Foundation of Faith and Morals', published in 1936, Malinowski cited 'Belief in Providence' and 'Belief in Immortality' as the only two universally held religious affirmations, but stated his own belief that it was in the latter, that is in the conviction that beyond the brief span of natural life there is a compensation in another existence that the essence of religious understanding of the world was to be found. As he wrote in one of the last pieces of writing to come from his pen: 'Religion is … the affirmation that death is not real, that man has a soul and that this is immortal, [and] arises out of a deep need to deny personal destruction.'[35]

S. F. Nagel has claimed that Malinowski was less sure of his ground when he was discussing religion than when he was discussing magic and this is certainly so, an uncertainty which arose from Malinowski's uncritical espousal of Frazer's distinction between magic and religion. This said, however, there is no justification for saying, as Nagel does, that Malinowski simply demonstrates that 'religion was little more than a bigger and better kind of magic', for there are times when, as Malinowski explicitly recognised, religion meets needs in individual and in social life which magic cannot meet, as for example in the telling of myths, in the proclamation and legitimisation of values, and, supremely, in reconciling men and women to death.

One of the chief merits of Malinowski's work was the respect that it showed to the religious data of the peoples whose way of life and outlook on the world Malinowski was seeking to understand. Though Malinowski himself thought that the understanding of the working of the world found in small-scale, primitive societies was a mistaken one, it was, for him, an understandable one. After Malinowski students of primitive societies – even armchair ones – could no longer approach primitive religion in the patronising, dismissive way that had characterised so many eighteenth- and nineteenth-century approaches. The task of anthropological study of religion became, after Malinowski, one of understanding the role of religion within the lives of the peoples who were being studied with the consequent abandoning of the question how people actually came by the particular beliefs that constituted their religious understanding of the world.

Another thinker who did much to change the focus of anthropological study of religion was A. R. Radcliffe-Brown, whose study of *The Andaman Islanders* was published in 1922, the same year in which Malinowski published his *Argonauts of the Western Pacific*. Though differing from Malinowski on topics such as totemism, Radcliffe-Brown's approach to the understanding of religion was much closer to Malinowski than either of them realised at the time for, like Malinowski, Radcliffe-Brown maintained that each element in a religion functions as an integral and component part of a socio-cultural system. But if Radcliffe-Brown's approach is sociological, it is also psychological in that the intervening variable between religious ritual and society is what he called 'sentiments'. He wrote:

> I have tried to show that ceremonial customs are the means by which society acts upon its individual members and keeps alive in their minds a certain system of

sentiments. Without the ceremonial, sentiments would not exist and without them the social organisation in its actual form could not exist.[36]

A view which he reiterated thirty years later when he wrote in *Structure and Function in Primitive Society* that:

> Rites can be seen to be the regulated symbolical expression of certain sentiments. Rites can, therefore, be shown to have a specific social function when, and to the extent that, they have as their effect to regulate, maintain, and transmit from one generation to another sentiments on which the constitution of society depends.[37]

Qualified support, however, for an intellectualist approach to primitive culture, despite the fact that he was a vigorous critic of the speculative theories of Tylor and Frazer on the origin of religion, came from the British anthropologist Sir Edward Evans-Pritchard, Radcliffe-Brown's successor in the chair of Social Anthropology at Oxford. As his pupil Mary Douglas wrote in her study of his thought for the Fontana Modern Masters series:

> If he could alter the categories of his own generation's universe so that primitive peoples would rank in it as fully rational beings, that change would entail others, among them a higher status for religious knowledge in sociological thinking.[38]

Holding that men and women in primitive societies were neither pre-logical, nor a-logical, Evans-Pritchard argued that what was wrong with the thought of men and women in primitive societies was not that their thinking was pre-logical, but that in certain areas it was unscientific in that it was not in accord with the way in which the world actually worked. Relating in his now classic work *Witchcraft, Oracles and Magic among the Azande* how odd the curious explanations of misfortune given by the Azande in terms of bewitchment seemed to him when he first lived among them when, to him, such misfortunes more often than not had obvious natural causes, he gradually, he tells us, learned the idiom of their thought and 'applied notions of witchcraft as spontaneously as themselves in situations where the concept was relevant'.[39] Having thought himself into the logic of their language – and Evans-Pritchard's point was that there was logic in Azande thinking – he too could play the game, but, of course, for Evans-Pritchard it was just a game. Recognising that world-views in both traditional societies and in modern societies are socially transmitted, his overall judgement was that those living in traditional societies were simply operating on inherited false premises. He wrote:

> The fact that we attribute rain to meteorological causes alone whilst savages believe that gods or ghosts or magic can influence the rainfall is no evidence that

our brains function differently from their brains. It does not show that we 'think more logically' than savages, at least not if this expression suggests some kind of hereditary psychic superiority. It is no sign of superior intelligence on my part that I attribute rain to physical causes. I did not come to this conclusion myself by observation and inference … I merely accept what everybody else in my society accepts … This particular idea formed part of my culture before I was born into it and little more was required of me than sufficient linguistic ability to learn it. Likewise a savage who believes that under suitable natural and ritual conditions the rainfall can be influenced by use of appropriate magic is not on account of his belief to be considered of inferior intelligence. He did not build up this belief from his own observations and inferences, but adopted it in the same way as he adopted the rest of his cultural heritage, namely by being born into it. He and I are both thinking in patterns of thought provided for us by the societies in which we live. … It would be absurd, therefore, [he continues] to say that the savage is thinking pre-logically (or mystically) and that we are thinking logically about rainfall. In either case like mental processes are involved and, moreover, the content of thought is similarly derived. What, however, we can say is that the social content of our thought about rainfall is scientific, is in accord with objective facts, whereas the social content of savage thought about rainfall is unscientific since it is not in accord with reality and may also be mystical where it assumes the existence of supra-sensible forces.[40]

The distinction which Evans-Pritchard draws between 'logical' and 'scientific' is given in another article written in 1934, where he wrote:

Scientific notions are those which accord with objective reality both with regard to the validity of their premises and to the inferences drawn from their propositions … Logical notions are those in which, according to the rules of thought, inferences would be true were the premises true, the truth of the premises being irrelevant. A pot has been broken during firing. This is probably due to grit. Let us examine the pot and see if this is the cause. That is logical and scientific thought. Sickness is due to witchcraft. Let us consult the oracles and see who is the witch responsible. That is logical and unscientific thought.[41]

What Evans-Pritchard is saying is that primitive peoples are as rational and logical as men and women in the modern West. The difference lies in the fact that they operate on different premises to those on which the majority of those living in the modern West operate. Here, Evans-Pritchard contended, language often misleads for, as he demonstrated in his study of *Nuer Religion*, the language of the Nuer, as with most primitive peoples, is rich in analogies, figures of speech, symbols and metaphors – something which has often misled prosaic anthropologists such as Tylor, Frazer and Lévy-Bruhl.

Yet there is no gainsaying the fact that primitive peoples, like premodern European peoples, operate on different ontological premises than do modern Western peoples. How they came by these premises is a question that, for Evans-Pritchard, as he stated in his study of *Theories of Primitive Religion*, admits of no firm answer. His position with regard to the place of theories of religion is, however, interesting for, far from rejecting all such theories, he calls for more not less theorising about the role of religion in human life. Religion, for Evans-Pritchard, is not an alternative theory of the working of the world to that put forward by science, but a complimentary discourse which asks and seeks to answer different questions to those asked by science, although he recognises that in primitive societies these are often confused. Standing firm on the ontology of his own Western, scientific understanding of reality he sees religion as essentially a 'construct of the heart' which offers human beings meaning and purpose and makes them, in Mary Douglas's term, socially 'accountable' so that, for him, whilst no society can survive without science, neither can it survive without religion or an ideological substitute for religion.[42]

– ROBIN HORTON –

Another thinker to whom the stark contrast between primitive and scientific thought – or, as he himself prefers to express it, between traditional and modern thought – is anathema, is the historian of science turned anthropologist Robin Horton, who, on the basis of a first-hand acquaintance with traditional societies in Nigeria stretching over thirty years, offers a revised version of what he takes to be the truth in the approach to primitive thought found in the writings of Tylor and Frazer, both of whom, as we have seen, saw primitive religion as essentially an exercise in explaining, predicting and controlling the workings of the world. Horton has sought in a number of papers written between 1960 and 1990, and now conveniently collected in his book *Patterns of Thought in Africa and the West*, to reassert the inherent rationality of the world-view of those living in so-called 'primitive' societies, thus continuing, as he himself recognises, the work of Tylor and Frazer. In the introduction to *Patterns of Thought in Africa and the West* he writes: 'If there is one thesis that unites the essays assembled in this volume, it is that of the deep-seated similarity between much of the world's religious thought, past and present, and the theoretical thought of modern science.'[43] Horton, however, is no post-modern relativist, for, in the last resort, for him, it is science that offers our best hope of understanding and controlling events in the world.

Horton has introduced much needed common sense into the anthropological understanding of religion pointing out the bizarre nature of much that passes for an explanation of religion among many of his fellow anthropologists. He is particularly severe in his criticism of those such as Edmund

Leach who, following Durkheim and Radcliffe-Brown, see religion as little more than a symbolic representation of social relationships, 'a species of poetic jollification rather than as a system of theory and practice guided by the aims of explanation, prediction and control'.[44] He is equally scathing of the Wittgensteinian Fideists who hold that all religious life is 'the expression of an autonomous commitment to communion with Spiritual Being'.[45]

In contrast to symbolical and fideistic interpretations of religion Horton, taking his lead from Tylor, defines religion as belief in 'extra-human personal beings and action in relation to such beings', and he identifies two types of relationship to such beings – those of 'manipulation' and 'communion'.[46] By using the term 'manipulation' Horton seeks to call attention to the way in which religion is used to explain, predict and control the forces which are believed to operate in the world. By 'communion' he seeks to designate that form of religion in which a believer's relationship to the divine is regarded as an end in itself. In religions, as in human relationships, Horton sees a wide range of variation between these two poles, with more or less pure manipulation at one extreme and pure communion at the other and a great many combinations lying between. His thesis is that primitive religion is more concerned with the former than it is with the latter and, as he points out, by using the term 'manipulation' he intends to draw attention to the 'explanation/prediction/control' role played by religions in the ongoing life of individuals and society.[47] It was the restating of this important function of religion in pre-modern societies that allowed Horton, in his well-known paper 'African Traditional Thought and Western Science' published in 1967, to draw attention to the similarity between traditional religious thought and Western science. Distinguishing between the 'explanation/prediction/control' and the 'communion' aspects of religion also allowed him to make sense, he claimed, of much that has happened in Western religious thought since the scientific revolution of the sixteenth century.

Distancing himself from Lévy-Bruhl's account of primitive thought processes, Horton allies himself with the intellectualist approach of Tylor and Frazer in whose understanding of primitive religious thought continuity rather than contrast between primitive and modern thought processes is emphasised.[48] Horton discerns a common quest behind both traditional African and Western thinking about the workings of the world, a quest which he describes as a quest for the unity underlying the apparent complexity of the world, for order underlying apparent disorder, and for regularity underlying apparent anomaly.[49]

In taking traditional African and much religious thought outwith Africa, including pre-modern European thought, at its face value, Horton claims that he is simply giving people the respect due to them by accepting what they say that they are doing rather than, as have so many anthropologists, sociologists, psychologists and indeed theologians, trying to deconstruct the beliefs and practices of such people as a prelude to reinterpreting these beliefs according to some preconceived (and often misguided) ideological notion of their own. This approach leads Horton to see much (though by no means all) religious belief and practice in Africa and, until recently, in the West also, as a theoretical explanation of the workings of the world, leading to attempts to manipulate and control it. In that science, on the whole, does a better job of this, Horton sees the 'manipulative, 'explanation/prediction/control' side of religion declining, both in the West and in traditional societies the world over, and being replaced by a growing emphasis on the 'communion' side of religion. However, as he states in his postscript to the collection of essays to which we have referred, for religion to survive both aspects need to be present and he detects a return to something approaching the explanation/prediction/control model in the writings of a number of contemporary theologians.[50]

This view of the nature of religion brings Horton into conflict both with the Symbolists, as he calls them, of whom the outstanding exponents are Raymond Firth and John Beattie and who see religion as essentially a symbolic way of talking about something else, and with those who, like Peter Winch, can be said to have presaged what at the end of the twentieth century would be called post-modernism and for whom all views are equally true and equally false. It has also brought him into conflict with those Christian theologians (Western and African) who have so over-emphasised certain elements of African traditional religion in an endeavour to make it conform to their own monotheistic understanding of the world as to have misrepresented it.

Despite the fact that the explanations of the working of the world in both African traditional religion and in the religion of pre-modern Europe are couched in the language of the personal activity of gods, goddesses, ancestral spirits, demons and other hidden entities, this does not, for Horton, as it did for Tylor and Frazer, make them any less rational than those offered by contemporary science. There is no inherent reason, says Horton, why an explanation couched in terms of the activity of personal agencies should be any less rational than an explanation couched in terms of the impersonal entities of modern science – atoms, electrons and so forth. If it be objected that personal entities are capricious in ways that the impersonal entities of modern science are not, Horton's reply is to point to the fact that the behaviour of the various gods and goddesses of traditional religion is not as capricious as is often thought. African traditional religion, he contends, espouses a limited number of categories of gods and of other supernatural agencies, such as ancestors and heroes. These agencies, he claims, have prescribed functions and operate in uniform ways. He writes:

> Each category of gods has its appointed functions in relationship to the world of observable happenings. The gods may sometimes appear capricious to the unreflective man. But for the religious expert charged with the diagnosis of spiritual agencies at work behind observed events, a basic modicum of regularity in their behaviour is the major premise on which his work depends.[51]

This is no doubt so, but it needs also to be added that an important feature of the primal understanding of the workings of the world is the sense that those living in traditional societies have of an underlying moral order in the world – offences against which carry near inevitable consequences in the realms of health, wealth and happiness. This is important because it is perhaps here that religion begins to separate itself off from what eventually will become science and offers answers to aspects of the working of the world not at the forefront of the concerns of modern science.

Horton is surely right to draw attention back to the explanation/control function of religion for, at the level of popular piety, this is one of the more obvious features of religion in the pre-modern period the world over, although he is wrong perhaps not to give due weight to the fact that religion also puts different questions to the world than those put by science and which have to do with meaning and purpose. But even if expanded in this way, Horton's understanding of religion, even of religion in so-called primitive societies, would still be limited. If Cantwell Smith, to whose remarks about the term 'religion' we made reference in the Introduction, is right in his contention that, prior to the advent of the modern world, religion was not an element in a culture, but the way in which cultures saw themselves and reality as a whole, then it would be surprising if the explanation/control model exhausted the role that religion plays in such cultures. It is here that what Horton has to say needs to be supplemented by due recognition being given to those features of religion on which the anthropologists who we have considered have laid stress. The reality of the situation is not that we have to choose between the differing roles upon which different anthropologists have focused their attention in studying the religious life of pre-modern peoples, but that we must decide what weighting to give these in our total understanding of religion. Unfortunately, anthropologists themselves have all too often written as if the particular feature on which they themselves focus attention excludes the insights of others and so exhausts the functions of religion not only within the societies they themselves are studying, but in all societies wherever they are found. But societies and cultures differ, and we should be careful not to generalise from the particular so that a prominent feature of the religious life of one society – more often than not the society studied by the anthropologist – is raised to the status of a feature of all societies.[52] For a balanced understanding of religion the insights of all the anthropologists we have considered need to be kept in view.

– NOTES –

1. E. B. Tylor, 'The Religion of Savages', *Fortnightly Review*, 15 August, 1866.
2. E. B. Tylor, *Primitive Culture*, London: John Murray, 1887, 4th revised edn, 1903, Vol. 1, p. 424f.
3. As Robert Segal has pointed out, Tylor never denies that religion is more than a theory about the workings of the world and towards the close of *Primitive Culture* he acknowledges that his task has been 'not to discuss religion in all its bearings, but to portray in outline the great intellectual doctrine of Animism'. C.f. *Primitive Culture*, Vol. 2, p. 445. Yet Tylor so downplays the non-theoretical side of religion as to make it appear to be of no significance whatever. C.f. Segal, 'Paralleling Religion and Science: The Project of Robin Horton', *Annals of Scholarship*, 10 (1993), p. 179.
4. Tylor, *Primitive Culture*, Vol. 2, p. 229.
5. Evans-Pritchard, *Theories of Primitive Religion*, Oxford: Clarendon Press, 1965, pp. 25–7.
6. At the University of Liverpool in 1907. Although Frazer accepted the chair, and although he resided in Liverpool from April to September 1908, giving his inaugural lecture on 'The Scope of Social Anthropology' in May of that year, he quickly realised his mistake in moving from Cambridge and moved back to that city later the same year. He did, however, return occasionally to Liverpool to give lectures. C.f. Robert Ackerman, J. G. *Frazer: His Life and Work*, Cambridge: CUP, 1987, pp. 207–9 and 333, note 39.
7. For a history of the development of *The Golden Bough* and of the influences on Frazer during its writing c.f. Robert Faser, *The Making of the Golden Bough: The Origins and Growth of an Argument*, New York: St Martin's Press, 1990.
8. Quoted Mary Douglas, *The Illustrated Golden Bough*, London: Macmillan, 1978, p. 251. The lines from Ovid are from his *Fasti*, 6. 756, and the lines from Macaulay read:
   The still glassy lake that sleeps
     Beneath Arcacia's trees –
   These trees in whose dim shadow
     The ghastly priest doth reign,
   The priest who slew the slayer,
     And shall himself be slain.
9. The subtitle of the second and third editions of *The Golden Bough* was *A Study in Magic and Religion*. The original subtitle had been *A Study in Comparative Religion*.
10. Sir James Frazer, *The Magic Art*, London: Macmillan, 1932, p. 222.
11. Sir James Frazer, *The Golden Bough*, abridged edn, London: Macmillan, 1922, p. 51.
12. Frazer, *The Magic Art*, p. 220.

13. Sharpe, *Comparative Religion: A History*, London: Duckworth, 1975, p. 92.
14. Frazer, *The Golden Bough*, abridged edn, p. 932.
15. Mary Douglas, *The Illustrated Golden Bough*, p. 11.
16. Frazer, *The Magic Art*, p. 233.
17. For a recent study of Australian Aboriginal religion c.f. Tony Swain and Garry Trompf, *The Religions of Oceania*, London: Routledge, 1994, pp. 19–47.
18. C.f. Wilhelm Schmidt, *The Origin and Growth of Religion*, 12 vols, London: Methuen, 1931.
19. Andrew Lang, *The Origins of Religion and Other Essays*, London: Watts and Co., 1908, pp. 110–11.
20. R. R. Marett, *The Threshold of Religion*, London: Methuen, 1914, p. xxxi.
21. R. H. Codrington, *The Melanesians*, Oxford: Clarendon Press, 1915, p. 532.
22. Lévy-Bruhl, *La Mentalité primitive*, Paris: Alcan, 1947, pp. 17–18. Quoted Evans-Pritchard, *Theories of Primitive Religion*, p. 81.
23. Lévy-Bruhl, *How Natives Think*, London: Allen & Unwin, 1926, quoted Gustav Jahoda, *The Psychology of Superstition*, Harmondsworth: Pelican Books, 1970, p. 101.
24. Lévy-Bruhl, *Les Fonctions mentales dans les sociétés inférieures*, Paris, 1912, p. 30.
25. Ibid., pp. 76–80.
26. Ibid., pp. 33, 426, 452–4.
27. Guthrie, *History of Greek Philosophy*, Cambridge: CUP, 1962, Vol. 1, p. 26.
28. F. M. Cornford, *From Religion to Philosophy*, New York: Harper Torch edition, 1957.
29. Bronislaw Malinowski, *Magic, Science and Religion*, New York: Doubleday Anchor edition, 1954, pp. 28–9.
30. David Hume, *The Natural History of Religion*, ed. A. Wayne Colver, Oxford: Clarendon Press, 1976, pp. 30–1.
31. Edmund Leach, Introduction to Malinowski, *Coral Gardens and Their Magic*, Bloomington: Indiana University Press, 1965.
32. Glick, 'The Anthropology of Religion: Malinowski and Beyond', in C. Y. Glock and P. E. Hammond (eds), *Beyond the Classics*, New York: Harper & Row, 1973, p. 185.
33. Malinowski, *Magic, Science and Religion*, p. 48.
34. Ibid., p. 51.
35. Malinowski, article on 'Culture' in *Encyclopaedia of the Social Sciences*, vol. IV (1931), pp. 634–42.
36. A. R. Radcliffe-Brown, *The Andaman Islanders*, New York: The Free Press, 1922, p. 324.
37. A. R. Radcliffe-Brown, *Structure and Function in Primitive Society*, New York: The Free Press, 1952, p. 157.
38. Mary Douglas, *Evans-Pritchard*, Fontana Modern Masters series, London: Collins, 1980, pp. 88–9.
39. E. E. Evans-Pritchard, *Witchcraft, Oracles and Magic among the Azande*, Oxford: The Clarendon Press, 1937, p. 65.
40. E. E. Evans-Pritchard, 'Lévy-Bruhl's Theory of Primitive Mentality' in *Bulletin of the Faculty of Arts*, University of Egypt, 1934. Quoted by Peter Winch, 'Understanding a Primitive Society', in D. Z. Phillips (ed.), *Religion and Understanding*, Oxford: Basil Blackwell, 1967, pp. 10–11.
41. Ibid., p. 11.
42. C.f. E. Evans-Pritchard, *Theories of Primitive Religion*, p. 115; Mary Douglas, *Evans-Pritchard*, p. 11.
43. Robin Horton, *Patterns of Thought in Africa and the West*, Cambridge: CUP, 1993, p. 347.

44. Ibid., p. 306.
45. Ibid.
46. Ibid., pp. 19–49.
47. Ibid., p. 5.
48. Ibid., pp. 80–8.
49. Ibid., p. 198.
50. Ibid., p. 377.
51. Ibid., p. 199.
52. Nancy Sanders called attention to just this error in the writings on religion of the great historian of Sumaria and Assyria, Thorkild Jacobsen, as well as in the writings of the social philosopher and psychologist Erich Fromm. She wrote: 'The danger with these, as with all systems, is that they may be taken for universals, when in fact much of the evidence used is peculiar to one locality and one situation.' N. K. Sanders, 'The Religious Development of Some Early Societies', in P. R. S. Moorey (ed.), *The Origins of Civilization*, Oxford: Clarendon Press, 1979, p. 106.

CHAPTER 7

Religion as Psychological Construct

The explanations of religion which we shall consider in this and the follow-ing chapter have this in common that they see religion as an essentially human construct having its origins either within the individual or in society, origins of which religious believers themselves are largely unaware. For Feuerbach, Nietzsche and Freud, as for Marx, Weber and Durkheim, religion is essentially a 'projection', an 'objectification', an 'externalisation', a 'reification' – the language varies from thinker to thinker – of some attribute or other of human nature which, once it has been 'objectified', is mistakenly taken to have an autonomous existence independent of its human creators. Thus understood, religion, for these thinkers, is a coded way by means of which human beings talk about themselves, about their hopes and fears and about the possibilities inherent in human nature and in human society. It is a way of understanding religion which has its origins in Hegel's philosophy of Spirit, but in Hegel's philosophy of Spirit as this was transformed by Hegel's one-time disciple, Ludwig Feuerbach.

– Ludwig Feuerbach –

Feuerbach was born in 1804 at Landshut in Bavaria, the son of a well-known jurist. In 1823 he began the study of theology at the University of Heidelberg, but dissatisfied with the lectures which he heard there, and which he described as 'a web of sophistry', he transferred in 1825 to the University of Berlin where he attended the lectures of Hegel and Schleier-macher. However, owing to difficulties in his family's finances, he was forced to leave Berlin to finish his studies at the less expensive university at Erlangen, to which university, in 1828, he successfully submitted a doctoral dissertation and where, until 1832, he taught as a *Privatdozent* – a freelance lecturer. The controversy aroused by the publication of his *Thoughts on Death and Immortality* in 1830, in which he denied the Christian doctrine of personal immortality, was such that professional advancement within the university world of the time was out of the question and, after marrying a comfortably well-off lady who owned a pottery factory, he retired with her to the small town of Bruckberg and there lived the life of a rural recluse devoting his time to developing his highly original philosophy and to studying the natural sciences. Despite his growing fame as a radical thinker his friends were unable to lure him away from this country idyll back into academic life, although during the revolutionary fervour of 1848 he was persuaded by the students of Heidelberg University to give a series of public lectures in the Town Hall in that city – lectures which were published in 1851 as *Lectures on the Essence of Religion*. In 1860 Feuerbach's wife's pottery factory went into liquidation and he and his family were forced to move to a small village near Nüremberg where he lived in genteel poverty until his death in 1872.

A student of both theology and philosophy, Feuerbach was disillusioned by the way these were pursued in the German universities of his day where the professors had, he felt, left the world inhabited by real men and women to inhabit an ethereal world of their own abstractions. His own philosophical programme sought to bring both theology and philosophy back to earth.

Although he had published a history of modern philosophy, a study of the French freethinker Pierre Bayle, and a critique of Hegelian philosophy, it was with the publication of *The Essence of Christianity* in 1841 that Feuerbach came to public attention. Its leading idea – that it is men and women who create religion – was not, of course, new: it had been advanced in the ancient world by Xenophanes, Lucretius and Euhemer, and in later centuries by Giambattista Vico and David Hume.[1] What was striking was the way in which Feuerbach worked out this idea. He himself summed up his programme in a single sentence in his *Principles of the Philosophy of the Future*, where he wrote that his intention was 'to transform theology into anthropology'.[2] Religion was only important, for Feuerbach, for what, albeit by means of what he termed a 'detour' (*Umweg*), it told us about men and women. Whereas, for Hegel, all the stages in the development of human culture were but 'moments' in the progressive unfolding of Absolute Spirit or God, for Feuerbach, human history is the story of men and women's coming to a truer understanding of themselves and the possibilities inherent in their own human nature. He wrote:

> When religion – consciousness of God – is designated as the self-consciousness of man, this is not to be understood as affirming that the religious man is directly aware of this identity; for, on the contrary, ignorance of it is fundamental to the peculiar nature of religion. To preclude this misconception, it is better to say,

religion is man's earliest form of self-knowledge. Hence, religion everywhere precedes philosophy, as in the history of the race, so also in that of the individual. Man first sees his nature as of *out of* himself, before he finds it in himself ... Religion is the childlike condition of humanity ... But the essence of religion, thus hidden from the religious, is evident to the thinker.[3]

Gregor Nüdling, in a sadly neglected study of Feuerbach's religious philosophy, has shown that Feuerbach made at least three attempts to explain religion: all, however, were variations on the theme outlined in the quotation given above.[4] In the first, and most well-known explanation, put forward in *The Essence of Christianity* (1841), Feuerbach sought to reduce God to the essence of human nature; in the second, put forward in *The Essence of Religion* (1845), he sought to reduce God to the essence of nature; and in the third, put forward in his *Theogonie* (1857), he sought to reduce God to the essence of human desire.

This last theory, in which religion is held to arise out of human desire – or to be more specific out of *Glückseligkeitstrieb* or the desire for happiness – has recently been resurrected by Van A. Harvey, who has argued that, after the publication of *The Essence of Christianity*, Feuerbach jettisoned his neo-Hegelian theory of the origin of religion in favour of a very different theory and moved from being a sympathetic interpreter of religion to become one of its severest critics. Harvey wrote:

> By abandoning the Hegelian objectification-alienation-reappropriation schema, Feuerbach could no longer claim to be a charitable and friendly interpreter of religion because he no longer regarded theism as mystified truth but, rather, as a tissue of errors, a misinterpretation of nature based on ignorance and superstition ... Like Marx, Nietzsche and Freud, Feuerbach no longer wanted to uncover some truth hidden in religion; rather he wanted to clear the religious rubble away in preparation for a new and completely secular philosophy.[5]

This latter theory, which Harvey terms the 'naturalistic-existentialist' theory, is found, Harvey contends, in Feuerbach's study of Luther, published in 1846, and in his *Lectures on the Essence of Religion*.[6] We shall consider it in due course.

Feuerbach began his explanation of religion from what Hegel had said about Absolute Spirit, but instead of saying, as had Hegel, that Absolute Spirit or God achieves self-knowledge by objectifying itself in the world, Feuerbach suggested that a truer way of viewing things would be to see finite spirits (i.e. human beings) coming to self-knowledge by externalising or objectifying themselves or, more particularly, objectifying what he termed their 'species nature' – that is, human nature as such – in the idea of God or in whatever non-theistic religions take to constitute ultimate reality.

Religion is the form in which the human spirit discovers its own essential nature. He wrote:

> Man – this is the mystery of religion – projects (*vergegenständlicht sich*) his being into objectivity, and then again makes himself into an *object* to hide his own projected image of himself thus converted into a subject; he thinks of himself as an object to himself, but as *the object of an object*, of *another* being than himself.[7]

Feuerbach saw the process whereby men and women create religion as a historical one which developed and matured as the religious consciousness developed and matured. However, the religious consciousness was not, for Feuerbach, an undifferentiated consciousness. Feuerbach was well aware of the variety of religious expression found in the world, but he believed that there are certain fundamental patterns of development and that the whole process is grounded in a human nature which is common to all men and women. This essential and universal human nature – men and women's 'species nature' as he called it – is the true subject-matter of religion. The productions of the religious consciousness, that is, the various theologies found in the world, must, therefore, be reduced to anthropology and the religious consciousness – which, for Feuerbach, is not the same thing as theology – must be deconstructed so as to extract from it what it has to say about the human feelings, needs, desires, ideals and yearnings out of which it arises.

Religion, said Feuerbach, is the consciousness that men and women have of their own infinite nature.[8] He also asserted that the proper constituent elements of human nature are the absolute, self-authenticating attributes of reason, will and love. He wrote:

> That alone is true, perfect, divine, which exists for its own sake. But such is love, such is reason, such is will. Reason, will and love are not powers which man possesses, for he is nothing without them, he is what he is only by them; for they are the constituent elements of his nature, which he neither has nor makes, the animating, determining powers – divine absolute powers – to which he can oppose no resistance.[9]

Whatever our individual limitations, Feuerbach is saying, we recognise reason, will and love as in themselves infinite, unqualified perfections – objects of absolute worth. 'The absolute to man,' he wrote, 'is his own nature.'[10] But men and women, as individuals, do not properly comprehend their infinity and they are all too prone to ascribe their own individual limitations to the species as such and to project the infinite possibilities of their own nature onto an external object – that is onto God. He wrote:

All divine attributes, all the attributes which make God God, are attributes of the species – attributes which in the individual are limited, but the limits of which are abolished in the essence of the species ... My knowledge, my will, is limited; but my limit is not the limit of another man, to say nothing of mankind; what is difficult to me is easy to another; what is impossible, inconceivable, to one age, is to the coming age conceivable and possible. My life is bounded to a limited time, not so the life of humanity.[11]

Religion is thus a form of self-knowledge in which men and women contemplate their own nature as though it were extrinsic to themselves. Religious men and women are thus alienated men and women, for they make that which is their own creation – God – into an authority over themselves and thus throw away their natural sovereignty and reduce themselves thereby to servile and miserable beings. 'Religion', wrote Feuerbach:

is the disuniting of man from himself; he sets God before him as the antithesis of himself. God is not what man is – man is not what God is. God is the infinite, man the finite being; God is perfect, man imperfect; God eternal, man temporal; God almighty, man weak; God holy, man sinful. God and man are extremes: God is the absolutely positive, the sum of all realities; man is the absolutely negative, comprehending all negations.[12]

If the integral humanism which was the real goal of Feuerbach's philosophy was to be achieved, this false antithesis had to be resolved and resolved in a way which allows men and women to realise for themselves the infinite possibilities inherent in their human nature. Hegel's philosophy of Spirit, Feuerbach contended, had failed to do this, in that the self-alienation of men and women of which it spoke was, in the last resort, but the self- realisation of Absolute Spirit working through them. Men and women must begin, therefore, by rejecting both Hegel and traditional religion, or rather they must see religion for what it is, then the truth will become clear – theology is anthropology and God simply a projection of unenlightened men and women. Marx, in his now famous *Theses on Feuerbach* had, as we shall see in the next chapter, some pertinent criticism to make of this programme and of what he took to be Feuerbach's wrong-headed methodology for achieving social reform, maintaining that Feuerbach had got things the wrong way round. What was needed, said Marx, was a change in social conditions rather than a change in consciousness. Only then would the alienation of men and women from their own humanity, as evidenced in religion, be finally overcome.

Feuerbach, like many nineteenth-century thinkers who rejected religion, was at heart a humanist concerned to enhance the quality of life for men and women in this world and who believed that religion, and the Christian religion in particular, worked against this objective. In a concluding appraisal of what he believed himself to have achieved in *The Essence of Christianity* he wrote:

> We have reduced the superhuman, supernatural nature of God to the elements of human nature and its fundamental elements. Our process of analysis has brought us again to the position with which we set out. The beginning, middle and end of religion is MAN.[13]

Feuerbach's second attempt to get at the nature of religion can be found in *The Essence of Religion*, published in 1845 and in the *Lectures on the Essence of Religion*, published in 1851.[14] It is not incompatible with the first explanation, but whereas *The Essence of Christianity* had dealt, as the title indicates, almost exclusively with the Christian religion, Feuerbach now widened the scope of his enquiry to offer an explanation for the existence of natural religion as well. Natural religion, Feuerbach says, arises from a feeling of dependence on nature so that God becomes not hypostatized human nature, as in *The Essence of Christianity*, but hypostatized nature. 'Nature,' he now wrote, 'is the first and originating object of religion.'[15] Further, by the time he came to write *The Essence of Religion*, he had abandoned Hegel's philosophy of Spirit and now characterised human beings more concretely than he had earlier when he saw their essential attribute as simply that of self-consciousness. Whilst this latter attribute is not denied, human beings are now seen as embodied beings (*dasein*) possessing a range of natural instincts. Natural religion is seen by Feuerbach, as it had been seen by Schleiermacher, as originating in a feeling of dependence, but this is not thought of by Feuerbach as an abstract feeling, but as one that has, as he put it, 'eyes and ears, hands and feet'. There is now no mention of the 'infinity' of human nature, for what now interested Feuerbach were real men and women who desire, will and feel. Further, whilst originally he had envisioned that the overthrow of religion would put an end to human egoism, he now reverted to the view, common in the thought of the eighteenth century, that men and women are naturally egoistic. In *The Essence of Christianity* he described the process whereby human beings created 'God', but had not explained its causes. This he now tried to do, although he went no further than stating that the source of religion is men and women's ignorance of their situation in nature. Realising their dependence on nature, men and women devise anthropomorphic fancies to express their fear of Nature's caprice and the positive feelings of gratitude and hope that Nature arouses in them. Religion, for Feuerbach, as Kolakowski has put it, 'is an ersatz satisfaction of human needs that cannot be met in any other way'. Men and women 'seek to compel nature to obey them by using magic or appealing to divine goodness, i.e. they try to achieve by imagination what they cannot have in reality'.[16] As science proceeds, religion will yield to a rational world-view and men and women will utilise science and its attendant technology to control the world for their good. Religion arises out of the human imagination and of the very nature of the cognitive process which can think only in abstractions. Human beings have a tendency, says Feuerbach, to credit these with an existence independent of the human beings who create them. In the same way 'God' and other figments of the human imagination personify human ideas, feelings and abilities. He wrote:

> The idea or generic concept of God in the metaphysical sense is based on the same necessity and the same foundations as is the concept of things or fruit … the gods of polytheists are nothing but the names and collective or generic concepts imagined as actual beings, but, in order to understand the meaning of the general concepts it is not necessary to deify them and turn them into independent beings that differ from individual essences. We can condemn wickedness without at once personifying it as the devil.[17]

This, of course, is to revert to views that were common in the thinkers of the Enlightenment, and which had, as we saw in Chapter 5, been put forward in Classical Antiquity, but in the Germany of Feuerbach's day, dominated by the thought of Kant and Hegel, were, as Kolakowski notes, something of a novelty.

Feuerbach's third and last attempt to clarify the human basis of religion returns to his earlier focus on human beings as beings with desires who invent gods who are able to fulfil these desires. The fundamental human desire, Feuerbach now argues, is a desire for happiness (*Glückseligkeitstrieb*) and what religions offer is, if not happiness in this life, then the promise of happiness in the life to come. He wrote, 'Where desire arises, there too the gods arise and make their appearance'; and, 'In every desire a god is hidden, but conversely behind every god there is only a desire'; and 'a divinity is essentially an object called forth by desire; it is represented, thought, believed only because it is demanded, called for, desired'.[18] Desire, he maintains, arises out of deprivation and men and women create the gods to offer them what they themselves lack. For Feuerbach, as for Nietzsche and Freud, religion is born of wish fulfilment. It is, as he put it, desire fulfilled.

As we have seen, Feuerbach, by the time he came to give the *Lectures on the Essence of Religion* at Heidelberg in 1848, had all but abandoned his earlier neo-Hegelian view of the origin of religion so that religion is now seen, not as a necessary stage in the growth of human self-knowledge, but as an erroneous interpretation of the encompassing mysterious powers impinging on human beings and upon which they are dependent. Commenting on this new theory, Harvey, in the study to which we have referred, writes:

> This new theory religion in the nature of the case is less systematic and elegant than the earlier. There are no successive and necessary Hegelian 'moments' in the spirit's objectification of itself, no necessary dialectical moves that lead, finally, to self-realisation. Rather, religion is, as it were, an overdetermined phenomenon, and it varies from culture to culture, depending upon how this 'not-I' is symbolised. It is grounded in both subjective and objective factors. It springs from the self's differentiation from others and nature, but it has as its object the powers of nature that can harm, bless or kill it. This is no less clear in the so-called religions of nature than it is in the monotheisms of the so-called higher religions in which the nexus of secondary causes is regarded as the action of God. With Schleiermacher, Feuerbach argued that *Dasein* [the embodied, self-conscious human being] desperately wants to believe that 'in, with, under' all that impinges on us, there is a Subject who acknowledges, loves, and affirms the individual.[19]

Unable to accept necessity, chance and death, human beings people reality with a host of supernatural beings whom they believe are able to help them overcome these anxiety-causing factors in the human condition and, in the case of monotheism, they reify that most abstract of all abstractions – Being itself. Religion is simply an instance of the endemic anthropomorphism in human nature – an understanding of religion which the anthropologist Stewart Guthrie has recently articulated with a wealth of supporting evidence in his book *Faces in the Clouds*.[20]

This is not, however, a particularly deep theory of religion and it is hard to see why Harvey sees it as marking an advance on what would appear *prima facie* to be the more sophisticated theory put forward in the *Essence of Christianity* and which no less a scholar than Sidney Hook considered 'the most comprehensive and persuasive hypothesis available for the comparative study of religion',[21] for there is little that is new in Feuerbach's later theory. It is a way of accounting for the origin of the gods that, as we have seen, was not unknown in Classical Antiquity, and it was restated in early modern Europe by Francis Bacon in a famous passage in his *Magno Instauratio* (The Great Instauration), written in 1620, where he lists what he calls the 'Idols and false notions which are now in possession of the human understanding' and which prevent human beings from arriving at a clear understanding of the world in which they live. The first two of the four 'idols' which Bacon identifies as working against the new scientific understanding of the workings of the world are what he terms the 'Idols of the Tribe', so called 'because they have their foundation in human nature itself' and which are responsible, he says, for an innate tendency to attribute human significance to natural phenomena, populating the universe with human intelligence and desire, from the anthropoid totems of traditional religion to the casual poetry of 'ranging tempests', and the 'Idols of the Cave' which govern individual temperament, predisposing it to find particular patterns of significance in the contingency of things. Every one, he wrote, 'has a cave or den of his own, which refracts and discolours the light of nature'.

The impulse that drives men and women to create these 'idols' will be explored in depth, certainly, by those such as Freud and Becker whose discussions of the origin of religion Harvey sees Feuerbach as presaging. What is not so certain is that what Feuerbach, Freud and Becker have to tell us about the helplessness of men and women in the face of nature and of death and of their need for the comforts supposedly provided by religion, tells us anything about human nature that wasn't well known, if, perhaps, not so well articulated, before their time. The theory also presupposes that religions are, indeed, comforting which, as Lucretius was aware when he wrote his *De Rerum Naturum* in the last century BCE, is not necessarily the case.

Feuerbach's later writings on religion passed virtually unnoticed in his lifetime and despite Harvey's valiant attempt to re-establish the later Feuerbach as an undervalued figure in the study of religion, it is not hard to understand why. What impressed his contemporaries was the neo-Hegelian theory put forward in the *Essence of Christianity*, and yet this theory too has not been without its critics, the question most frequently raised being why it is that human beings began and continued to project their own deficiencies onto a being thought of as being extraneous to themselves and to their world? 'Religion,' wrote Feuerbach, 'immediately represented the inner nature of man as an objective, external being.'[22] Yet nowhere in his writings does he tell us why this should have been so.

Feuerbach's distinction between finite and infinite human nature has also been called into question and particularly his use of the term 'infinite' to characterise 'the species nature' of human beings. Is the term 'infinite', it has been asked, the correct term to describe the possibilities inherent in human nature and is the term being used in precisely the same sense in which theologians have sought to use the term of God? The Christian theologian Marcel Neusch certainly thought not. He wrote:

> the whole argument is evidently fallacious because 'infinite' is given two meanings. As applied to the species Feuerbach's 'infinite' refers to a virtual infinity: the species prolonging itself indefinitely in a gradual growth through space and time; this is Hegel's 'false infinity'. Can the infinity which is predicable of the species be applied to God? Feuerbach unhesitatingly uses the same term, but … the infinity predicated of God is an infinity in act, an infinity that is already fully real.

Feuerbach's infinity is still something finite, and finitude suggests at least one question: what is its ground? Whence does it derive its being, since it is incapable of explaining itself?[23]

But Feuerbach had little interest in metaphysics as such. His questions were of a different order and the answers which he gave were meant to be answers to what he saw as the over-riding problem of the nineteenth century which was how men and women might recover what he believed had been taken away from them by religion. He wrote:

Today we are still living in a situation of troublesome contradiction between religion and culture. Our religious teachings and customs are utterly opposed to our contemporary point of view in matters material and spiritual ... The elimination of this contradiction is an indispensable condition for the re-birth of the human race, the only condition, we might say, for the existence of a new race and a new age ...[24]

Nietzsche thought likewise.

– FRIEDRICH NIETZSCHE –

Nietzsche was born in 1844 at Röcken in Saxony, where his father was a Lutheran minister. His father, however, died when he was four and he was brought up by his mother. In the expectation that he would follow in his father's footsteps and become a minister Nietzsche was educated at Schulpforta, the most famous Protestant boarding-school in Germany, and at the universities of Bonn and Leipzig, where he read theology, classics and philosophy. However, it was whilst studying at Bonn, and after reading David Strauss's attempt at a truly historical biography of Jesus, *The Life of Jesus*, which had been published in 1835, that Nietzsche finally abandoned Christian faith and became what he called a 'searcher after truth'. As he wrote to his sister, Elizabeth, on the occasion of his refusing to attend Easter communion with her and his mother: 'Here the ways of men divide. If you want to achieve peace of mind and happiness, then have faith; if you want to be a disciple of truth, then search.'[25] Nietzsche now abandoned his theological studies and devoted himself to classical philology and was so successful that, at the age of 24, he was appointed to a chair in classical philology at the University of Basel. It was soon after taking up the chair at Basel that he met and came under the influence of the composer Richard Wagner, who lived in the nearby town of Tribschen, and whom he hoped would bring about the cultural renewal which he believed both Germany and Europe sorely needed. However, he soon became disillusioned with Wagner and sought thereafter to offer his own solution to the catastrophe to which he believed European and Western culture was heading.

As is the case with all nineteenth-century thinkers after Hegel, Nietzsche too had a story to tell about the development of human understanding of the world, but it was a very different story to that told either by Hegel or by Nietzsche's English contemporaries Tylor and Frazer who, as we saw in a previous chapter, saw the culmination of history in the triumph of the scientific rationalism of the eighteenth-century *Aufklärung* or Enlightenment. Nietzsche's story is, in fact, a counter-narrative to that told by the apostles of Enlightenment.

Nietzsche's story, like that of Tylor and Frazer, begins with myth, but for Nietzsche myth is not, as it was for Tylor and Frazer, a form of primitive error, but the very life-blood of culture. As he wrote in his very first work *The Birth of Tragedy*: 'Without myth every culture loses its healthy, creative natural power. Only a horizon enclosed by myths gives unity to a whole cultural movement.'[26] It is, however, in a work written towards the end of his active life, *The Twilight of the Idols* published in 1889, that Nietzsche summarises his view of the development or, as he sees it, the degeneration of Western men and women's understanding of themselves and of their relationship with the world. In a series of notes entitled 'How the "True World" Finally Became a Fable: The History of an Error', Nietzsche tells how, under the combined influence of Platonism and Christianity, the harmonious relationship between the world and human beings which had characterised the archaic age in human culture gradually gave way, at least in the Western world, to that division into the natural world and the supposedly more 'real' transcendent world which has dominated Western thinking for over two thousand years. In the archaic age the 'true world', he says, was identical with the sensual world. The archaic world was not one in which religious ideals were remote and 'transcendent', but one in which men and women were existentially at one with their ideals. He wrote:

1. The true world – attainable for the sage, the pious, the virtuous man; he lives in it, *he is it*. (The oldest form of the idea, relatively sensible, simple and persuasive. A circumlocution for the sentence, 'I Plato *am* the truth.')[27]

The true world, Nietzsche is saying, was not, at this stage in human thinking, other than the world which men and women ordinarily inhabited. It had not yet been alienated into the object of a metaphysical doctrine or of moral striving.[28] It is what historians of religion call 'the primal world' and it is a world for which Nietzsche felt considerable nostalgia.

The second stage in Western men and women's relationship with the world occurs when 'the true world' is thought to lie outwith the ordinary world, so that the sensible world is no longer in and of itself the meaningful world, for the meaning of the world is now seen as lying 'beyond' the ordinary world. In Nietzsche's words:

> 2. The true world – unattainable, for now, but promised for the sage, the pious, the virtuous man, for 'the sinner who repents'. Progress of the idea: it becomes more subtle, insidious, incomprehensible – *it becomes female* [i.e. seductive], it becomes Christian.

The cause of this cleavage between men and women and the world, says Nietzsche, is religion and, where the Western world is concerned, Christianity, aided by Platonism, introduces a morality which denigrates life in this world and urges the sage, the pious, those who would be virtuous, to shun this world and to live with the object of achieving the true object of life in the hereafter – parallels, he felt, could easily be found in all post-archaic religions.

The third stage takes this cleavage further: it is the cold, bleak, northern world of Protestantism. Nietzsche wrote:

> 3. The true world, indemonstrable, unpromisable; but the very thought of it – a consolation, an obligation, an imperative. (At bottom, the old sun, but seen through mist and scepticism. The idea has become elusive, pale, Nordic, Königsbergian [i.e. Kantian].)

This, for Nietzsche, is also the stage in human understanding which sees the rise to pre-eminence in Western thinking of the world-view of modern science.

The fourth stage in the history of the Western world brings us nearer to Nietzsche's own day, for it is the stage in which the consequences of the third stage begin to work themselves out. It is a stage which can no longer accept the consolations of religion and it might seem that Nietzsche would have welcomed this stage in the development of Western culture, but the words that he used to describe it are anything but welcoming. He wrote:

> 4. The 'true' world – unattainable? At any rate, unattained. And being unattained, also *unknown*. Consequently, not consoling, redeeming, or obligating: How could something unknown obligate us? (Grey morning. The first yawn of reason. The cock-crow of positivism.)

It is difficult to say whether Nietzsche saw the fifth stage as having already arrived or whether he saw it as lying in the future, for in this stage all forms of transcendentalism have disappeared and men and women rely only on the testimony of their senses: reason's battle has been won. He wrote:

> 5. The 'true' world – an idea that is no longer good for anything, not even

obligating – an idea which has become useless and superfluous – *consequently*, a refuted idea: let us abolish it! (Bright day; breakfast; return of *bon sens* and cheerfulness …

Yet, as Nietzsche notes here and elsewhere in his writings, men and women are anything but cheerful. The Enlightenment dream of a rational world founded on science and natural law will, Nietzsche believed, turn into a nightmare and in *Zarathustra* and his notes for *The Will to Power* he draws a nauseating picture of what he terms 'the last man', a picture presaged, as Francis Fukuyama has noted, by Alex de Tocqueville in *Democracy in America*.[29] As Max Weber, paying tribute to Nietzsche, said in his famous lecture 'Science as a Vocation':

> although a naïve optimism may have celebrated science – that is the technique of the mastery of life founded on science – as a path which would lead to happiness, I believe that I can leave this entire question aside in the light of the annihilating critique which Nietzsche made of 'the last men' who 'have discovered happiness'.[30]

Nietzsche ends his story with an account of the future for mankind in which, so he hopes, some of those who have heard his message will finally come into their own. These are what he calls the over-men (*übermenschen*), that is, those who have overcome their human all too human selves as to stand out from the majority of their fellow human beings by reason of their capacity to say 'yes' to life, to create values, and to live cheerfully in a godless world. Nietzsche wrote:

> 6. The true world – we have abolished. What world has remained? The apparent one perhaps? But no! *With the true world we have also abolished the apparent one.* (Noon. Moment of the briefest shadow; end of the longest error; high point of humanity; INCIPIT ZARATHUSTRA.)

As J. P. Stern, on whose understanding of Nietzsche I have drawn liberally, has noted, the dissolution of the dualistic world-view, which is fundamental to all forms of post-primal religion, calls for something entirely new. There can be no simple return to the past. Yet as Stern also notes, there is a terrible ambiguity in the formulation of this final stage. What it expresses is not the joy of intellectual and existential liberation, but a sense of deprivation and loss, as in the famous passage, to which we shall be referring shortly, in which Nietzsche proclaims the death of God, the question which Nietzsche raises, and never wholly resolves, is the question of the future of mankind in a godless world. Is it to be the serene life of men and women who are freed from ancient illusions and false comforts, or a world empty of all purpose and meaning? Perhaps, as Stern suggests, it depends, for Nietzsche, on what you are, or rather whether you are capable of becoming what you are.[31]

Walter Kaufmann, who did more than anyone to rehabilitate Nietzsche from his expropriation by the Nazis and to establish him as one of the seminal influences on contemporary European thought, claimed that Nietzsche was the great diagnostician of the ills of the modern European culture, its greatest psychologist and its profoundest prophet. His reasons for this judgement were that Nietzsche diagnosed the coming crisis in Western culture and its causes with an accuracy unequalled by any other thinker. Like the Hebrew prophets, Kaufmann claims, Nietzsche had the capacity 'to experience his own wretched fate so deeply that it became the allegory of something larger'. He felt, Kaufmann continues, 'the agony, the suffering, the misery of a godless world so deeply and intensely at a time when others were still blind to its tremendous consequences, that he was able to experience in advance, as it were, the fate of a coming generation'.[32]

As will be evident from what has been said so far, Nietzsche was unable to share the triumphalism of his age, an age in which science and technology were beginning to make spectacular and hitherto unheard-of advances, where schemes for social reform were rife and where optimism was common. All this was as nothing when put alongside of the one thing that, for Nietzsche, alone mattered, but to which his contemporaries were blind and deaf, namely, that 'God is dead'. The well-known passage is worth quoting:

Have you not heard of the madman who on a bright morning lit a lantern and ran into the market place and cried out unceasingly 'I seek God, I seek God!' As many of those who do not believe in God were standing around he provoked much laughter. 'Why, is he lost?', said one. 'Has he lost his way like a child?', said another. 'Or is he hiding?' Thus they yelled and laughed. The madman jumped into their midst and transfigured them with his glances. 'Whither is God?', he cried. 'I shall tell you. We have killed him – you and I. All of us are his murderers. But how have we done this? How were we able to drink up the sea? Who gave us the sponge to wipe away the entire horizon? What did we do when we unchained this earth from its sun? Whither are we moving now? Away from all suns? Are we not plunging continually? Backward, sideward, forward, in all directions? Is there any up and down left? Are we not straying as through an infinite nothingness? Do we not feel the breadth of empty space? Has it not become colder? Is not night and more night coming on all the while? ... God is dead. God remains dead. And we have killed him. What was holiest and most powerful of all the world has yet owned has bled to death under our knives. Who will wipe this blood off us? Is not the magnitude of this deed too great for us? Shall we not have to become gods merely to seem worthy of it? ...' Here the madman fell silent and looked again at his hearers, and they too were silent an looked again at him in astonishment. At last he threw his lantern on the ground and it broke and went out. 'My time is not yet come. This tremendous event is still on its way ... It has not yet reached the ears of men ...' It is further stated that the madman made his way into different churches on the same day and there sang his *requiem in aeternam deo*. When led out and called to account he always gave the same reply: 'What are these churches now if they are not the tombs and monuments of God?'[33]

'God is dead' says Nietzsche, but he does not say this on a note of triumph for, as the imagery in the passage just quoted makes plain, 'the death of God', which for Nietzsche is an indisputable cultural fact, is one which is fraught with the most terrible consequences both for individuals and for humanity. Certainly men and women were now free in ways in which they had not been free before, but whether they could bear that freedom and what they would do with it were questions which would preoccupy Nietzsche for the rest of his life. For Nietzsche the joy of liberation is tempered by the terror at men and women's unprotectedness. Freud, as we shall see shortly, expressed similar worries about the ability of men and women to live without the consolations of religion although, on the whole, he was more hopeful of the outcome than was Nietzsche.

Yet fearful for a future without religion as he was, Nietzsche saw the demise of the Christian religion as a cause for rejoicing, for Christianity is, as he argued in *The Anti-Christ*, not just erroneous, but harmful. Christianity, like Platonism, is in fact 'a crime against life'. As we have seen in the notes quoted above from *The Twilight of the Idols*, Nietzsche saw Christianity, as he saw all post-archaic religions, as having propagated a dualistic world-view in which life in this world was something from which men or women needed to be redeemed. This leads, Nietzsche argued, to the espousal of an ascetic ideal which denigrates life in this world and which recommends flight from it – an attitude to which Nietzsche, like Feuerbach, was vehemently opposed. Thus in *Thus Spoke Zarathustra* Nietzsche entreats men and women to remain faithful to the earth and not to believe those who speak to them of superterrestrial hopes. They are, he says, 'poisoners whether they know it or not. They are despisers of life, atrophying and self-poisoned men of whom the earth is weary'.[34] And in *The Will to Power* he writes: 'I regard Christianity as the most fatal seductive lie that has yet existed, as the great unholy lie ... I reject every compromise position with respect to it – I force a war against it.'[35]

To get at Nietzsche's understanding of religion and particularly at his negative evaluation of Christianity, and of all forms of post-archaic religion, it will be necessary to look not only at what he has to say about the historical origins of religion, but also at what he calls its 'genealogy', that is at its source in the souls of men and women.

On the historical origin of religion Nietzsche, like the later Feuerbach, has little that is original to say. Gods, he says, owe their existence 'to a state of human intellectuality which was as yet too young and immature' to conceive of reality otherwise than in personal and anthropomorphic terms.[36] Men and women, bewildered both by the forces of nature and by the forces welling up within themselves, looked for a causal explanation of these outwith both the world and themselves. The important passage is in *The Will to Power*. It reads:

> *On the origin of religion*. In the same way as today the uneducated man believes that anger is the cause of his being angry, spirit the cause of his thinking, soul the cause of his feelings – in short, just as there is still thoughtlessly posited a mass of psychological entities that are supposed to be causes – so, at a yet more naïve stage, man explained precisely the same phenomena with the aid of psychological person entities. Those conditions that seem to him strange, thrilling, over-whelming, he interpreted as obsession and enchantment by the power of a person … A condition is made concrete in a person, and when it overtakes us is thought to be effected by that person. In other words: In the psychological concept of God, a condition, in order to appear as effect, is personified as cause …
> …The naïve *homo religiosus* divides himself into several persons. Religion is a case of '*altération de la personnalité*'.[37]

In creating religion men and women are thus seen as the victims of their own imaginations and the consequence, for Nietzsche as for Feuerbach, is that they end by belittling themselves and their own achievements and possibilities.

Nietzsche's originality comes to the fore when he is discussing the 'genealogy' of religion, that is when he seeks to uncover what it is in human beings that motivates them to keep religion in being, often long after explanations of natural and human phenomena in religious terms have ceased to be tenable.[38] Religion, he says, is born of and is kept in being by *ressentiment*. Echoing Hegel, Nietzsche divides human beings into two psychological types – the strong and the weak, the latter of whom exhibit what he calls 'a slave mentality'. It must be emphasised that these categories are not to be thought of in terms of social class. For Nietzsche they indicate two different approaches to life – the one life-affirming and value-creating in which the individual is driven by an inner will to power, shown supremely, for Nietzsche, in cultural creativity in which the individual continually transcends whatever he or she might be at any given time; the other dependent, obedient, re-active rather than pro-active, and driven by *ressentiment* against the power of the strong. It is these latter people who need and create religion and, Nietzsche claims, where they abandon religion, espouse either socialism or some other ideology which, like religion, raises equality and the values of compassion, selflessness and social justice, which are the weapons the weak use against the strong, to the status of absolute values.[39] Christianity is the supreme example, for Nietzsche, of the slave mentality, although he did on occasion in his attacks on religion cite Buddhism as a further example. Of Christianity he wrote:

> In Christianity, three elements must be distinguished: (a) the oppressed of all kinds, (b) the mediocre of all kinds, (c) the discontented and sick of all kinds. With the first element Christianity fights against the political nobility and the individual; with the second element, against the exceptional and privileged (spiritually and physically) of all kinds; with the third element, against the natural instinct of the healthy and happy.[40]

It is thus that, in the aftermath of 'the death of God', the moral values associated with religion, and with Christianity in particular, must be subject to that 'revaluation of all values' which Nietzsche believed should now take place. Thus the 'death of God' and the nihilism which initially ensues is, for Nietzsche, but the prelude to a new constructive philosophy – a philosophy which Nietzsche's begins to elaborate through the teaching of 'Zarathustra', the philosopher whom he casts as the herald of the future. The details of this positive post-religious philosophy need not detain us for to discuss it would take us far from the central concern of this book. It would, however, some forty years after Nietzsche's death in 1900, form the basis for the Existentialist philosophy of Jean-Paul Sartre. Its fundamental premise, as Sartre made clear at the outset of his famous lecture 'Existentialism and Humanism', is that the death of God and the demise of religion free men and women to create themselves, to live authentic lives.[41] 'Man,' Sartre claimed, 'is always a project in advance of himself.' The problem, however, as Nicholas Martin has pointed out, is that the *übermensch*, living as he or she is encouraged to do beyond conventional notions of good and evil – which for Nietzsche are the products of a slave mentality – is given something of a blank cheque with little or no directions for calling it in.[42] The same can, of course, be said of the Existentialist hero or heroine. It is a theme which has been developed by a number of French thinkers and in particular by Michel Foucault who has called into question the whole Western Humanist essentialist conception of 'Man' and its overarching conception of an ideal human nature.[43] As he wrote at the close of *Les Mots et les choses*, the work which brought him to public attention, 'As the archaeology of our thought easily shows, man is an invention of recent date. And one perhaps nearing its end.'[44] Foucault is not here expressing any disdain for men and women but, as his book shows, pointing out that the conception of human nature on which the high Humanist tradition (to which Hegel, Feuerbach and Marx were committed) is based was the product of a particular historical situation which, as he noted, 'arose at the time of the Enlightenment' but which 'if those arrangements were to disappear as they appeared ... then one can certainly wager that man would be erased, like a face drawn in the sand at the edge of the sea'.[45] The death of God leads inevitably to the death of humanity.

Freud's vision of life in a godless world, to which we now turn, is equally bleak, for Freud, like Nietzsche, sees religion as a human, all too human, construct which must now be superseded, and he too is none too sure that men and women will be able to live without the support which he believes religion has given in the past to human beings seeking to live their lives in a hostile environment.

– SIGMUND FREUD –

In 1929 the British psychologist Sir John Adams wrote:

> We have a body of newer psychologists who are out on the warpath against the very foundational principles of their seniors. It is not, of course, a matter of age, but of point of view, and these belligerent new psychologists are not in the least in doubt about what they believe and what they deny. They know exactly what they want and are quite clear about the way they propose to attain it. There is a lion in their path; they want that lion killed and decently buried. This lion is Consciousness, and they have the grave all nicely arranged for him.[46]

I quote this passage because it represents a common misapprehension of what Freud and his followers were about. It is a misapprehension because neither Freud nor his followers sought, as Adams implied, to denigrate, let alone 'slay', consciousness. In fact, quite the contrary, for Freud, and later Jung, went out of their way to emphasise the crucial role played by consciousness in the process of coming to knowledge of the truth about human beings and their situation in the world. What Freud and Jung did do, however, was to make men and women more aware than they had been hitherto of the fact that, in certain areas of life, belief and action are often influenced by mental and emotional activity of which they are largely unconscious, but which could, through techniques such as the interpretation of dreams, be brought to consciousness and then taken into account in the making of decisions. As Stuart Hampshire pointed out in his book *Thought and Action*, Freud saw himself, in fact, as a great liberator, in that he believed that in making human beings aware of the unconscious factors conditioning their behaviour and by bringing these unconscious and irrational factors to consciousness he was putting men and women in a better position than they had hitherto been to act in a more informed and therefore in a freer way,[47] and, for Freud, though not for Jung, one area from which men and women needed to be freed was that occupied by religion.

It must also be noted that Freud was adamantly opposed to the explanation of religion put forward by Tylor and Frazer, both of whom he had read, for he saw that if the intellectualist understanding of the origins of religion was true then, with the advance of scientific knowledge, it would be difficult, if not impossible, to account for the persistence and continuing influence of religion in human life. He wrote: 'It is not to be supposed that men were inspired to create their first system of the universe by purely speculative curiosity. The practical need for controlling the world around them must have played its part.'[48] And in *The Future of an Illusion*, he wrote: 'This is a fresh psychological problem. We must ask where the *inner force* of those doctrines lies and to what it is that they owe their efficacy, independent as it is of recognition by reason.'[49] What Freud sought to uncover were the ongoing, persistent springs of religion within the souls of men and women.

Freud was born in 1856 in the little town of Freiberg in Moravia, then part of the Austro-Hungarian empire, today situated in the Czech Republic. His father, a moderately successful wool merchant, was Jewish, but there is no evidence that Freud had anything but a minimal Jewish upbringing, and indeed the family had something of a reputation in Jewish circles for being freethinkers. In 1859 the family moved first to Leipzig and then to Vienna and it was in Vienna that Freud received his education, first at the gymnasium and then at the university where he read medicine. After graduating from the university he studied for a time in Paris under the famous neurologist Charcot. This was the great turning point of his life. Hitherto he had been largely concerned with histology or the anatomy of the nervous system, but after studying with Charcot his interests moved increasingly in the direction of psychopathology and it was his clinical work in this field, and from the techniques which he developed for recalling repressed memories to consciousness, that psychoanalysis was born. The 'royal road', as he called it, to uncovering these repressed memories was, for Freud, that of the interpretation of dreams.[50] Freud set himself up in private practice in Vienna and practised there until the anti-Semitic policies of the Nazis, who had occupied Austria in 1937, drove him to accept asylum in London where he died in September 1939.

Freud believed that psychoanalysis could uncover, among other things, the hidden springs of religion within the personality. Leaving aside as now totally discredited the bizarre theory that he put forward in *Totem and Taboo* (1915) in which he argued that religion arose during the pre-history of the human race as an act of expiation for a primeval murder of the male father by the male adolescents of the primal horde desirous of possessing their mother,[51] the essence of what Freud had to say about the origin of religion can be found in a passage written late in his life in a psychoanalytical study of Leonardo da Vinci where he wrote:

> Psycho-analysis has made us aware of the intimate connection between the father-complex and the belief in God, and has taught us that the personal God is psychologically nothing other than a magnified father; it shows us every day how young people can loose their religious faith as soon as their father's authority collapses. We thus recognise the root of religious authority as lying in the parental complex.[52]

Freud's numerous remarks on religion are all of them variations upon this theme of God as the magnified father. Freud, who was 'a natural atheist', believed, with Feuerbach, that religion was the result of a projection onto external reality of what are no more than psychological processes.[53] Well before he had embarked upon psychoanalysis he had made up his mind that religious claims were false and that the only task remaining was to explain both how religion originated and why it had persisted for so long in human evolution. He came to believe that his experience in psychoanalysis provided him with the answer to both of these questions.

To appreciate the answer that Freud gave to the question of the origin and persistence of religious belief we need to know a little about his general theory of human development. For Freud the human infant is a bundle of instinctual desires, which he called the *id*, which undergo a process of gradual modification, both in the light of experience – whether they find or fail to find satisfaction – and, more particularly, in the light of parental encouragement and criticism. The course of this development follows a well-marked path and, with individual modifications, all children pass through certain well-marked phases of development. The details of this development need not concern us: what, for Freud, is important is that no child passes from one stage to another completely smoothly; difficulties and conflicts occur and those which are too painful for the conscious mind to bear are pushed into the unconscious, that is repressed, to emerge into the light of day only in dreams, slips of the tongue and, if severe, in neurotic symptoms. All of us bear such marks of maladjustment to a greater or lesser extent as the case may be. If in the course of life we come across, as most of us do, situations which place too great a strain on our personalities then the chances are that we shall fall back – Freud's term is 'regress' – into a response appropriate to a stage in our development to which we never satisfactorily adjusted. Quite simply, for Freud, most of us never grow up.

The relevance of this to what Freud says about religion is that, for him, the religious response to the world is just such a regression to childhood as has been described, which allows him to see religion as an essentially 'infantile' response to the world. For Freud, the religious man or woman is someone who has never quite grown up and who consequently falls back on infantile modes of response as a 'defence mechanism' – another phrase coined by Freud – against an alien and hostile world. In theistic religions, which are the only religions of which Freud takes cognisance, this takes the form of postulating a kind and all-powerful God reminiscent of the real, or imagined or wished-for parent of our childhood. In a passing remark in *The Ego and the Id* he wrote that the ego-ideal is a substitute for the early longing for a loved father, the germ from which all religions have evolved,[54] and in *Civilisation and Its Discontents* he wrote:

> Man cannot imagine Providence in any other form than that of a greatly exhalted father, for only such a one could understand the needs of the sons of men, or be softened by their prayers and placated by the signs of their remorse.[55]

God is the magnified father and thus the religious believer continues into adult life a form of dependence which is really only appropriate to childhood. Such was Freud's answer to Schleiermacher. That not all religions postulate such a deity, nor the fact that, even in Judaism, Christianity and Islam, there is rather more to the God whom these religions believe to have revealed himself to them than that of a kindly parent, seems to have escaped the attention of Freud, as does the fact that not all families the world over are the patriarchies which his theory of religion seems to presuppose.

The gist of what Freud had to say about the role of religion in human life can also be got from two books which he published towards the end of his life – *The Future of an Illusion* published in 1927 and *Civilisation and Its Discontents*, published three years later in 1930.

In *The Future of an Illusion* religion, which is, of course, the illusion of the title, is defined as consisting of 'certain dogmas, assertions about facts and conditions of external (and internal) reality, which tell one something that one has not discovered oneself, and which claim that we should give them credence'.[56] These beliefs, for Freud, arise out of what he terms 'the most insistent wishes of mankind' – and which he further defines as the desire to escape from the hard facts of reality. Religion is wishful thinking, as it is also a regression, as we have seen, back to the secure world of childhood. For Freud, men and women project the earlier security of their childhood and particularly the security centred on the patriarchal father – Freud himself, of course, was brought up in just such a Jewish family in Vienna – on to external reality. That there actually is in reality an almighty, righteous and loving Father, or even that the universe is in any way in harmony with the striving and hopes of men and women, is for Freud an illusion, although he believes that for many men and women it is a necessary illusion.

A word should be said about Freud's use of the term 'illusion' for he took great care in *The Future of an Illusion* to distinguish between 'illusion' and 'error'. He wrote:

> An illusion is not the same as an error, it is indeed not necessarily an error. Aristotle's belief that vermin are evolved out of dung ... was an error. On the other hand, it was an illusion on the part of Columbus that he had discovered a new sea-route to India. The part played by his wish in this error is very clear ... It is characteristic of the illusion that it is derived from man's wishes ... Thus we call a belief an illusion when wish-fulfilment is a prominent factor in its motivation, while disregarding its relations to reality, just as the illusion itself does.[57]

Religion, being the product of wish-fulfilment is, therefore, an illusion, although it need not, on that count, be an error, although Freud privately thought that it was in that it failed the crucial test of being in accord with reality as Freud understood reality. Freud remained all his life an un-reconstructed positivist. In the *Psychopathology of Everyday Life* he wrote: 'I believe that a large part of the mythical view of the word, which extends a long way into the most modern religions, is nothing but psychology projected onto the external word'[58] – a statement which, as a contemporary Freudian psychoanalyst, Paul Pruyser, readily acknowledges ,'rests on a view of reality which takes the obvious world of the senses for granted and gives it the status of an uncontroversial reference point for all sane people'. Pruyser continues: 'Freud did not attempt to define reality in any ultimate sense; he stuck to the position of positivism, if not naïve realism, when he spoke of the reality principle, outer world, body, perception, internalisation, and projection.'[59] On such an epistemology the issue of the truth or otherwise of religious affirmations is, of course, foreclosed from the very outset of the enquiry. Freud could never have contemplated, as we shall see in the next chapter, Peter Berger, a contemporary sociologist, contemplating that the 'projections' spun from the human psyche might correspond to something 'out there' in a reality beyond both the individual human being and his or her society. It was, perhaps, for this reason that Freud never seems to have seriously considered that religion, unlike other cultural productions – art, music, literature and so on – could ever be the outcome of the process that he called 'sublimation', the process whereby the sexual and aggressive drives in human nature are diverted to other, more socially tolerable and acceptable ends. Yet despite the inbuilt limitations in Freud's understanding of religion, it could still be, as we shall see shortly, that some of the things that he says about religion and religious behaviour offer genuine insights into what a Christian psychoanalyst, R. S. Lee, has called 'the pathology of religion'. Certainly, as Lee recognises, there are people who do, at times, thrust their cares on God in just the way that Freud imagines. Freud's mistake is to imagine that all people at all times and places have and continue to do this.[60]

Freud restated the argument of *The Future of an Illusion* in *Civilization and Its Discontents*, which he published three years after *The Future of an Illusion* in 1930, but in the new book he added what he took to be a new psycho-analytic insight into those religious rites and rituals – in the opinion of Freud the vast majority of such rituals – which were designed either to assuage guilt or bring about desired results in the world, claiming that these bore a remarkable resemblance to the obsessive behaviour of neurotics – an insight which led him to describe 'the observances by means of which the faithful give expression to their piety' as 'a universal obsessional neurosis'.[61] The fact that the behaviour of scientists in their laboratories, where the exact performance of the minutiae of accepted procedures is necessary for the successful replication of experiments, follows a not dissimilar pattern, seems to have escaped him, for nowhere in his writings does he describe science in such derogatory terms.

Yet despite his overall negative view of the role of religion in human life, he did, in *Civilization and Its Discontents*, admit that humanity was, perhaps, not yet ready to throw off the consolations which religion had to offer and face the realities of life (and death) without them. Yet he remained confident, in a way that Nietzsche could not, in the ability of science finally to overcome all resistance and to offer, if not a heroic, then at least a decent future for the majority of human beings. Thus at the close of *The Future of an Illusion* he wrote of human beings that:

> Their scientific knowledge has taught them much since the days of the Deluge, and it will increase in power still further. As for the great necessities of Fate, against which there is no help. They will learn to endure them with resignation. Of what use to them is the mirage of wide acres of the moon, whose harvest no one has yet seen? As honest smallholders on this earth they will know how to cultivate their plot in such a way that it supports them. By withdrawing their expectations from the other world and concentrating all their liberated energies into their life on earth, they will probably succeed in achieving a state of things in which life will become tolerable for everyone and civilization no longer oppressive to anyone. Then, with one of our fellow unbelievers, they will be able to say without regret: *Den Himmel überlassen wir//Den Engeln und den Spatzen* ('We leave Heaven to the angels and the sparrows': Heine).[62]

Yet despite this perhaps to our modern (and post-modern) ears over-confident faith in science, Freud did, on occasion, express caution with regard to the ability of science to answer all questions and he was aware, at times, that what he said about religion might not be an exhaustive explanation of that phenomenon. Early in his life, in *Totem and Taboo*, he wrote:

> There are no grounds for fearing that psychoanalysis, which first discovered that psychical acts and structures are invariably over-determined, will be tempted to trace the origin of anything so complicated as religion to a single cause. If psychoanalysis is compelled – and is, indeed, duty-bound – to lay all the emphasis on one particular source, that does not mean it is claiming either that the source is the only one or that it occupies first place among the numerous contributory factors. Only when we can synthesise the findings in the different fields of research will it become possible to arrive at the relative importance of the part played in the genesis of religion by the mechanism discussed in these pages. Such a task lies beyond the means as well as beyond the purpose of the psychoanalyst.[63]

And towards the end of his life, in *The Future of an Illusion*, he wrote: 'It does not lie within the scope of this enquiry to estimate the value of religious doctrines as truth.'[64] Freud was, however, all too inclined to forget these caveats so that, as we have noted, whilst in *The Future of an Illusion* he distinguished very carefully between 'illusion' and 'error', he took it for granted that religion was both an illusion, that is, the product of wishful thinking, and an error, that is, false. Yet nowhere in his writings does he argue this. Freud was a child of the Enlightenment and he, therefore, accepted uncritically the Enlightenment assumption that the claims of religion no longer merit serious discussion. Therapy and not argument was what was needed when confronted by the phenomenon of religion, although Freud was under no illusions as to the difficulty such therapy would encounter. 'It is painful to think', he wrote, 'that the great majority of mortals will never be able to rise above this [infantile] view of life [that religion offers].' Science might not prevail, 'but an illusion it would be', he continued, 'to suppose that what science cannot give us we can get elsewhere'.[65]

What then are we to make of Freud's account of the genealogy of religion? The first thing that strikes the historian of religion when confronted by Freud's writings on religion is the limited nature of his knowledge of religion – a knowledge which is confined almost entirely to Judaism and Christianity and to a limited and selective use of such knowledge of so-called primitive religions as was available to him. Freud has nothing at all to say about polytheism, nor about those religions where worship of the feminine predominates, just as he has nothing to say about non-theistic forms of religion. Even his characterisation of the Judaic and Christian God is something little short of a travesty to anyone – believer or unbeliever – acquainted with their theologies.

Freud's description of the psychic forces at work in human beings that lead them to create and sustain religions has recently come under intensive criticism both from his fellow psychologists as well as from philosophers and sociologists. Indeed it would not be too strong a statement to say that the entire psychoanalytical enterprise associated with Freud is today being questioned in ways that would have been inconceivable a generation ago.[66] What will survive the current reassessment of Freud's legacy it is not within the scope of our enquiry here to speculate. All we can note is that his legacy seriously calls into question any theory of religion based upon it.

The conclusion to be drawn is that whilst Freud might have some insights to offer to the question why certain individuals are drawn to certain particular forms of religion, the claim that he in any sense offers a theory that explains the existence of all forms of religion cannot be sustained and in his more sanguine moments Freud, as indicated in the quotation given earlier from *Totem and Taboo*, would have agreed.

'I have not the courage,' Freud wrote towards the end of his life, 'to rise up before my fellow men as a prophet. I bow to the reproach that I can offer them no consolation.'[67] Carl Gustav Jung had no such inhibitions.

– CARL GUSTAV JUNG –

Jung was born in Kesswil in the canton of Thurgau in Switzerland in 1895, the son of a Zwinglian pastor. After reading medicine at the University of Basel he began his career as a psychiatrist at both the Burghölzi Mental Hospital and the Psychiatric Clinic in Zurich. Initially impressed by the work of Freud, he gradually became increasingly critical of Freud's theory of infantile sexuality and began to develop his own lines of enquiry which first entered the public domain with the publication of his *Psychology of the Unconscious* in 1912. Extended trips abroad, first in North Africa then to Arizona, New Mexico, East Africa and India, led him to take an interest in primal religions and the primal mentality, and his friendship with Richard Wilhelm, the Director of the China Institute in Frankfurt, led to a lifelong interest in Chinese culture. His friendship with the German Indiologist Zimmer and the Hungarian folklorist Karl Kerényi extended his awareness of cultural diversity yet further. He also had a lifelong interest in the occult and in the data of the history and comparative study of religions, and more particularly in comparative mythology. Jung could claim, therefore, with justification, that his work on the human mind and on human culture was more broadly based than was that of Freud. He was also, however, as the researches of Richard Noll have shown, deeply influenced by Nietzsche and by some of the more bizarre figures of the various life-philosophies (*lebensphilosophie*), occult and *völkische* movements which were prevalent in *fin de siècle* Germany and Switzerland – figures such as Otto Gross, Count Keyserling and Johann Bachofen.[68]

With Freud, Jung accepts the division of mental life – of the *psyche* as he calls it – into conscious and unconscious parts, and although his account of both differs radically from that given by Freud, like Freud, he sees the origin of religion, as well as of art, music, literature and indeed of all cultural production, as having its ultimate origin within the unconscious realm of the mind. However, Jung's account of the unconscious is richer, broader and much more positive than that given by Freud, and, unlike Freud's, it is not biologically reductive, for the *psyche*, for Jung, is a reality with its own structure and its own laws and it plays, or can play, a positive part in the life of human beings. His term for it is *libido*, but with little of the sexual overtones that the term has now acquired. The *libido* is the source of men and women's deepest and most enduring longings and Jung is quite severe in his strictures on those who speak of its manifestations disparagingly as 'merely subjective' or as 'nothing but imagination'. The life of the *psyche*, he asserts, is dynamic, and, when properly regulated, rewarding. The *libido* is the source of psychic energy and its primary role is to serve the purposes of life including the creation of culture. This, for Jung, is achieved, largely through the surplus energy of the *libido* being redirected towards the creation of symbolic activities – many of which are associated with mythology and religion. Jung has a much more positive appreciation of the role of religion in human life than had Freud, and his work has inspired the work of many theologians and historians of religion, although, as we shall also see, there remains a teasing and indeed irritating ambiguity about what Jung understands by the truth of religion.[69]

Before we turn to look in detail at Jung's theory of religion, it will be necessary, as it was with Freud, to look at Jung's general view of human nature in order that we might place what he says about religion in context. We must also bear in mind what Jung means by 'symbol' and by 'symbolic expression', for his use of these expressions is extremely precise. In particular he draws a clear dividing line between a sign and a symbol. A sign, he says, is simply a substitute for, or a representation of, the real thing, whilst a symbol expresses a psychic fact that cannot easily be represented in any other way.[70]

Jung's view of the unconscious is much more positive than the views of those who see the unconscious as but the repository of everything bestial and infantile within us or of all we want to forget and have repressed. The unconscious certainly contains such things, but it also contains the germs of new life possibilities. Jung, in fact, sees the unconscious as consisting of two different aspects – 'the personal unconscious' which contains the repressed and suppressed elements of consciousness and 'the collective unconscious' which is the unconscious in the fullest sense of the word and the positing of which represents Jung's most well-known and most controversial contribution to psychology. The personal unconscious belongs to the individual. It contains his or her repressed wishes, suppressed subliminal perceptions and forgotten experiences. Some of these can be recalled by the methods pioneered by Freud – by means of dreams, association tests and so on – others surface in neurosis and like illnesses. The collective unconscious, however, lies at a deeper level of the un-conscious – hence the term 'depth psychology' often used to describe Jung's psychology – but can be inferred from observation of instinctual behaviour, defined by Jung as 'impulses to action without conscious motivation', although it was only certain instinctual actions which, owing to their universality, Jung termed 'inherited and unconscious' and which he found 'uniformly and regularly occurring everywhere', so much so that, for him, these belonged properly to what he termed 'the collective unconscious'.[71] What impressed Jung about instinct was not just the fact that human beings appeared compelled to certain broad lines of action in specific circum-stances, but that they appeared to experience and understand life in a way that could only be accounted for by postulating some form of genetic inheritance. Jung did not mean by this that the experiences themselves were inherited. What he suggested was that the brain itself had been shaped by the remote experiences of mankind. As he himself puts it:

> Although our inheritance consists in physiological paths, still it was mental processes in our ancestors that created the paths. If these traces come to con-sciousness again in the individual, they can do so only in the form of mental processes; and if these processes can become conscious only through individual experience and thus appear as individual acquisitions, they are none the less pre-existing traces, which are merely filled out by the individual experience. Every 'impressive' experience is such an impression, in an ancient but unconscious stream bed.[72]

This tendency to apprehend experience in a manner conditioned by the past history of mankind Jung calls 'archetypal' and the 'archetypes' them-selves he describes as 'the pre-existent forms of apprehension' (that is, existing before consciousness) or 'congenital conditions of intuition'.[73] Jung's more well-known term for them is 'the archetypes of the collective unconscious'. His earlier term, taken from the Swiss cultural historian Jacob Burckhardt, was 'primordial images' (urtümliche Bilder). They are the result of the many recurring experiences of life – the rising and setting of the sun, the cycle of the seasons, the search for sexual satisfaction, the experiences of birth and death, the experience of danger, the search for food and so on – all of which find expression, for Jung, in powerful, recurring images or symbols which are found not only in the mythologies of the world, but also in dreams and (abnormally) in the experiences of schizophrenics and other mentally disturbed individuals. Jung was impressed by the fact that many of the images which occurred in the dreams of his patients seemed to corresponded to images found in primitive and archaic mythology of which he was certain they could have had no prior knowledge. These archetypal images – of the earth-mother, the wise old man, the trickster, the sun-god and so on – which, according to Jung, reoccurred in the dreams of his patients, his friends, and, indeed, in his own dreams, were to be regarded as fundamental expressions of human nature which modern men and women, obsessed as Jung believed they were by rational understanding, ignored at their peril, for these emotionally charged images would not forever remain unexpressed and whilst, for the most part, they inhabited what he called the 'shadow' side of our mental and spiritual life, in moments of acute crisis they could come forth with terrible consequences for both the individual and, as in the case of Nazi Germany, for Europe and the world. Both psychic and social health, therefore, demanded that we recognise the existence of this 'shadow' side of human nature and seek to come to terms with it. Further, the collective unconscious and its archetypes inspired not only destruction but also creation. It was, said Jung, 'the buried treasure from which mankind has ever and anon drawn, and from which it has raised up its gods and demons and all those potent and almighty thoughts without which man ceases to be man'.[74]

Here we begin to touch on what Jung had to say about the origin and role of religion in human life for, for Jung, the 'shadow side' of the human psyche contains the greatest of all the archetypal images – that of the Self, which Jung identifies with God. God, for Jung, was a psychic reality and the way to knowledge of the Divine and of the salvation which a proper and harmonious relationship with the Divine had to offer, lay within. Here we can begin to detect the influences that Jung had absorbed from his study of the religions of the East.

For Jung, men and women were naturally religious, and psychic health and stability– as Jung argued in the most well-known of all his many books, the collection of essays which he published in 1933 as *Modern Man in Search of a Soul* – lay in the proper expression of this religiosity every whit as it did in the proper and regulated expression of the instincts and here, to mitigate the charge of irrationalism which has often been levelled at Jung,

the conscious mind, aware of and working over the contents of the unconscious, had a major role to play.

Jung defines religion as:

an attitude of the human mind, which could be formulated in accordance with
the original use of the term 'religio', that is a careful consideration and observation of certain dynamic factors, understood to be 'powers', spirits, demons,
gods, laws, ideals or whatever name man has given to such factors as he has found
in his world, powerful dangerous, or helpful enough to be taken into careful
consideration, or grand beautiful, and meaningful enough to be devoutly adored
and loved.[75]

The important word in this definition is 'dynamic' and what must be of
interest to the student of religion is where Jung locates such powers, for of
their reality he has no doubts. The answer is, of course, that Jung locates
these powers in the psyche itself. They are, in fact, 'the archetypes of
the collective unconscious'. The task of the psychotherapist, as of the
theologian, is, therefore, to help the individual to express these 'powers' in
socially acceptable and individually satisfying ways. This process Jung calls
'individuation'. This is a state of being where individuals achieve peace and
harmony with themselves by reconciling the conscious and the unconscious aspects of their being. Jung wrote:

Consciousness and unconsciousness do not make a whole when either is suppressed or damaged by the other. If they must contend, let it be a fair fight with
equal rights on both sides. Both are aspects of life. Let consciousness defend its
reason and its self-protective ways, and let the chaotic life of the unconscious be
given a fair chance to have its own way, as much of it as we can stand. This means
at once open conflict and open collaboration. Yet, paradoxically, this is pre-
sumably what human life should be. It is the old play of hammer and anvil: the
suffering iron between them will in the end be shaped into an unbreakable whole,
the individual. This experience is what is called – the process of individuation.[76]

The manner in which this 'process of individuation' is accomplished
varies, according to Jung, with the age of the person involved. The coming
to terms with the archetypes will be different for the young than for those
who are in the second half of their lives for it is in the second half of life
that we are much more likely to meet with the archetypes of the collective
unconscious – a meeting fraught with danger as men and women face the
perils of succumbing to their peculiar fascination. The fortunate, however,
will discover what Jung, drawing on his knowledge of Buddhist and
Chinese religious thought, calls 'the Diamond Body' or 'the Golden Flower'
– the archetypes of psychic wholeness. He wrote:

Though everything is experienced in image form, symbolically, it is by no means a question of playhouse dangers, but of very real risks, upon which the fate of the whole life may depend. The chief danger is that of succumbing to the uncannily fascinating influence of living archetypes. If we do, we may come to a standstill either in a symbolic situation or in an identification with an archetypal personality.[77]

Jung is moving, in passages such as this, from the language of science to the language of religion, and a passage from the strangest of all his writings – his book on *Psychology and Alchemy* – provides further illustration of the way in which he mixes the language of science and the language of religion. He wrote:

It is absolutely necessary to supply those fantastic images that rise up so strong and threatening before the mind's eye with a sort of context so as to make them more intelligible. The psychological elucidation of these images, which cannot be passed over in silence or blindly ignored, leads logically into the depths of religious phenomenology. The history of religion in its widest sense (including therefore mythology, folklore and primitive psychology) is a treasure house of archetypal forms from which the doctor can draw helpful parallels and enlightening comparisons for the purpose of calming and clarifying a consciousness that is all at sea.[78]

Religion, in some form or other, is necessary, argues Jung, if men and women are to be made whole and to achieve peace with themselves and with the world.

Reactions to Jung have ranged from those who see him as the father of all psychological gobbledegook to those who, like the student of comparative mythology Joseph Campbell, see him as a great thinker and healer who offers the way forward to a truer understanding than hitherto of the place of mythology and religion in the lives of men and women. Others have questioned the very existence of the archetypes and have doubted or denied the physiological and genetic base required to substantiate Jung's claim that they are inherited, whilst yet others have asked, why, if the archetypes are but the deposit of a more primitive experience of the world, we should take them seriously. Yet, as Joseph Campbell has shown in his monumental study of comparative mythology *The Masks of God*, the archetypal images which lie at the root of all mythology are not easily dismissed. Denied one route of access they will most surely find another and often more devastating way of expression – as, to cite Campbell's own example at the outset of the first volume of *The Masks of God*, the mythology underlying the world outlook of National Socialism in Germany in the first half of the present century.[79]

Whilst many theologians have welcomed Jung's support for religion, others, perhaps showing more perception, have been worried by what Jung understands by religion for, whilst recognising that the myths of religion, including belief in God, are psychic facts, and whilst recognising also the pragmatic value that religion can have in human life, Jung's attitude to the truth of religions remained somewhat gnomic. Working as he did with all religious traditions, his criterion for truth would appear to be a pragmatic one. Religion works in that it has obvious therapeutic value for some, though by no means all, individuals. The ultimate ontological status of the claims made by the religions of the world is not something upon which Jung passes judgement.

More worrying for adherents of established religions is the fact that, as Richard Noll has shown in his controversial study of Jung entitled *The Jung Cult*, a case can be made for seeing Jung as consciously seeking to found a new religion. His influence on what has been termed 'New Age Spirituality' has been profound and Noll recognises this, but goes further and argues that Jung himself actively sought to establish a new religion with himself as its founder. This is not the place to discuss this charge. Of itself it need not tell against the truth of Jung's understanding of the religion anymore than it tells against that of Jesus of Nazareth, Muhammad or Buddha. If Jung sought to establish a new religion then this must be examined on its merits. This is not our concern. Our concern is with what Jung had to say about religion in general and his view is that religion – all religions – have their origin in the collective unconscious and in the desire on the part of human beings for deification or divinisation – Jung's own preferred term is god-likeness. Whilst the first of these positions is tenuous to say the least, the latter is one which finds an echo throughout the history of religions – East and West.

Jung's theory can be seen as in some ways a variation on both Feuerbach and Freud's theories of religion as a projection onto the universe of that which properly appertains to human nature, although what is projected, for Jung, are the archetypes of the collective unconscious rather than, as for Feuerbach, the human attributes of reason, will and love. Jung has a very different conception of what is to be a human being and thus of what constitutes human fulfilment than had Feuerbach and Freud and it is a conception, as Jung acknowledges, which owes much, though by no means all, to certain movements in the Indian religious tradition. Much depends on the ontological status Jung accords to the archetypes of the collective unconscious, for Jung can be seen as doing what a number of contemporary Christian theologians have been doing and that is to move from a model where the supernatural realm is thought of as being outwith the world to one in which it is related to the interior life of human beings. It need not, for that reason, be any the less objective. Much depends on the ontological status accorded to the archetypes of the collective unconscious.

There is, of course, more to the complex phenomena of religion in human life than those aspects of religion upon which Jung focused his attention, but what Jung offers is not a general theory of religion, but an interpretative theory which tells us what, in his opinion, religion is really about. This, of course, is the case with Feuerbach, Nietzsche and Freud. The difference is that Jung sees positive virtues in religion and offers therefore, unlike Nietzsche and Freud, a sympathetic interpretation of religion. In fact Jung's theory is, at bottom, a religious theory of religion rather than a naturalistic one and it is one that has inspired theologians in a variety of traditions to rethink the fundamental premises of their own tradition. Its scientific status, however, remains problematical.

All the thinkers we have considered in this chapter sought in their own way to reintegrate men and women back into the world and to rescue them from the alienation which they saw as having been brought about by religious traditions which teach that the world is not men and women's true home and which urge them to seek redemption from it. A similar criticism of religion can be found in the thought of those who see religion as a social as well as a psychological construct. However, where religion is considered a psychological construct, this need not mean, although in the case of the thinkers whom we have considered, with the exception of Jung and the early Feuerbach, it certainly has involved, the total rejection of religion. Seeing religion as a psychological construct might, however, presage new forms for old religions – forms in which the traditional Abrahamic model of a God 'out there' is replaced by something approximating to the model put forward in certain movements within the Hindu tradition of 'the God within'. This would also involve a radical reinterpretation of what it is to be a human being.

A variation on the theory that religion is a psychological construct is the theory that it is a social construct. The two need not be at variance: indeed, in that society is made up of individuals, the social construction of reality cannot be other than a psychological process even where, as in the case of thinkers to whom we now turn, what is emphasised are the social (psychological) forces behind the construction of religion.[80]

– NOTES –

1. For a brief history of the naturalistic understanding of religion c.f. J. Samuel Preus, *Explaining Religion*, New Haven: Yale University Press, 1987.
2. Feuerbach, *The Principles of the Philosophy of the Future* in *The Fiery Brook: Selected Writings of Ludwig Feuerbach*, ed. Z. Hanafi, New York: Doubleday Anchor Books, 1972, p. 177.

3. Ludwig Feuerbach, *The Essence of Christianity*, trans. George Eliot, New York: Harper & Row, 1957, p. 13.
4. Gregor Nüdling, *Ludwig Feuerbachs Religionsphilosophie*, Paderborn: Schöningh, 1936.
5. Van A. Harvey, *Feuerbach and the Interpretation of Religion*, Cambridge: CUP, 1995, p. 211.
6. Feuerbach, *The Essence of Faith According to Luther*, trans. Melvin Cherno, New York: Harper & Row, 1967; *Lectures on the Essence of Religion*, trans. Ralph Manheim, New York: Harper & Row, 1967.
7. Feuerbach, *Essence of Christianity*, p. 29.
8. Ibid., p. 23.
9. Ibid., p. 3.
10. Ibid., p. 5.
11. Ibid., p. 152.
12. Ibid., p. 33.
13. Ibid., p. 184.
14. L. Feuerbach, *Das Wesen der Religion* in *Gesammelte Werke*, ed. Werner Schuffenhauer, Berlin: Akademie-Verlag, 1981–93, Vol. X.
15. Feuerbach, *Lectures on the Essence of Religion*, para. 2, p. 4.
16. Leszek Kolakowski, *Main Currents of Marxism*, Oxford: Clarendon Press, 1978, Vol. 1, p. 117.
17. Quoted ibid., pp. 117–18.
18. Feuerbach, *Lectures*, p. 202.
19. Harvey, *Feuerbach*, p. 230.
20. C.f. Ernest Becker, *The Denial of Death*, New York: The Free Press, 1973; Stewart Elliot Guthrie, *Faces in the Clouds: A New Theory of Religion*, New York: OUP, 1993.
21. Sidney Hook, *From Hegel to Marx: Studies in the Intellectual Development of Karl Marx*, Ann Arbor: University of Michigan Press, 1966, p. 221.
22. Feuerbach, *Essence of Christianity*, p. 198.
23. Neusch, *The Sources of Modern Atheism*, trans. Mathew J. O'Connell, New York: Paulist Press, 1977, pp. 48–9.
24. Feuerbach, cited in Marcel Xhaufflaire, *Feuerbach et la théologie de la Sécularisation*, trans. M. Neusch, Paris: Cogiratio fidei 45, Cerf. 1970, p. 259.
25. Nietzsche, letter of 11 June 1865 in *Selected Letters of Friedrich Nietzsche*, ed. and trans. C. Middleton, Chicago: Chicago University Press, 1969, p. 7.
26. Nietzsche, *The Birth of Tragedy*, trans. Francis Golffing, New York: Doubleday Anchor, 1956, §23.
27. Nietzsche, *The Twilight of the Idols*, in Walter Kaufmann, *The Portable Nietzsche*, New York: The Viking Press, 1954, p. 485.
28. J. P. Stern, *Nietzsche*, London: Collins/Fontana, 1978, p. 53f.
29. Francis Fukuyama, *The End of History and the Last Man*, London: Hamish Hamilton, 1992, pp. 308–10.
30. Max Weber, 'Science as a Vocation', in H. H. Gerth and C. Wright Mills, *From Max Weber: Essays in Sociology*, New York: Oxford University Press, 1946, p. 143. Nietzsche's picture of 'the last man' can be found at various places in his writings. A concise exposition, with examples drawn from contemporary society, of Nietzsche's criticism of the rational bureaucratic society can be found in chapter 28 of Fukuyama's *The End of History and the Last Man*.
31. Stern, *Nietzsche*, pp. 57–8.

32. Walter Kaufmann, *Nietzsche: Philosopher, Psychologist, Antichrist*, New York: Meridian Books, 1956, p. 82.

33. Nietzsche, *The Gay Science*, sect. 125, in Kaufmann, *Portable Nietzsche*, pp. 95–6.

34. Nietzsche, *Thus Spoke Zarathustra*, trans. R. J. Hollingdale, Harmondsworth: Penguin Classics, 1961, p. 42.

35. Nietzsche, *The Will to Power*, trans. W. Kaufmann and R. J. Hollingdale, New York: Random House, 1967, p. 117.

36. Nietzsche, *The Dawn of the Day* in *The Complete Works of Friedrich Nietzsche*, trans. J. M. Kennedy and ed. O. Levy, New York: Russell & Russell, 1964, Vol. 9, §91.

37. Nietzsche, *The Will to Power*, ed. Walter Kaufmann, New York: Random House, 1967, §135, pp. 85–6.

38. For a discussion of what Nietzsche means by 'genealogy' c.f. Richard Schacht, *Nietzsche*, Routledge & Kegan Paul, 1983, pp. 127–30.

39. Nietzsche, *The Will to Power*, §29, p. 123.

40. Ibid., §215, p. 126.

41. J.-P. Sartre, *Existentialism and Humanism*, trans. Philip Mairet, London: Methuen, 1948.

42. Nicholas Martin reviewing Michael Tanner, *Nietzsche*, Oxford: OUP, 1996 in the *Times Literary Supplement*, 19 April 1996, p. 27.

43. For a discussion of the anti-humanism of Foucault and other French thinkers c.f. Tony Davies, *Humanism*, London: Routledge, 1997, pp. 32–4, 35–6, 47–50, 131 and more especially pp. 69–71. C.f. also Eric Matthews, *Twentieth-Century French Philosophy*, Oxford: OUP, 1996, pp.147–56.

44. Michel Foucault, *The Order of Things: An Archaeology of the Human Sciences*, London: Tavistock, 1970, p. 387.

45. Ibid., p. 387.

46. Adams, *Everyman's Psychology*, London, 1930, p. 17.

47. Stuart Hampshire, *Thought and Action*, London: Chatto & Windus, 1982, pp. 132, 133. Walter Kaufmann made essentially the same point when he wrote: 'Much has been made of his [Freud's] "determinism"; but the whole purpose of his therapy was to restore their freedom to people who had become unable to do what they wanted to do, or to stop doing what they wanted to stop doing.' *From Shakespeare to Existentialism*, New York: Doubleday Anchor Books, 1960, p. 330.

48. Freud, *Totem and Taboo*, trans. James Strachey, New York: Norton, 1950, p. 78.

49. Freud, *The Future of an Illusion*, trans. James Strachey, New York: Norton, 1961, p. 29.

50. C.f. Freud, *The Interpretation of Dreams*, London: Allen & Unwin, 1900.

51. For a detailed account and critique of this theory c.f. Edward Evans-Pritchard, *Theories of Primitive Religion*, Oxford: Clarendon Press, 1965, pp. 41–3. A more sympathetic assessment can be found in the Freudian psychoanalyst Paul Pruyser's contribution to C. Y. Glock and P. E. Hammond (eds), *Beyond the Classics: Essays in the Scientific Study of Religions*, New York: Harper & Row, 1973, 'Sigmund Freud and His Legacy: Psychoanalytic Psychology of Religion', pp. 243–90. A somewhat bizarre post-modernist attempt to see Freud as a religious thinker and *Totem and Taboo* and *Moses and Monotheism* as religious texts can be found in Regina Schwartz's chapter 'Freud's God' in *Post-Secular Philosophy*, ed. Phillip Bond, London: Routledge, 1998, pp. 281–304.

52. Freud, *Leonardo da Vinci*, London: Kegan Paul, 1932, p. 103.

53. Ernest Jones, *The Life and Work of Sigmund Freud*, Harmondsworth: Pelican Books, 1964, p. 55.

54. Freud, *The Ego and the Id*, London: Hogarth Press, 1962, p. 37.

55. Freud, *Civilization and its Discontents*, London: Hogarth Press, 1939, p. 23.
56. Freud, *The Future of an Illusion*, London: Hogarth Press, 1934, p. 45.
57. Ibid., pp. 53–4.
58. Freud, *The Psychopathology of Everyday Life*, Harmondsworth: Pelican Books, p. 258.
59. Pruyser, 'Sigmund Freud and His Legacy', p. 262.
60. R. S. Lee, *Freud and Christianity*, Harmondsworth: Pelican Books, 1967, pp. 9, 11.
61. Freud, *Collected Papers*, New York: Basic Books, 1959, Vol. 2, p. 34.
62. Freud, *The Future of an Illusion*, trans. James Strachey, New York: Norton, p. 82.
63. Freud, *Totem and Taboo* in *The Complete Psychological Works of Sigmund Freud*, ed. James Strachey and Anna Freud, London: Hogarth Press, 1953– , Vol. XIII, p. 100.
64. Freud, *The Future of an Illusion*, New York: Norton, 1961, p. 57.
65. Freud, *Civilization and its Discontents*, p. 21; c.f. also *The Future of an Illusion*, p. 92.
66. The challenge to psychoanalysis's claim to be a science has been put particularly forcibly in Arthur Grünbaum, *The Foundations of Psychoanalysis*, Berkeley, CA: University of California Press, 1984, and in his *Validation in the Clinical Theory of Psychoanalysis: A Study in the Philosophy of Psychoanalysis*, Madison, CT: International University Press, 1993. For a more rounded appreciation and critique of Freud c.f. Frank Sulloway, *Freud: Biologist of the Mind: Beyond the Psychoanalytic Method*, New York: Basic Books, 1979. Criticism of Freud's arguments by (dubious) analogy can be found in Malcolm Macmillan, *Freud Evaluated: The Completed Arc*, New York: North Holland, 1991. For trenchant criticism of Freud's understanding of primitive religion c.f. Evans-Pritchard, *Theories of Primitive Religion*, pp. 41–3.
67. Freud, *The Complete Psychological Works*, Vol. XXI, p. 145.
68. Richard Noll, *The Jung Cult: Origins of a Charismatic Movement*, London: Harper Collins/Fontana, 1996, part I.
69. E.g. Victor White, *God and the Unconscious*, London: Collins/Fontana, 1960.
70. Jung, *Contributions to Analytical Psychology*, London: Kegan Paul, 1928, p. 47.
71. Ibid., pp. 271 and 273.
72. Ibid., p. 61.
73. Ibid., p. 276.
74. Jung, *Two Essays on Analytical Psychology*, London: Hogarth Press, 1953, para. 104.
75. Jung, *Psychology and Religion: West and East*, London: Hogarth Press, 1958, p. 5.
76. Jung, *The Integration of the Personality*, London: Kegan Paul, 1940, p. 27.
77. Ibid., p. 90.
78. Jung, *Psychology and Alchemy*, London: Hogarth Press, 1953, para. 38.
79. Campbell, *The Masks of God*, Vol. I: *Primitive Mythology*, Harmondsworth: Penguin Books, 1976, pp. 11–12.
80. It is thus hard, for example, to see the point of Evans-Pritchard's criticism of Durkheim that he breaks his own rules of sociological method by putting forward a psychological rather than a sociological explanation of religion for it is hard to see what a purely sociological explanation that did not involve some reference to collective, if not necessarily individual, psychology might be. C.f. Evans-Pritchard, *Theories of Primitive Religion*, pp. 67–8.

CHAPTER 8

Religion as Social Construct

We turn finally to those who see religion not as the creation of individuals but of society. The foremost representatives of this approach are Karl Marx and his collaborator Friedrich Engels, Émile Durkheim, Max Weber and, more recently, and in a qualified way, Peter Berger.

– MARX AND ENGELS –

Marx was born in 1818 at Trier in the Rhineland into an ethnically Jewish but formally Christian although somewhat freethinking family. Educated at the universities of Bonn and Berlin, Marx realised that his radical political opinions precluded him from the academic career to which he felt drawn and, after successfully sustaining his doctoral dissertation, he entered the field of radical journalism instead. Owing to his involvement in radical causes, he had to move, first to Paris, then to Brussels and Cologne, and finally, in 1849, to London to escape prosecution. There he lived out the remainder of his life devoting himself to writing – writing in which he sought to expose the unsatisfactory nature of capitalism and show the necessity for its revolutionary transformation first into socialism and then into communism. He died in London in March 1883.

Engels was born at Barmen in the Wuppertal valley not far from Düsseldorf in 1820 the son of a rich textile manufacturer. His education was very different from that of Marx in that he left school before his final year to work in his father's factory. He had grown up in a stifling atmosphere of narrow-minded evangelical pietism and only managed to escape from this when he was sent to Bremen to gain business experience. It was here that his interest in social questions was first aroused and he embarked on a course of private study which led him to make contact with the Young Hegelian radicals one of whom was Karl Marx. He was attracted for a time to Schleiermacher's sentimental pietism, but, on reading Strauss's *Life of*

Jesus, he abandoned Christianity completely and embraced atheism. Like Marx he began to contribute to the radical journals of his day. In 1842 he went to work in one of his father's factories in Manchester and it was during this initial two-year stay in England that he did the research for his book *The Condition of the English Working Class* published in Leipzig in 1845. His meeting with Marx in Paris in August 1844 and later in England where Engels had taken up permanent residence marked the beginning of forty years of friendship and collaboration between the two men which came to an end only with Marx's death. Engels lived on for a further twelve years during which he wrote a number of important works of his own. He died in 1895.

Although there is evidence that in adolescence Marx had moments of fervent, if somewhat sentimental religious fervour, by the time he became a student in Berlin, in 1836, such religious beliefs as he might have once held had been abandoned. In a letter to his father in 1837, in which he describes his spiritual Odyssey, he wrote:

> From the idealism which, by the way, I had compared and nourished with the idealism of Kant and Fichte, I arrived at the point of seeking the idea in reality itself. If previously the Gods dwelt above the earth, now they became its very centre.[1]

And in the introduction to his doctoral thesis *On the Difference between the Natural Philosophy of Democritus and the Natural Philosophy of Epicurus*, written in 1841, he wrote:

> Philosophy makes no secret of it. The confession of Prometheus: 'In simple words I hate the pack of gods' is its own confession, its own aphorism against all gods who do not acknowledge human self-consciousness as the highest divinity. It will have none other besides.[2]

Marx had read his Feuerbach and his atheism was not, as some have maintained, accidental, but integral to the vision of the revolutionary transformation of humanity to which, in the early 1840s, he was beginning to commit himself. Feuerbach had placed human self-consciousness, that is the way in which human beings viewed themselves, at the very centre of his philosophy and Marx, as the quotation given above makes clear, did likewise. With Feuerbach and the 'left' Hegelians Marx, at this stage in his thinking, believed that a change in the way human beings viewed themselves was all that was needed to take human nature, and hence human society, out of the alienated state into which it had fallen during the long course of human history. As he wrote to his collaborator on the *Deutsch-Französische Jahrbücher*, Arnold Ruge, in 1843:

The self-confidence of the human being, freedom, has first of all to be aroused again in the hearts of these people. Only this feeling, which vanished from the world with the Greeks, and under Christianity disappeared into the blue mists of the heavens, can again transform society into a community of human beings united for their highest aims, into a democratic state.[3]

Although Marx began his critique of religion and of society at the point where this had been left by Feuerbach, he soon came to realise that transforming human consciousness was insufficient of itself to bring about change in the real world, and both he and Engels also came to see that the philosophical anthropology espoused by (the early) Feuerbach was no less abstract and no less remote from the real concerns of the majority of men and women – from poverty, exploitation and political tyranny – than was the Hegelian notion of Spirit which Feuerbach had criticised. Feuerbach saw human beings as alienated from themselves because they were subject to what he saw as the creations of their own consciousness and in particular to the images of themselves enshrined in and re-enforced by religion. Feuerbach's solution was to relocate these images and restore human beings to themselves. This, argued Marx and Engels, did not get to the heart of the political and social problems with which they were beginning to become concerned. For them it was existing economic and social conditions and not religion that was the true cause of human alienation. Whilst the re-jection of religion was a prerequisite for the liberation of men and women, religion, they argued, was not the real enemy, for it was but the symptom of a deeper malaise. This is made clear in the well-known passage from Marx's *Notes Towards a Critique of Hegel's Philosophy of Right*, in which he described religion as the 'opium of the people', a passage which, whilst it begins from the position taken by Feuerbach that men and women make religion, goes on to ask the further question, *why* do men and women do this? He wrote: 'The basis of irreligious criticism is: Man makes religion, religion does not make man. Religion is the self-consciousness and self-esteem of man who has either not yet found himself or has already lost himself again.' But he immediately adds that 'Man is no abstract being encamped outside the world, Man is the world of man, the state, society. This state, this society produce religion, an inverted world-consciousness because they are an inverted world.'[4]

What Marx is saying is that men and women are essentially social beings who live in particular historical circumstances – something which has important consequences for the way in which he understood human alienation, for alienation, for Marx, does not originate, nor does it operate, in the restricted area of the spiritual life, that is in religion and philosophy, but in the total world which men and women inhabit and, above all, in the world of political, economic and social reality, and he saw that under existing political, social and economic conditions, robbed of the fruit of their labour, the majority of men and women had become the victims of a universal perversion. Whilst Feuerbach has seen alienation as rooted in religious perversion – the oppression of men and women, the real creators, by God, their own creation – Marx saw alienation as rooted in existing socio-economic and political relationships. It is here that men and women are enslaved by their own productions and so alienated on every side. Thus the religious form of alienation was secondary for Marx, for it was but a symptom of the far more important forms of alienation which produced it. He wrote:

> Religion is the general theory of that world, its encyclopaedic compendium, its logic in a popular form, its spiritualistic *point d'honneur*, its enthusiasm, its moral sanction, its solemn complement, its universal source of consolation and justification. It is the fantastic realisation of the human essence because the human essence has no true reality. The struggle against religion is therefore indirectly the fight against the world of which religion is the spiritual aroma. Religious distress is at the same time the expression of real distress and also a protest against real distress. Religion is the sigh of the oppressed creature, the heart of a heartless world, just as it is the spirit of spiritless conditions. It is the opium of the people.[5]

Religion, as we see from the above quotation, plays a twofold role for Marx: it is both an expression of and a protest against real distress, and it is also a means whereby those who are distressed find consolation. It is, however, for Marx, a false consolation and the consequence which he drew from this was that the real struggle is not with religion, but with the world which produces religion. He wrote:

> To abolish religion as the illusory happiness of the people is to demand their real happiness. The demand to give up illusions about the existing state of affairs is the demand to give up a state of affairs that needs illusions. The criticism of religion is therefore in embryo the criticism of the vale of tears, the halo of which is religion.[6]

And he continued:

> The task of history, therefore, once the world beyond the truth has disappeared, is to establish the truth of this world. The immediate task of philosophy, which is at the service of history, once the holy form of human self-alienation has been unmasked, is to unmask self-alienation in its unholy forms. Thus the critique of heaven turns into the critique of earth.[7]

The critique of religion was, therefore, for Marx, but the first step in a wider critique, although in certain circumstances it might well be an important first step to take, for the trouble with religion, as Marx saw it, is that it distracts men and women from their true goal and, as he also saw, is often used as such by those whose interests are best served by such distraction. Religion is both a fantasy of alienated men and women and the ideology of the ruling class. Any account of Marx and Engels's mature theory of religion must give due weight to both of these insights. I shall deal with each in turn.

Marx continues his criticism of religion in his *Notes Towards a Critique of Hegel's Philosophy of Right* as follows:

> Criticism has plucked the imaginary flowers from the chain not so that man will wear the chain without any fantasy or consolation but so that he will shake off the chain and cull the living flower. The criticism of religion disillusions man to make him think and act and shape his reality like a man who has been disillusioned and has come to reason, so that he will revolve around himself and therefore round his true sun. The criticism of religion ends with the doctrine that man is the highest being for man, hence with the categorical imperative to overthrow all conditions in which man is a degraded, enslaved, neglected, contemptible being.[8]

Nietzsche would not have disagreed, although, as we saw in the last chapter, he drew very different conclusions as to what it was to think and act like 'a man'. Marx, in placing the struggle against religion within the wider context of the struggle for the total liberation of mankind, showed that, for him, the negative denial of religion is not enough, and he was far from ascribing to the struggle against religion the importance that it tended to assume in the writings of the 'left' Hegelians. Marx was, in fact, continually surprised, and on occasion not a little annoyed, by the persistent attacks on religion by Feuerbach and Bruno Bauer. As he saw it, religion in general, and the Christian religion in particular, were already *in extremis*, and the attacks on it by the 'left' Hegelians reminded him, as he said, of Sancho Panza in Cervantes's *Don Quixote*, who mercilessly beat the harmless attendants at a funeral procession. For Marx, the attack on religion was as unnecessary as it was misplaced – unnecessary because religion was a spent force; misplaced, because the real enemy was not religion but the society which produced religion. To criticise religion without criticising its secular basis advanced the liberation of man not one whit. As Marx, now writing in collaboration with Engels, wrote in *The German Ideology*:

> The 'liberation of man' is not advanced a single step by reducing philosophy, theology, substance and all the trash to 'self-consciousness' and by liberating man from the domination of these phrases ... it is only possible to achieve real liberation in the real world only by employing real means ... liberation is an historical and not a mental act.[9]

Further, to criticise religion without criticising its secular basis is to persist in a standpoint which is as theological as the religious standpoint itself, for an atheism which takes itself as an end in itself is only the negation of religion and does not succeed in transcending the religious level. As Marx wrote in his *Economic and Philosophic Manuscripts of 1844*:

> But since for the socialist man the entire so-called history of the world is nothing but the creation of man through human labour, nothing but the emergence of nature for man, so he has visible, irrefutable proof of his birth through himself, of his genesis. Since the real existence of man and nature has become evident in practice, through sense experience, because man has thus become evident for man as the being of nature, and nature for the being of man, the question about an *alien* being above nature and man, a question which implies the admission of the unreality of nature and man, has become impossible in practice. Atheism, as the denial of this unreality, has no longer any meaning, for atheism is a negation of God, and postulates the existence of man through this negation; but socialism as socialism no longer stands in need of such mediation.[10]

It was thus that Marx and Engels saw themselves bringing to fruition the process begun by German critical philosophy. In the resolution of that process philosophy itself was transformed and became, what it had not been in either Hegel or in Feuerbach, namely, revolutionary praxis. As Marx put it in the last of his *Theses on Feuerbach*: 'Philosophers have only *interpreted* the world ..., the point, however, is to *change* it.'[11]

Marx's criticism of Feuerbach was that, although he had seen rightly that religion is an alienation of the human essence, he had failed to see that the real cause of this act of self-alienation, and hence the true source of religion, lies in the fact that men and women are compelled to create the fantasy world of religion by the very nature of the society in which they live and had thought, therefore, that it would be sufficient for them to get rid of the illusions of religion for them to come to themselves. This for Marx was too simple. As he wrote in the fourth of his *Theses on Feuerbach*:

> Feuerbach starts out from the fact of religious self-estrangement, of the duplication of the world into a religious, imaginary world and a real one. His work consists in resolving the religious world into its secular basis. He overlooks the fact that after completing his work, the chief thing remains to be done. For the fact that the secular basis lifts off from itself and establishes itself in the clouds as an independent realm can only be explained by the inner strife and intrinsic contradictoriness of this secular basis. The latter must itself, therefore, first be understood in its contradictoriness and then, by the removal of the contradiction, revolutionised in practice.[12]

Feuerbach had also, in Marx's opinion, ignored the fact that man himself is a social product and that, as a consequence, religion too is a social product. He wrote;

> Feuerbach resolves the essence of religion into the essence of man. But the essence of man is no abstraction inherent in each single individual. In its reality it is the ensemble of social relations. Feuerbach, who does not enter upon a criticism of this real essence, is hence obliged ... to abstract from the historical process and to define the religious sentiment (*Gemüt*) regarded by itself, and to presuppose an abstract, isolated individual ... Feuerbach, consequently does not see that the 'religious sentiment' is itself a social product, and that the abstract individual that he analyses belongs to a particular society.[13]

Although Marx and Engels accepted Feuerbach's basic insight that religion is an illusory form of human fulfilment, they took his analysis much further by searching out the roots of religion – its secular basis – not only in human nature but in society. For Feuerbach, men and women make religion by setting up an illusory world onto which they project what the real world denies them. Marx and Engels accepted this analysis of religion but posed the further question, why do men and women create such an illusory world? – and they found the answer in the fact that society has been and still is a society in which men and women are not truly themselves. Henceforth their search for the sources of religion and their efforts to eradicate it were subsumed under what, for them, was the more important question of humanity's self-inflicted imprisonment in its own world – that is, on the problem of alienation, although, as we shall see, they also believed (rightly or wrongly) that religion was kept in being as the legitimating ideology of the ruling classes in society.

The role of 'alienation' in the philosophy of Marx is, however, difficult to determine, for the problem is that the concept functions in a variety of ways in his early writings and then disappears to re-emerge only in the manuscripts upon which he was working when he died.[14] As used in the early writings the concept is vague, ambiguous and confused.

As a concept 'alienation' is, of course, rooted in German Idealism and in the philosophy of Hegel in particular, although the mood which it sometimes appears to indicate is one which is as old and universal as humanity itself. As John Plamenatz has said:

> Theologians, poets, and ordinary men in reflective mood have spoken of man as if he were lost in the world, or as if he were oppressed by it, or have said of him that he is his own enemy, the victim of his own actions. Man at odds with himself and man a stranger in a hostile world are themes as old as poetry and myth. A human condition which is part of what Hegel and Marx refer to when they speak of alienation has long been familiar to the introspective who see that condition revealed in themselves.[15]

No part of Marx's thought owes as much to Hegel as his conception of human nature. In the third of his *Economic and Philosophical Manuscripts of 1844* Marx acknowledged his debt to Hegel in this respect as follows. He wrote:

> The outstanding achievement of Hegel's *Phenomenology* is, first, that Hegel grasps the self-creation of man as a process ... and that he, therefore, grasps the nature of labour, and conceives objective man (true, because real man) as the result of his own labour. The real, active orientation of man to himself as a species-being, or the affirmation of himself as a real species-being (i.e. as a human being), is only possible in so far as he really brings forth all his species-powers (which is possible only through the co-operative endeavours of mankind and as an outcome of history).[16]

Marx also acknowledged that Hegel understood what it is for man to suffer alienation – an understanding that takes us to the root of most social and psychological ills. He wrote:

> *The Phenomenology* is a concealed, unclear and mystifying criticism but in so far as it grasps the alienation of man ... all the elements of criticism are contained in it, and are often presented and worked out in a manner which goes far beyond Hegel's point of view. The sections devoted to the 'unhappy consciousness', the 'honest consciousness', the struggle between the 'noble' and 'base' consciousness, etc., etc., contain the critical elements (though still in an alienated form) of whole areas such as religion, the state, civil life, etc.[17]

Hegel, Marx is saying, understood what alienation is and how it is related to religion, the state and other areas of social life, although his understanding was vitiated by his desire to go beyond human beings to talk about Infinite Spirit. For Marx two facts about men and women stood out in Hegel's philosophy: that they are 'self-creative' and that they suffer 'alienation'. Men and women are the products of their own labour and become properly human only as a result of their own activities. This they do in the course of history. What is true about Hegel's understanding of human nature, Marx tells us, is that he 'grasps the self-creation of man as a process', and sees that this applies not just to individual men and women, but to humanity as a whole.

Yet Hegel's conception of what it is to be human forms part of an outlook which Marx rejected, for Marx, like Feuerbach, wanted nothing to do with Hegel's metaphysical speculations regarding Infinite Spirit or Consciousness. Men and women themselves, and not the Absolute, Infinite Spirit or Consciousness, were, for him, the true subject of the historical process. This, in Marx's own eyes, was the essence of his reform of the Hegelian dialectic. Feuerbach had argued that Hegel had succeeded in projecting human qualities, determinate predicates, into some metaphysical realm, thus elevating them to the status of 'moving subjects', so that predicates had been transformed into substantives, self-moving 'mystical subjects' and a person's determinate traits reduced thereby to the status of predicates of the Absolute Spirit. In Hegel's philosophy men and women were nothing but by-products in the life-history of the self-moving Infinite Spirit, and in rejecting this view Marx agreed with Feuerbach. But if, as Feuerbach had perceived, men and women and not Spirit are the true subject of history, then the cosmic objectification of Spirit, that is alienation in the metaphysical realm, must be translated into their real counters and ascribed to the true subjects of history, namely to men and women in the real world of time and history. This was the task which Marx set himself when he claimed to have found Hegel standing on his head and to have set him the right way up.[18] Much in Hegel's understanding of men and women and of alienation would, however, survive this process.

Marx recognised that although men and women are produced by nature they are in many crucial respects different from the rest of nature. Mental activity, for Marx, was inconceivable apart from the bodily behaviour in which it was manifested, and inconceivable except within the context of an environment external to persons, yet persons are unique, for Marx, not only because they are self-creative, but also because they are self-conscious in ways that other animals are not, and their self-consciousness and self-creativity are, for Marx, intimately connected. He wrote:

> The animal is one with its life-activity. It does not distinguish the activity from itself. It is its activity. But man makes his life activity itself an object of his will and consciousness ... Conscious life activity distinguishes man from the life activity of animals. Only for this reason is he a species-being. Only for this reason is his activity free activity.[19]

The conclusion which Marx drew from this was that men and women have, over and above their biological needs, needs peculiar to themselves as self-conscious and self-creative beings, in particular the need for self-affirmation and recognition, needs which depend on the quality of their relations with others and with themselves. Men and women are social beings, produced by, yet at the same time producing, society. They also act on and humanise nature and so produce their life world. When people recognise this fact they can be said to have come of age, to have attained their majority. They see that, as rational, moral and creative beings, they are the product of their own activities, of a long course of social and cultural change which consists of what they themselves have done. They also see that they no longer need to postulate a creator external to themselves, for there are in the world no higher purposes than their own; 'Man', in Marx's well-known words, 'is the highest being for man'.[20] People's aspirations and ideas must, however, be kept within the bounds of their powers, though they have at times grossly underestimated and undervalued these, but when they come to see themselves as they truly are they will be satisfied and secure in a godless world, for their idea of the world will then be congenial to They will, in John Plamenatz's words, 'be fully human in a humanised world'.[21]

Marx was also influenced, as Norman Birnbaum has argued, by Robert Owen's utopian vision of a 'New Moral World' which contained a critique of capitalism's destruction of human dignity and human community, as well as by the writings of the French utopians led by St Simon and the German religious-socialist thinker Weitling, all of which were motivated by the vision of a humanity come into possession of its religious heritage by realising new social forms which would restore to men and women the dignity and the human relationships which capitalism and industrialisation had destroyed. Marx, as Birnbaum put it, 'envisaged the self-realisation of humanity as the creation of a new and true community. This was to develop from human need and through extreme conflict; it was to be produced, briefly, by the intolerability of its absence, by the self-destruction of its negation, the class society.'[22] Marx, again following Hegel, held that the *raison d'être* of this was immanent in the historical process itself and it was therefore, for him, if not for Hegel, free of theological content in the sense that theological terms could be and must be translated into profane and secular ones. The question that might be put to Marx at this point is whether this translation can be made from the discourse of religions other than Christianity, for, if it cannot, then in no way can it be considered a general theory of religion. A further question would be whether such a translation would be exhaustive, in the sense that once it had been made, there would be nothing that religions of the world had to offer that could not be better and more realistically offered by the kind of society that Marx was committed to establishing in the wake of the collapse of capitalism.

Marx recognised that Hegel had grasped the important truth that men and women develop their powers through activities which involve alienation and the overcoming of alienation. In the passage already referred to, in which Marx paid tribute to Hegel for grasping the self-creation of man as a process, Marx went on to claim, with Hegel, that, as he put it, 'Man's affirmation of himself as a real species-being (i.e. as a human being) is only possible in so far as he brings forth all his species-powers … *which can only be done at first in the form of alienation*'.[23]

As they work together with others men and women adapt their natural environment to their needs, and in the process of doing so produce their social environment, although, again, without realising what they have done. Society, therefore, which men and women have themselves created, appears as something external to them and they feel towards it as they would to a thing alien to themselves which has them in its thrall. They feel oppressed by it, despite the fact that they have created it by their own activity. When men and women fully understood this they will, Marx believed, be in a position to do something about it.

But although Marx took much of his early understanding of alienation from Hegel, he believed that Hegel had not fully appreciated the full range of human activity, nor had he understood the most fundamental human activity of all, that is material human labour. 'Hegel,' he wrote, 'understands labour as abstract and mental labour'.[24] Whether this was so is open to question, but Marx certainly believed that both Hegel and Feuerbach had underestimated the role of productive relations in human life and had, therefore, failed to discern the true cause of human alienation. Hegel had rightly seen mankind as passing from stage to stage in a historical process in which men and women continually developed their specifically human powers. But this, for Marx, is only part of the truth about men and women. There is indeed a movement, intellectual, moral and aesthetic, from less to more adequate views of the world, from less to more satisfying attitudes to it, but this movement is not autonomous. It depends, Marx claimed, in ways which he never, unfortunately, made clear, on more fundamental movements in the socio-economic sphere. Hegel had seen men and women as subject to needs peculiar to self-conscious beings, but in Marx's opinion, he had never fully appreciated the earthy, material basis of these needs, had never, in fact, taken fully into account the full range of human needs and had certainly never appreciated the material substratum upon which all the higher needs were based. Hegel had passed too quickly, Marx thought, to what he regarded as the fundamental human need, the need for recognition. Marx did not ignore this need; he fully appreciated that man has a sense of what is due to him as a human being and that when the fulfilment of this need is denied him, he feels diminished in his own eyes, but he was aware, as perhaps few before him were aware, of the importance of the equally fundamental human needs for clothing, shelter, food, etc.[25] He agreed with Hegel, however, that progress is related to need, and that it was in the course of history that men and women became aware of their needs and developed new ones. History, for Marx as for Hegel, is a process of self-discovery.

But Marx, like Hegel, was also aware that men and women are often dissatisfied, often unfulfilled, and that the unsatisfied, the essentially human needs (for material well-being, for self-affirmation and for recognition) persist. It is out of this alienated condition, for Marx, that the illusions of religion are born. Alienated in this world, men and women come to believe in another world in which they will be truly at home. Religion, for Marx, is thus a fantasy of alienated men and women.

Unless we see that, for Marx, human needs are more than biological, that they are what may be called 'spiritual', we shall not fully appreciate the depth of Marx's analysis of religion as a fantasy of alienated men and women, and although Marx himself obscured this analysis of the human condition by writing, at times, as if men and women's needs were wholly material, his writings taken as a whole leave us in no doubt that, overall, he recognised that the needs of self-conscious, rational creatures are wider than these material needs. Whether Marx recognised the full range of human needs is, of course, open to question, as is, as we have said, the related question whether there might, perhaps, be human needs that no human society, however well structured, could ever satisfy, which is to raise the question that is being asked with renewed urgency today about what it is to be human. Some words that J. S. Dunne wrote in his book *The City of the Gods* are worth recalling at this point. He wrote: 'The history of hitherto existing society is the history of the struggle for life. This struggle though, has not been the struggle among races, or among classes, which it is supposed to have been ... Rather it has been the struggle of all human beings against the common nemesis of every human life, a struggle to overcome death. The shadowed figure of Gilgamesh roaming over the wasteland ... is the figure of man himself wandering through these many centuries in quest of immortality.'[26] This is to go to the other extreme, but it is nearer the truth of religion than those who see men and women as motivated wholly by the pursuit of material self-interest.

Marx's answer to the question of how it is that human beings become alienated can be found in a passage in the *1844 Manuscripts* where he wrote that: 'Man is not merely a natural being. He is a being for himself (i.e. self-conscious) and is, therefore, a species-being; and as such has to express and authenticate himself in being as well as in thought.'[27] Thus, to explain how men and women become alienated, we must look, says Marx, at how, in society as it exists in the present, men and women are denied their all-round development as human beings, how they are thwarted in their attempts to express, affirm and authenticate themselves, and how, in religion above all else, they seek a substitute satisfaction for the authenticity denied to them in reality.

In the philosophy of Hegel there are two distinct but related ideas – externalisation (*Entaüsserung*) and estrangement or alienation (*Entfrem-*

dung). Externalisation is the process whereby Absolute Spirit (and human beings as that in which Spirit is manifested) brings into being a world – especially a social and cultural world – through which Spirit strives to come to full self-realisation. Alienation, on the other hand, is the sense which the majority of human beings have of being restricted or oppressed in this world, or at odds with it and with themselves, and yet without which the onward dialectical process of the self-realisation of Spirit would not take place. Much confusion has been caused by a number of Hegel's (and Marx's) interpreters who have used 'alienation' to cover both the process of externalisation and the condition of alienation. Yet the two must be kept logically distinct, for there can, as a matter of logic, be externalisation without alienation: indeed, there must be in Hegel's Rational State and in Marx's Communist Society where alienation is overcome without men and women ceasing to be human. Thus, for Hegel, as for Marx, while self-externalisation is integral to the human condition, alienation is not, or at least need not be so. As a matter of historical fact, however, Marx claims that all societies have been characterised by varying degrees of alienation and hence have been dominated by a religious outlook on life. But this, for Marx, is a contingent fact and not a logical or a metaphysical necessity. Alienation can and will be transcended, with the consequence that for Marx, if not for Hegel, religion, as a mistaken spiritual response to the condition of alienation, will disappear.

But, for Marx and Engels, religion is more than a fantasy of alienated men and women for, in societies structured into classes, and in which each class pursues its own interests, religion can further be seen as a way in which those in power seek to legitimate and justify their position. In other words religion is a form of what Marx and Engels call 'ideology', a term which for them always had pejorative connotations. Exactly what Marx and Engels understood by 'ideology' is difficult to determine,[28] but, overall, ideology, for them, is the limited view of a class presented as if it were a universal truth. Thus, when they call religion a form of ideology, what they are saying is that religion is presented, by those whose interests are served by so doing, as the truth about the world, when it is, in fact, nothing more than ideology serving to legitimate the social status quo in the interests of those so presenting it. The way in which religion does this is to claim that the existing order of society reflects the will of God or, in primitive society, of the gods and/or ancestral spirits.

That religion has served this conservative function in society no-one with any acquaintance with the history of religions (or with anthropology) can doubt. Hindu society, for example, is organised around the caste system and Hinduism claims that this ordering of society represents the will of the gods. Thus in the Bhagavadgita, the great God Vishnu speaks, through his *avatar* Krishna, as follows:

> The four-caste system did I generate
> with categories of constituents and works;
> Of this I am the doer, know thou this.[29]

And to take an example from the Christian religion: a passage in the catechism in the Anglican *Book of Common Prayer* reads as follows:

> Question: What is thy duty towards thy neighbour?
> Answer: To honour and obey the Queen and all that are put in authority under her. To submit myself to all my governors, teachers, spiritual pastors and masters. To order myself lowly and reverently to all my betters.

And to give a final example from religion in the Germany of Marx's own day: the German theologian Helmut Gollwitzer has written:

> Where in his wanderings could the taylor's apprentice Weitling, or the turner's apprentice Bebel, have found a manse in the Germany of that day in which a sermon would not have been preached to him on the submission to his fate and humble acknowledgement of the divinely decreed order as the bearing which God required of him? ... Where was there any sign that the church did not identify itself with the programme of a 'Christian State' under Friedrich Wilhelm IV, and did not greatly profit from it.[30]

Marx and Engels saw religion as a fantasy of alienated man and as a form of ideology. They did not exempt from this verdict the religions of primitive peoples, even though what they took to be the major cause of alienation and a prerequisite of all ideology – the division of labour – is not found among such peoples. Their ideas about religion and alienation do not therefore fit easily together to form a consistent whole, for there were also, as they recognised, elements in the religious response to the world which are outwith the division of labour and the development of the class-system, although they did not say as much about these as those of us seeking to ascertain their opinion on this matter might wish.

Their views regarding the sources of religion which lie outside the socio-economic sphere are found in what they surmise about the origin of religion in pre-class society. In *The German Ideology*, in the context of a discussion of the inter-related phenomena of human language and consciousness, Marx and Engels put forward a theory of the twofold aetiology of religion to explain what they termed 'natural religion' and 'religion in civil society'.

The question whether 'natural religion' continues to exist as a constituent element in the religion of civil society, and so as an element in religion at the present time, was, unfortunately, not a question which Marx and Engels discussed although Engels, in some of his later writings, did hint that this might be so. The question has, however, proved to be important in discussion of the Marxist critique of religion, for if we broaden the sources of 'natural religion' in the way, as we saw in Chapter 6, that anthropologists such as Malinowski have suggested, then it may well be that religion arises from sources other than those identified by Marx and Engels.

Immediately after identifying 'natural religion' as an instinctual response to the awe-inspiring phenomena of nature Marx later added, as a marginal note, that the behaviour which 'natural religion' signified was 'determined by the form of society and vice versa'. He wrote:

> We see here immediately: this natural religion or this particular attitude to nature is determined by the form of society and vice-versa. Here, as everywhere, the identity of nature and man also appears in such a way that the restricted attitude of men to nature determines their restricted attitude to one another, and their restricted attitude to one another determines men's restricted attitude to nature.[31]

Nature is, as yet, hardly altered by history, but:

> It is man's consciousness of the necessity of associating with the individuals around him, the beginning of the consciousness that he is living in society at all. This beginning is as animal as social life itself at this stage. It is mere herd consciousness …[32]

This herd consciousness, which Marx and Engels identified with tribal consciousness, develops in history through productivity, increased needs and the growth of the population. With these developments division of labour occurs and evolves through differences in strength, abilities, needs, and so on, until the all-important division between mental and physical labour comes about. Within the Marxian scheme of things, the division of labour, leading as it does to the breakdown of the original organic unity which characterised primitive society in the thought of Marx and Engels, plays a very similar part to that played by the doctrine of 'The Fall' in the Christian scheme of things. From this moment on society is characterised not by unity but by conflicts of interests. For the development of ideology the important step, of course, was the division between mental and physical labour. As Marx and Engels wrote:

> From this moment onward, consciousness can really flatter itself that it is something other than consciousness of existing practice, that it really represents something real; from now on consciousness is in a position to emancipate itself from the world and to proceed to the formation of 'pure' theory, theology, philosophy, morality, etc. But even if this theory, theology, philosophy, morality, etc. come into contradiction with the existing social relations, this can only occur

because existing social relations have come into contradiction with existing social forces.

But although the realm of ideology can be thought to exist independently of the social realm, ultimately, as Marx and Engels saw it:

> It is self-evident ... that 'spectres', 'bonds', the 'higher being', 'concept', 'scruple', are merely idealist, speculative, mental expressions, the concepts of apparently isolated individuals, the mere images of very empirical fetters and limitations, within which move the mode of production of life, and the form of intercourse coupled with it. [33]

From these passages we see that, for Marx and Engels, the basis of 'natural religion' and the basis of 'religion in civil society' are very different: 'natural religion' is an animal, instinctual response to natural forces; 'religion in civil society' is a reflection in consciousness of the 'contradictions' of social life . 'Natural religion' and the highly articulate, theologically construed 'religion of civil society' are discontinuous, but not necessarily opposed; both could co-exist in any living religion, although Marx and Engels nowhere say that this they do.

But whatever might or might not be the case with regard to the historical origins of religion, religion as it now exists is, as we have seen, for Marx and Engels, both a fantasy of alienated men and women and a form of ideology arising out of and kept in being by conditions of social alienation.

Although in his later works Marx had certain things to say about religion and society on the basis of the theoretical position we have outlined, he never again returned to theoretical matters with regard to religion except to summarise what he had already said, but as Delos B. McKown has shown in his book *The Classical Marxist Critiques of Religion*, whatever might be the case with Marx's views on other things, the position which he had taken up with regard to religion in his early writings never changed. With the single exception of the consolatory function of religion, to which Marx had referred in his *Contribution Towards a Critique of Hegel's Philosophy of Law*, every point which Marx made *vis-à-vis* religion in his early works can be documented exclusively from works published after 1847.[34]

Engels, on the other hand, who was always more interested in religion and in religious controversies than was Marx, sought, in a number of works which he published independently of Marx, and in particular in *Socialism: Utopian and Scientific* (1877), *Anti-Dühring* (1878) and *Ludwig Feuerbach and the End of Classical German Philosophy* (1886), to amplify the position which he and Marx had set forth in *The German Ideology*.

In *Anti-Dühring*, Engels dealt with the origin of religion much as he and Marx had dealt with it in *The German Ideology*. Although he does not re-employ the term 'natural religion', it is clear that he had the substance of what he and Marx had earlier so described in mind when he claimed that 'All religion is nothing but the fantastic reflection in men's minds of those forces which control their daily life, a reflection in which terrestrial forces assume the form of supernatural forces.' But he now widened the basis of 'natural religion' to include threatening social forces for he continued:

> It is not long before, side by side with the forces of nature, social forces begin to be active – forces which confront man as equally inexplicable, dominating him with the same apparent necessity as the forces of nature themselves. The fantastic figures, which at first only reflected the mysterious forces of nature, at this point acquire social attributes, become representative of the forces of history.

And he added:

> In this convenient, handy, and universally adaptable form, religion can continue to exist, that is, the sentimental form of men's relation to the alien natural and social forces which dominate them, so long as men remain under the control of these forces.[35]

Engels thus answers in the affirmative the question left open in *The German Ideology* as to whether the springs of 'natural religion' continue to operate in the 'religion of civil society', although later, in *Anti-Dühring*, he so plays down the continued existence of uncontrollable forces – natural as well as social – that he can look forward to the day when they and religion will vanish from the society of the future altogether. He wrote:

> When therefore man no longer merely proposes, but *also disposes* – *only* then will the last alien force which is still reflected in religion vanish; and with it will vanish the religious reflection itself, for the simple reason that there will be nothing left to reflect.[36]

Eight years later, in *Ludwig Feuerbach*, Engels had more definite things to say about the origin of religion; things which marked a fairly radical departure from the theory which he and Marx had earlier put forward and which he himself had repeated in *Anti-Dühring*. Having become interested in the new science of anthropology, he now utilised views put forward by the leading anthropologist of the day, Sir Edward Tylor, and offered an 'animistic' aetiology of religion. He did not cite Tylor by name, but there is evidence from his correspondence that he was not unacquainted with Tylor's writings. The following passage from his *Ludwig Feuerbach* is, in fact, a summary of what Tylor says in chapters 11–17 of the second volume of *Primitive Culture*:

From the very early times when men, still completely ignorant of the structure of their own bodies, under the stimulus of dream apparitions, came to believe that their thinking and sensation were not activities of their bodies, but of a distinct soul which inhabits the body and leaves it at death – from this time men have been driven to reflect about the relation between this soul and the outside world. If upon death it took leave of the body and lived on, there was no occasion to invent yet another distinct death for it. Thus arose the idea of immortality, which at that stage of development appeared not at all a consolation but as a fate against which it was no use fighting, and often enough, among the Greeks, as a positive misfortune. Not religious desire for consolation, but the quandary arising from the common universal ignorance of what to do with this soul, once its existence had been accepted, after the death of the body, led in a general way to the tedious notion of personal immortality. In an exactly similar manner the first gods arose through the *personification of natural forces. And these gods in the further development* of religions assumed more and more an extra-mundane form, until finally by a process of abstraction, I might almost say of distillation, occurring naturally in the course of man's intellectual development, out of the many more or less limited and mutually limiting gods there arose in the minds of men the idea of the one exclusive god of the monotheistic religions.[37]

This highly intellectualistic theory marks a quite considerable departure from the view that religion arose from instinctual fear of the forces of nature and developed as a 'reflex echo' of man's real life process, for here religion is grounded in primitive man's intellectual reflections – as reconstructed by a nineteenth-century anthropologist. Engels, unfortunately, did not relate his new theory to his earlier theory and we can only guess that he saw the two theories as complementary – religion arising out of both instinctual fear and out of primitive intellectual speculation. Neither did Engels attempt to bring this new theory into relationship with the theory of the social origin of religion which had been such a distinctive element in his and Marx's earlier writings on religion, and again, in the absence of evidence, we can only surmise that Engels thought of developed religion as arising from all of these things. We must, therefore, conclude that Engels espoused no single theory of religion, but that, overall, his explanation of the persistence of religion was that religion persists in developed society because it continually draws sustenance from the 'contradictions' which still persist in such societies. That the various causes which initially gave rise to religion also continue to operate in developed society, Engels would seem to have allowed when he wrote to his friend Schmidt in 1890 that:

As to the realms of ideology which soar still higher in the air – religion, philosophy, etc., – these have a prehistoric stock, found already in existence by and taken over in the historical period, of what we should today call bunk. These various false conceptions of nature, of man's own being, magic forces, etc., have for the most part only a negative economic element as their basis; the low economic development of the prehistoric period is supplemented and also partially conditioned and even caused by the false conceptions of nature. And even though economic necessity was the main driving force of the progressive knowledge of nature and has become even more so, it would surely be pedantic to try to find economic causes for all this primitive nonsense.[38]

Religion, for Engels, was little more than a survival, from a more primitive age having little, if any, socio-economic basis and destined to disappear as man's understanding of the world and of himself progressed. Such a survival does, however, as Engels had pointed out in *Anti-Dühring*, take on more and more of a determined social form:

The fantastic figures, which at first only reflect the mysterious forces of nature ... acquire social attributes, become representative of the forces of history. At a still further stage of evolution, all the natural and social attributes of the numerous gods are transferred to one almighty god, who is but the reflection of abstract man.[39]

Thus, towards the end of his life, did Engels broaden the basis of religion, whilst seeking to keep intact the theory he and Marx had put forward in *The German Ideology*.

We have now completed our survey of what Marx and Engels have to say about the essence, the origin and the social role of religion. Five points have emerged and may be summarised as follows:

1. Religion is a human product and must be analysed as such.
2. Religion arises out of fear before the awesome phenomena of nature and out of ignorance of the workings of the world and of human society.
3. Religion in developed societies 'reflects' existing forms of social relations and the human self-alienation inherent in them.
4. Religion has served, within all hitherto existing forms of society, as (a) a disguised means of protest against existing conditions; (b) a fantasy of alienated men and women and a false means of consolation for the lack of human fulfilment inherent in all hitherto existing forms of society; and (c) a means whereby one class – the ruling class – has sought to maintain and legitimate the *status quo* and so sought to keep other classes in subjection to itself.

These are the guiding principles which have governed traditional Marxist understanding of religion. Their adequacy is, of course, another matter.

It must, however, be noted that not all Marxists have been as antithetical to religion as were Marx and Engels. Drawing on what Marx said about religion in the *1844 Manuscripts* rather than on the legacy of Plekhanov and Lenin, a number of 'modern' Marxists, as they have chosen to describe themselves, sought, a generation ago, to portray religion as a necessary step in the evolution of human understanding about the world. What the religions of the world – and particularly the Judaeo-Christian tradition – had seen but dimly, these Marxists claimed to make plain.

Thus Leszek Kolakowski, writing at a time when he was still a Marxist, acknowledged the fact that fundamental to both Judaeo-Christian and Marxist conceptions of history was the possibility of eschatology. He wrote:

> We put it otherwise, to all appearances non-theologically: Can the human values we accept attain complete realisation? Does history evolve in a definite direction that promises ultimate equalisation and universal justice? ... This secular eschatology, this belief in the future elimination of the disparity between man's essence and his existence (in the deification of man), presupposes, obviously, that essence is a value, that its realisation is desirable, and that the wisdom of history will bring about its realisation. Secular eschatology trusts in the final judgement of history.

And making what was an important point with regard to Marxism's claim to bring religion, and Judaeo-Christian forms of religion in particular, to fulfilment, he continued:

> Once historical eschatology had demonstrated its possibilities, human history became a cogent argument for atheism, for it had become known that another force could take the burden of God upon itself and lull with a vision of a happy ending its unfortunate subjects toward which their torment and efforts tend.[40]

The point that Kolakowski was making was that Marxism, in replacing God by the on-going, forward, teleological movement of history, had not broken as completely with the Judaeo-Christian outlook as many Marxists and Marxist-Leninists liked to think – nor had it broken entirely with the Hegelian understanding of history. When Marxism is looked at from outside the Western cultural tradition it is seen to be more firmly within that tradition than it itself has realised, for the eschatological dimension of history, characterised as it is by terms such as 'hope' and 'fulfilment', is fundamental to Jew, Christian and Marxist in a way in which it is not fundamental to Hindu, Buddhist or Taoist. Marxism, despite its claim to that universality which characterises science, took its fundamental outlook, in fact, from a particular cultural tradition in which history was conceived as moving towards an *eschaton* or *telos*, even if, for Marxism, this was something which would take place within, rather than beyond, time and history.

The recognition of a basic affinity between Jewish, Christian and Marxist conceptions of history led a number of non-Soviet Marxists to explore the biblical sources of their world-outlook. Foremost among these was the

German Ernst Bloch – whose book *Controversy over the Biblical Heritage* was seminal to the discussion – the Czechoslovaks Milan Machovec and Vitezslav Gardavsky, and the Swiss thinker Konrad Farner.

Gardavsky was in no doubt that Marxism drew its basic historical outlook from the Judaeo-Christian tradition. Contrasting, in his book *God Is Not Yet Dead*, the Jewish understanding of history with that of the Greek, he wrote:

> The point at issue in Genesis is man in a time system, not in the cosmic system, within which everything becomes fluctuating and uncertain, and in which man must fight all the time, over and over again, to defend his existence, must make up his mind between various possibilities, choosing and rejecting, erring and being punished …

This open-mindedness, said Gardavsky, devoid of any degree of certainty, is the exact opposite of the self-contained and well-rounded image held by classical antiquity, and he urged his readers to look again at Genesis and to grasp the point that:

> not only Genesis but The Old Testament as a whole contains something which is exceedingly important for the whole of European thought in general and for contemporary socialist and Marxist thought in particular: this is the first appearance of the idea of transcendence, of a step beyond all that has so far been achieved – and although it is revealed here [he adds] in a pre-scientific and mythological form, it is nonetheless perfectly clear; the dream of a personal identity in the midst of Time begins to show itself … for the first time.[41]

But although Gardavsky was prepared to acknowledge the Judaeo-Christian roots of Marxism, the qualification which he introduced into his remarks to the effect that the message inherent in the Judaeo-Christian tradition was expressed 'in a pre-scientific, mythological form', shows that he, like most Marxists, still saw Marxism as an essentially scientific outlook on the world. Marxists, even liberal Marxists, although they openly acknowledged their Judaeo-Christian heritage, claimed to transpose that inheritance into a truer key. This, of course, as we have seen, had been the Marxist way with religion from the beginning, for Marx himself did not so much reject religion as seek to transform what he took to be its essentially human yearnings into a scientific account of the way in which they would actually be fulfilled. When seen within the context of the variety of religions in the world, this claim may well be doubted and the culture-bound nature of the fundamental premises of Marxism made evident. One thing that also becomes clear is that Marxism, far from breaking with mythology, unconsciously substituted a new mythology of its own – a mythology whose active elements were those somewhat mysterious 'forces of history' upon which the foundation, and thus the ultimate plausibility, of Marxism as a world-outlook rested. In the final analysis, Marxism turns out to be not the exhaustive, scientific transformation of the religious into the secular that Marxists claimed, but a partial secularisation of one particular form of religion, namely, that found in the Judaeo-Christian tradition.

Thus, although Marxism had no overt transcendental reference outside this world, the question might fairly be raised (especially in the light of the Marxist conception of history) whether Marxism did not, in fact, need something like the Hegelian notion of an 'immanent transcendent'? The case for asking this question is strengthened when doubt is cast on the validity of Marx's self-proclaimed transformation of Hegel's philosophy of history into a science of history, for if Marx did not succeed in creating a science of history – and the failure of almost all of his historical predictions, and the subsequent failure of Marxist societies the world over, would seem well nigh conclusive proof of this – then the question that can be put to Marxism is: what are these 'forces' which you believe to be inherent in history and in which you place so much faith and hope? And the conclusion must be that if they were not natural forces – amenable to scientific analysis – then they were either no forces at all, or they were non-natural forces – the active forces of a Marxist mythology of history. They need, of course, be nonetheless powerful for that: indeed, as historians of religion and depth psychologists, as well as the experience of the past half-century or so, have shown, such ideologies may be even more powerful, and evoke deeper responses, than can any scientific theory. As Peter Berger has noted: 'ideologies derive their power from those realms of the mind where the gods used to dwell'.[42]

The fundamental question, however, which can be put to Marxist theories of religion concerns the viability of its claim that the hopes and aspirations of human beings can be truly fulfilled in this world. Can, we must ask the Marxist, any form of society bring about the fulfilment of human nature in the way that you envisage or is it not the case, perhaps, that human beings can only be satisfied, as Kant argued, with a meaning that transcends the everyday world? This is, as we have seen earlier, essentially a question about what it is to be a human being, and it is a question to which we will be returning when we come to consider the understanding of religion in the thought of Peter Berger. But before turning to Berger there are two further thinkers who, like Marx and Engels, see religion as primarily a social phenomenon and to whom we must pay some attention – Émile Durkheim and Max Weber.

– ÉMILE DURKHEIM –

Durkheim, whom many regard as the founder of the academic discipline of sociology, saw religion, as had Marx and Engels, as a social construct, but Durkheim's account of the origin, essence and social function of religion is very different from theirs. Durkheim did, however, agree with Marx, Engels and, indeed, with Freud, that religion was too potent a force in human culture to be explained away simply as a primitive misunderstanding of the world. He wrote: 'It is inadmissible that systems of ideas like religions, which have held such a considerable place in history, and to which, in all times, men have come to receive with the energy which they must have to live, should be made up of a tissue of illusions.'[43] Yet, with Marx, Engels and Freud, Durkheim too acknowledged that the religious believer did not understand the true origin of the forces with which he or she believed themselves to be in contact. He wrote: '[Religion] does not know itself. It knows neither what it is made of, nor what need it satisfies. Far from being able to dictate to science, it is itself the subject of scientific investigation …'[44] And Marx, Engels and Freud would have agreed with Durkheim when he wrote at the outset of his monumental study of religion, *The Elementary Forms of the Religious Life*, that:

> One must know how to go underneath the symbol to the reality which it represents and which gives it its meaning. The most barbarous and most fantastic rites and the strangest myths translate some human need, some aspect of life, either individual or social. The reasons with which the faithful justify them may be, and generally are, erroneous, but the true reasons do not cease to exist, and it is the duty of science to discover them.[45]

In *The Elementary Forms of the Religious Life*, published in 1912, Durkheim sought to do just that.

Durkheim was born in 1858 in Éspinal, a small town near Strasbourg in north-eastern France. Although his father was a rabbi, and although he had a traditional Jewish upbringing and had himself at one time thought of becoming a rabbi, by the time he entered the *École normale supérieure* in Paris in 1879 to study history and philosophy he was openly professing agnosticism with regard to the doctrines of religion. After completing his undergraduate studies in 1882 he taught for a time in various *Lycées* in the Paris region before in 1885 gaining a government scholarship to study in Berlin under the psychologist Wilhelm Wundt. In 1887 he was appointed to a lectureship in social sciences and education at the University of Bordeaux and spent the next fifteen years there. Building on the distinguished French tradition of social studies established by thinkers such as Saint-Simon, Montesquieu, de Tocqueville, Comte, and Fustel de Coulanges, Durkheim sought, in a series of studies which he wrote whilst at Bordeaux – *The Division of Labour* and *The Rules of Sociological Method* (1895), and *Suicide* (1897) – as well as in the journal which he founded and edited, *L'Année Sociologique*, to put the study of society on a more scientific basis than hitherto. In 1902 his growing academic influence was recognised when he was summoned to Paris, to the Sorbonne, and where he was eventually given a chair in the newly established science of sociology. It was whilst at the Sorbonne that he wrote his most influential work, *The Elementary Forms of the Religious Life*, published in 1912. Durkheim died in Paris in 1917.

Although an agnostic, Durkheim was fascinated by religion all his life and references to religion can be found throughout his early works. It was not, however, until he had read William Robertson Smith that, as he himself tells us, he came to realise the full sociological import of religion.[46] Smith who, as we saw in a previous chapter, had introduced Sir James Frazer to anthropology, was one of the first scholars to interpret religious beliefs and practices as part of a social matrix and, in principle, no different from other social and cultural products – language, law, morality, family relations, labour relations, science and technology and so on – so that for him religion, like other cultural productions, was first and foremost a social fact. For Durkheim, as for Marx, it was society and not the individual that constitutes the basic social unit and individuals, he believed, could thus be understood only in the context of the society in which they were situated. Whether individuals can be exhaustively explained in terms of society and whether all 'cultural production' is social are claims that can be challenged, although we should note that the causes of social change, and the role of the individual in bringing about social and cultural change, are not questions to which Durkheim devotes a great deal of attention. They are not, however, questions that can be lightly dismissed either in religion or indeed in any other sphere of cultural creation. The sociology of creativity remains, as yet, unwritten.

In seeking to get at the origin, essence and social function of religion Durkheim does not, as might have been expected, employ the comparative method, that is, he does not begin by looking at the information available with regard to religions in various parts of the world and then seek to distil from this what religions might be said to have in common: rather he looks for the essence of religion in the most primitive form of religion known and he believed that this was to be found among the native Australians or Aborigines whose religion was totemism. From an analysis of this and other primitive societies Durkheim believed that the perceptive observer could find all that could be known about religion, and the most important thing to be noted about such peoples was not, as Tylor and Frazer had supposed, that they divided the world into an ordinary natural world and a supernatural world peopled by divine spirits, but that they divided the world into the realms of the sacred and the profane.[47] The 'sacred' refers to those things which are set apart or forbidden, the 'profane' is the realm of the ordinary everyday world and is defined negatively as those things which are not set apart or forbidden. This is not, it must be emphasised, a moral distinction in the sense that it corresponds to notions of good and evil, for the sacred realm contains both good and evil, the divine and the demonic. A measure of the gulf which exists between the sacred and the profane, for Durkheim, are the rites and rituals that we find in primitive religion for those who wish to traffic between these two realms.

The essence of religion can also be seen, Durkheim argued, by differentiating magic from religion. Magic, for Durkheim, is essentially a transaction between individuals, between practitioner and client, whereas religion is an affair of the whole community, the 'church', as he calls such a community, and in Durkheim's own well-known words, 'There is no Church of magic.'[48] The communal nature of religion can be seen in totemism which, for Durkheim, as we have noted, was the earliest form of religion. Totemism is based upon the clan which is a sub-unit of the tribe. Although not related by descent, clan members regard themselves as a single kinship group by virtue of the fact that they share the same name which is invariably that of a species of plant or animal which is the clan totem. However, for Durkheim, the totem is not just a name or an emblem, it is the archetypal sacred thing and, after having described in some detail the way in which the Australian aborigines – and, indeed, other peoples for throughout *The Elementary Forms of the Religious Life* Durkheim cites in support of the points he is making a vast range of ethnography evidence – relate to their totemic emblems, Durkheim raises the question, what is really happening when the clans meet to celebrate their relationship to their totems? His answer is that what in fact the members of the clan are really doing (unbeknown, of course, to themselves) is to celebrate and worship the clan itself. This, for Durkheim, is what religion is ultimately about. Clan gatherings, he surmises, generate 'sentiments' which are directed towards the clan emblem, thought of as 'other' than the individual clan member, but which is, in reality, but a collective social force manufactured by society for its own benefit. Religion is, therefore, for Durkheim, 'a system of ideas by means of which people represent to themselves the society of which they are members and the opaque but intimate relations that they have with it'.[49] Durkheim's account of religion is almost wholly, but not exclusively, functional and the essential function of religion, as he sees it, is to carry social sentiments from one generation to another. It also provides the symbols and the rituals that enable the members of a society to express and re-enforce the emotions which bind them into a community, and as such, religion, or some substitute for religion, will always be necessary if the integrity of a society is to be preserved. It is for this reason that latter-day followers of Durkheim, such as Robert Bellah, have laid such emphasis on the need for societies to posses a civil religion.

Having described the essence and social function of religion Durkheim, like other nineteenth- and early twentieth-century thinkers, could not resist speculating on the origin of religion. Drawing on the ethnography of the Australian aborigines Durkheim saw the origin of aboriginal religion, and by extension of all religions, in the periodic gatherings of the various families that make up the clans. The 'moral density' arising from these gatherings generates, Durkheim speculates, a state of intense emotional excitement among the participants and it is under these emotionally charged conditions, where the participants loose all sense of control, that they become aware of being possessed by powers over which they appear to have no control. It is out of this 'effervescence', says Durkheim, that the religious idea is born. As Frank Parkin has put it: 'the origin of religion is to be found not simply in society, but society in a state of collective delirium'.[50] This bald statement, however, does less than justice to the vivid, evocative way in which Durkheim describes the generation of the basic religious notion of the sacred. Reading Durkheim we get the impression that he personally had witnessed such ceremonies, but, of course, Durkheim was simply rewriting the more prosaic ethnographic accounts of others, and more recent and more precise observations have rather overtaken what he tells us about these.

There is little or no place in Durkheim's account of the origin of religion for the charismatic leader, for the shaman, the prophet or the sage and it is, perhaps for this reason that Durkheim's account of religion, unlike Weber's with which we shall be concerned shortly, has little to say about belief and doctrine – a severe omission on the part of a theory that claims to explain religion. Yet Durkheim's reply would no doubt be that to allow doctrine a place in any explanation of the origin and essence of religion would be to overlook that which religions have in common on the grounds that it is doctrine, above all else, that divides believers. Yet Durkheim does little to explain the growth and development of religions beyond reiterating the evolutionary schema of the English anthropologists in which belief in an impersonal force gradually evolved into a belief in personal forces and then evolved further into a belief into the single unified force characteristic of monotheism or monism. Of the claims to revelation found in the world's religions and of the intellectual arguments advanced to support the various religious views of the world he has nothing to say.

Yet *The Elementary Forms of the Religious Life* is, as a number of commentators on Durkheim have pointed out, a treatise in the sociology of knowledge, for, as Durkheim notes, not only have religions been 'systems of ideas which tend to encompass the universality of things and to give us a complete representation of the world', they have also been the source for all subsequent thought, including scientific thought, which has grown by a process of differentiation and elaboration from the basic primeval awareness of the all-powerful unobservable force of which men and women became aware in the clan ceremonies of primal religion. Initially men and women conceived of this force using material symbols – supremely the totem – but later came to conceive of it in terms of the immaterial and unobservable gods, goddesses, ancestral and other spirits that people the primal world. Religion, for Durkheim, as later for Horton, provides the earliest explanation for the workings of the world. Yet for Durkheim, the explanatory function of religion was destined to be overtaken by empirical science, although he recognises that there will remain a residue of questions which science, ever more cautious in its claims than religion, would not feel competent to answer. But this, for Durkheim provides only a temporary respite for religion. He wrote:

> Having left religion, science tends to substitute itself for this latter in all that which concerns the cognitive and intellectual functions ... but the world of the religious and the moral life is still forbidden. The great majority of men continue to believe that there is an order of things which the mind cannot penetrate except by very special ways. Hence comes the active resistance which is met with every time that someone tries to treat religious and moral phenomena scientifically. But in spite of these oppositions, these attempts are constantly repeated and this persistence even allows us to foresee that this final barrier will finally give way and that science will establish herself as mistress even in this reserved region ....

Durkheim's own answer, however, was somewhat ambivalent for he continues:

> Since there is no proper subject for religious speculation outside that reality to which scientific reflection is applied, it is evident that this former cannot play the same role as in the past. However, it seems destined to transform itself rather than disappear ... For faith is above all else an impetus to action, while science, no matter how far it may be pushed, always remains at a distance from this. Science is fragmentary and incomplete; it advances but slowly and is never finished; but life cannot wait. The theories which are destined to make men live and act are therefore obliged to bypass science and complete it prematurely.[51]

Weber, to whose understanding of religion we now turn, had similar misgivings about the ability of science to offer anything by way of an answer to questions about the meaning and purpose of human life.

– MAX WEBER –

Weber was born in Erfut in 1864 into a prosperous family of German industrialists and textile manufacturers. His father was a lawyer and man of affairs, a municipal counsellor and a member of the recently established Reichstag, which necessitated the family moving to Berlin where Weber grew up. Whilst his father was a somewhat worldly *homme moyen sensuel*, his mother, Helene Fallenstein Weber, was a cultured and pious woman who had grown up in Heidelberg where she had been tutored by the well-known historian Gervinus who lived in the family house. Weber's family life was not a happy one and Weber, from an early age, was aware of this and suffered from it. The first of a series of severe nervous breakdowns occurred after his father's death which came about shortly after a heated exchange between himself and his father over his father's overbearing treatment of his mother. Not that Weber felt particularly drawn to his mother and to what he regarded as her excessive emotional Lutheran piety and good works. His was a lonely childhood in which, as so often at the time, refuge was taken in books.

Whilst he could accept neither his father's philistine approach to life nor his right-wing politics, he, nevertheless, on entering the University of Heidelberg in 1882 where he read law, economics and philosophy, immediately joined his father's old duelling fraternity and for two years, to the delight of his father and the disgust of his mother, lived the life of a duelling, beer-drinking, but, in Weber's case, far from idle student. He also made friends there with his Baumgarten cousin who was reading theology and, later whilst he was doing his national service in Strasbourg, where his uncle was Professor of History, with his parents. Here he found a family with more congenial intellectual and political tastes than those of his own family, and in which the burning political, cultural and theological issues of the day were earnestly discussed. After his military service he was made a reserve officer in the Prussian army, a position of which he remained all his life immensely proud. After his discharge he continued his studies in law and economics first at the University of Berlin and then at the University of Göttingen, where he graduated in law in 1886. Three years later he graduated with a doctorate from Berlin with a thesis on the history of trading companies during the Middle Ages and in 1891 he submitted his *habilitationschrift* – which entitled him to teach in a German university – on the history of agrarian institutions in the late Roman Empire to the same university. He was also by this time beginning to practise in the law courts in Berlin. In 1893 he married his cousin Marianne Schnitger. He was also at this time teaching law and economics at the University of Berlin, but in 1894 he was appointed to the chair of economics at the University of Freiburg and in 1896 to the chair of economics at the more prestigious University of Heidelberg where he remained, with long periods of absence owing to illness, until 1903. In 1904 he made his first and only visit to the United States and, unlike many of his fellow countrymen, was impressed by the vibrancy and dynamism of American capitalism. Henceforth, the central concern of his work in the sociology of religion would be to try to solve the problem why it was that Protestant Europe and not some other culture had produced this particular socio-economic revolution. In 1918 he returned briefly to teaching first at the University of Vienna and then at the University of Munich. He died in 1920.

In September 1918, less than two years before he died, Weber gave a lecture to the Union of Free Students at the University of Munich entitled 'Science as a Vocation'. In it he expressed his hopes and, more particularly, his fears for the future of Western civilisation. It was in this lecture that he put forward his now well-known view that:

> The fate of our age, with its characteristic rationalisation and intellectualisation, and above all the disenchantment of the world, is that the ultimate, most sublime values have withdrawn from public life, either into the transcendental realm of mystical life or into the brotherhood of immediate personal relationships between individuals.[52]

As will be clear from this quotation Weber did not exactly welcome this state of affairs and he was all too aware of what men and women had lost through the rationalising process, the origins and development of which he had spent the greater part of his life charting.[53] He was also aware that what men and women had lost could not be replaced by science, for science, he maintained, could not by its very nature create the kind of meaningful *Weltanschauung* that had been offered in the past by the religions of the world. He wrote:

> After Nietzsche's devastating criticism of those 'last men' who 'invented happiness', I may completely ignore the fact that science – that is the techniques of mastering life based on science – has been celebrated with naïve optimism as the way to happiness. Who believes that other than some overgrown children among the professoriat or in editorial offices?

And he continued:

The fact that science does not give us this answer [to the question: 'How should I live?'] is completely undeniable ... Science ... presupposes that what is produced by scientific work should be *important* in the sense of 'being worth knowing'. And it is obvious that all of our problems lie here, for this presupposition cannot be proved by scientific means. It can only be *interpreted* with reference to its ultimate meaning, which one must accept or reject according to one's own ultimate attitudes towards life.[54]

Yet a return to religion was not, for Weber, a serious option for modern men and women, although he recognised that for certain individuals it might be a necessity. Religious belief, as for Kierkegaard, was for Weber a matter for personal decision. It was a 'leap of faith', and whilst he himself was unable to make such a leap, he never condemned those who did, despite the fact that he regarded such a leap as a sign of weakness. He wrote:

One should tell somebody who cannot take this destiny of the age like a man that he would be better to return silently, without the usual public announcements of the renegade, but modestly and simply into the open, compassionate arms of the old churches. They will not make it difficult for him. To do so, he must give his 'sacrifice of the intellect' in some way – that is inevitable. We will not chide him, if he can really do it. For such a 'sacrifice' of the intellect in favour of an unconditional religious devotion is morally quite different from the evasion of straight intellectual integrity.[55]

In the same spirit he never castigated his pupil Georg Lukacs's decision to embrace Marxism, a decision which, as Weber knew, was born of metaphysical despair, even though he thought it a very foolish one.

Weber's own response to what in *The Protestant Ethic and the Spirit of Capitalism* he had called the 'iron cage' of material acquisition, scientific calculation, bureaucratic organisation and interpersonal instrumentalism in which modern men and women are condemned to live, was one of Stoical resignation.[56] He was not, however, an advocate of the thesis of the inevitable total secularisation of society and at the close of *The Protestant Ethic* he allowed for the possibility that the process of the increasing secularisation of society might be reversed. He wrote:

No one knows who will live in this cage in the future, or whether at the end of this tremendous development entirely new prophets will arise, or there will be a great rebirth of old ideas and ideals, or, if neither, mechanised petrifaction, embellished with a sort of convulsive self-importance.[57]

For all that he wrote much on religion, Weber was not interested in religion as such. He was, as he put it, 'religiously unmusical'. What interested him was the role that religions had played in cultural change and more particularly the role which Protestantism had played in the creation of the modern Western world. It is not surprising, therefore, that Weber, unlike Durkheim, offered no definition of religion. Yet it is possible from a study of his writings to get at what might be regarded as his working definition, for, for Weber, religions were before all else systems of meaning, human attempts to impose intellectual and moral order on the chaos of existence. They were also theodicies which sought both to reconcile men and women to their fate and to offer them salvation from that fate. Weber conceived of human beings as being driven to reflect on ethical and religious questions not, as Marx had argued, by material needs, but rather by an 'inner compulsion to understand the world as a meaningful cosmos'.[58] The tragedy of his own times, for Weber, was that such ways of reconciling men and women to their fate was no longer an option. Life could be lived only with such meaning as individual men and women could themselves impose on life. It is not surprising, therefore, that some have seen Weber as a proto-existentialist. Yet the fact that religious claims were no longer an option for modern men and women did not mean that Weber underestimated the role which religions had played in the creation, maintenance and development of culture.

Approaching religion without theological questions in mind – itself, at the time that Weber was writing, something of an innovation – Weber's overriding interest was in the empirical role which religious ideas had played in the creation of the modern Western world, and it is here that the crux of his argument with both Marx and Nietzsche is to be found, for Weber refused to see religious ideas merely as a reflection, an epiphenomenon of social or psychological interests. This is not to say that Weber was unaware of the role played by material and psychological interests in the ongoing development of society for he was not. Weber was as aware as Marx of the conservative, stabilising, legitimating function of religions, as his penetrating studies of the religiously legitimated caste system in Hindu society and of the role played by Confucianism in upholding the traditional religiously legitimated social structure of Chinese society show, but he was also aware of the dynamic, revolutionary role which religion had also played in the creation of culture and he was impressed above all by the role which he believed Protestantism to have played in the creation of the modern Western world. What he objected to in Marx and Nietzsche was their attempt to impose a monocausal interpretation of social change in society. In particular Weber refused to see religion as but an epiphenomenon of material and psychological forces. Weber agreed with Marx that religious ideas were powerless until they were fused with men and women's material interests and he shared Nietzsche's appreciation of the importance of ideas in the psychology of individuals.[59] Yet both Marx and Nietzsche, he believed, had simplified a complex situation and he was adamant that religion, in and of itself, had played a major role in the creation of the modern world. He did not, however, seek to substitute for Marx's materialistic understanding of history an equally monocausal spiritualistic or idealist understanding. He wrote:

> Modern man is in general, even with the best will, unable to give religious ideas a significance for culture and rational character which they deserve. But it is, of course, not my aim to substitute for a one-sided materialistic an equally one-sided spiritualistic causal interpretation of history. Each is equally possible. But each, if it does not serve as the preparation, but as the conclusion of an investigation, accomplishes equally little in the interest of historical truth.[60]

Whether Marx would have disagreed with this thesis is open to doubt. Passages can be found in Marx (and certainly in Engels) which appear to support the view that religion, once in being, did indeed, as Weber maintained, play an important part in both sustaining and developing of human cultures. Weber's disagreement with Marx and Nietzsche was that he saw religion as arising from forces other than those identified by these two thinkers – which brings us to the role played by the charismatic prophet in Weber's account of the genesis of religion.

Weber defined the 'prophet' as 'a purely individual bearer of charisma, who by virtue of his mission proclaims a religious doctrine or divine commandment'. And he drew no real distinction between what he termed 'a renewer of religion', that is one who preaches an old revelation, actual or suppositious, and 'a founder of religion' who claims a completely new deliverance.[61] The problem that has plagued interpreters of Weber is that of ascertaining exactly what Weber meant by 'charisma'. Weber's major interpreter in the United States of America, Talcott Parsons, has suggested that it is not very different from Durkheim's conception of the 'sacred' for, as Parsons pointed out, just as Durkheim contrasted the 'sacred' with the 'profane' so Weber contrasted 'charisma' with 'routine', and the conclusion that he drew was that 'charisma is … a quality of things and persons by virtue of which they are specifically set apart from the ordinary, the everyday, the routine'.[62] There is much to be said for this view for Weber did indeed apply the term 'charisma' to just those extraordinary powers, designated by such terms as 'mana', 'orienda' and the Iranian 'maga', that Durkheim designated by the term 'sacred'. It is this that allows Parsons to claim that 'charisma' is what distinguishes the religious from the secular and the profane and which is, in Weber's sociology of religion, the source of legitimacy in general. Yet Parsons also notes that within Weber's sociology of religion 'charisma' is also conceived in terms of a specific theory of social change, a theory where the most important empirical example is the role played by the charismatic prophet.[63]

Although, for Weber, charisma transcends the routine of ordinary life, it nevertheless depends for its effect on the active response of those engaged in the routine of ordinary life and for this it must relate to specific needs within a culture if it is to evoke enthusiasm. So much is obvious. The role of the charismatic prophet, therefore, is according to Steeman's understanding of Weber, to formulate 'the basic tension that exists between an established order ... on the one hand and the more spontaneous forces of human life and the inherent precariousness of social order on the other ... Charisma is the presence of that which does not fit the ordinary routine of life, is the continuous challenge of the established order.'[64] Parsons agrees. He wrote:

> The prophet is thus the leader who sets himself explicitly and consciously against the traditional order – or aspects of it – and who claims moral authority for his position, whatever the terms in which he expresses it, such as the divine will. It is men's duty to listen to him and follow his commands or his example.[65]

Nowhere in his writings, however, did Weber attempt to assess the truth of what any prophet proclaimed.

However, Weber's major contribution to the understanding of religion was to reassert the proactive role played by religious ideas in the creation and maintenance of cultures and in producing cultural change. This he did, above all, in his most well-known work *The Protestant Ethic and the Spirit of Capitalism* (1904–5) in which he examined the role which Protestantism in general and Calvinism in particular had played in the creation of the modern capitalist world. Weber did not, however, maintain that Protestantism alone created capitalist culture. He was as aware as was Marx of the role played by material, scientific, technological and social forces in the creation of the modern world, but he also saw that these alone did not explain the rise of capitalism and having examined cultures which had failed to develop in the direction of Western Europe and the United States, Weber concluded that the missing element was the general Protestant notion of an individual's sense of having been 'called' and the Calvinist 'inner-worldly ascetic ethic' – an ethic which, for reasons which Weber, using the method of *Verstehen* – sympathetic understanding – analysed with great psychological penetration, claimed not only encouraged hard and originally honest work, but which also forbade the self-indulgent use of the wealth which hard work created and which had, therefore, to be reinvested thus creating yet more wealth. There was, he maintained, an 'elective affinity' between this ethic and the spirit of modern rational capitalism –

an affinity which he analysed with great subtlety and psychological penetration – and that it was this which was responsible for the emergence of the modern capitalist state.

This is not the place to assess the theory that Weber advances in *The Protestant Ethic and the Spirit of Capitalism,* for it is not, and does not profess to be, a general theory of religion; it is a theory about a particular form of religion at a particular time and as such falls outwith our remit. If true, however, it is not without relevance to those seeking to understand religion, for it reasserts the role of the individual prophet in the production of religion and shows how religion can be a proactive force in the creation of culture. It should also be noted that in investigating the problem of the connection between religion and capitalism, Weber was the first sociologist to study the role of religion in the society and culture of non-Western societies and in the course of which he deepened Western Europe's understanding of the cultures of China and India.

Here we must leave Weber and look at a contemporary thinker who quite explicitly acknowledges his debt to Weber, as well as to Durkheim, the American sociologist Peter Berger.

– PETER BERGER –

For over a quarter of a century Peter Berger has been one of the most influential thinkers in the sociological study of religion. Whilst in his early published work he employed what he described in his book *The Social Reality of Religion* (1967) as a 'methodological atheism' in his approach to the study of religious phenomena, his work since the publication of that book has become increasingly less detached to the extent that many of his fellow sociologists see him today as more of a religious thinker than a sociologist. His early work drew heavily on the work of Durkheim, and Berger, like Durkheim, saw religion as a social construct designed to keep *anomie,* social disintegration, at bay. But Berger also drew on the work of Hegel and Feuerbach and with these thinkers in mind we are not surprised when we read that, for Berger, religion 'In all its manifestations ... constitutes an immense projection of human meanings into the empty vastness of the universe – a projection to be sure which comes back as an alien reality to haunt its producers.'[66]

The central argument of *The Social Reality of Religion* is that whilst religion had been one of the most effective bulwarks in human history against *anomie,* it has, at the same time, and directly related to its capacity to fulfil this function, also been one of the more alienating factors in human life, a very important form of 'false-consciousness'.[67]

At the time when Berger offered this explanation of religion his main interest was in the sociology of knowledge and the explanation which he offered was, he claimed, an attempt 'to apply a general theoretical perspective derived from the sociology of knowledge to the phenomenon of religion'.[68] This perspective was set out at length by Berger prior to the publication of *The Social Reality of Religion* in a work written in collaboration with Thomas Luckmann entitled *The Social Construction of Reality* and some knowledge of the argument of that earlier work is necessary if we are to appreciate fully the explanation of religion Berger advanced in *The Social Reality of Religion*.[69]

In *The Social Construction of Reality* Berger and Luckmann put the terms 'knowledge' and 'reality' in inverted commas to intimate their intention of leaving open the ultimate epistemological and ontological status of these terms. They defined 'knowledge', therefore, in terms of 'certainty', the certainty 'that phenomena are real and that they possess specific characteristics', a definition which allowed them to go on to say that the 'knowledge' that is the subject-matter of sociology is no more than what, in any society, ' passes for knowledge of reality'. 'Reality' was defined as 'a quality appertaining to phenomena that we recognise as having a being independent of our own volition (we cannot wish them away).'[70] Whether or not such recognition is justified was not, Berger and Luckmann claimed, a sociological question. The sociologist is as impressed as, it will be recalled, were the Greek Sophists, by the social relativity of such 'knowledge' of 'reality' as obtains in different societies, by the fact that:

> men in different societies take quite different realities for granted, that what may be real to a Tibetan monk may not be real to an American businessman, and is compelled by the logic of his discipline to go on to ask whether the difference between these different 'realities' may not be due to the differences between the societies which they inhabit. He will, therefore, concern himself with the ways by which realities are taken for granted in all human societies and so with the process by which any body of 'knowledge' comes to be socially established as 'reality', that is, with the social construction of reality.

Berger and Luckmann, as methodological relativists, unlike many whose views we have considered so far, claim that it is no part of the sociologist's task to be concerned with the truth or falsity of the 'knowledge of reality' whose construction it is the task of the sociologist of knowledge to investigate. The sociologist confines himself to telling us how 'knowledge of reality' comes about and how it is maintained. The process of constructing 'knowledge' is, Berger and Luckmann maintain, dialectical. Men and women are continually 'outpouring' themselves into the world in which they find themselves – something which they claim is endemic in the human biological makeup. Such 'outpouring' is an anthropological necessity. Unlike other animals, men and women are not wholly determined by instinct and so there is no human world prior to them, as it were in embryo, for them to inhabit. They must make the world for themselves and in the course of constructing their world, their 'reality', they produce and complete themselves. Thus do human beings create cultures – cultures which have no being, no reality apart from human activity. These, for Berger and Luckmann, are neither given in nature nor are they derivable from the nature of man. As they put it in *The Social Construction of Reality*:

> Social order is a human product, or more precisely, an ongoing human product. It is produced by man in the course of his ongoing externalisation. Social order is not biologically given or derived from any biological *data* in its empirical manifestations. Social order, needless to add, is not given in man's natural environment, though particular features of this may be factors in determining certain features of social order (for, example, its economic or technological arrangements). Social order is not part of the 'nature of things', and it cannot be derived from 'laws of nature'. Social order exists *only* as a human product. No other ontological status may be ascribed to it without hopelessly obfuscating its empirical manifestations. Both in its genesis … and in its existence at any instant of time … it is a human product.[71]

Whether society has ever been created in quite the free, almost arbitrary, way that Berger and Luckmann seem to suggest in the passage quoted might be open to question, but the gist of what they are saying will be familiar to those readers who have read what was said about Hegel and Marx in previous chapters. Yet Berger is no Marxist. In fact he goes out of his way to point out that what he is saying 'does not imply a sociologically deterministic theory of religion' and that 'it does not imply that any particular religious system is nothing but the effect or "reflection" of social processes'. The point that he is making, he says, is that the *same* human activity that produces society also produces religion with the relation between the two products always being a dialectical one.' He can thus allow, as did Weber, that it is just as possible that 'in a particular historical development, a social process is the effect of religious ideation, while in another development the reverse may be the case'. The conclusion that he draws is that the rootage of religion in human activity does not imply that 'religion is always a dependent variable in the history of society, but rather that it derives its objective and subjective reality from human beings who produce it in their ongoing lives'.[72] Why human beings have produced the particular religious systems they have produced and not some other system Berger does not say, although from hints thrown out and from what he has said in later writings, the answer to this problem would appear to lie in the realm of meaning and, therefore, in a societies' belief that some meanings are more meaningful than others.

But if the process of externalising human meanings creates social 'reality', the next step in this process is when this first step becomes forgotten and what is socially produced is seen to possess a (spurious) 'facticity' and so to stand over against men and women as an alien reality. Once this has occurred the socially objectified world begins to react back on those who produced it and the last stage in the dialectical process takes place as men and women reabsorb into consciousness the objectified world in such a way that the structure of that world comes to determine the subjective structures of consciousness itself.

To appreciate the role of religion in all this it is necessary to realise that 'realities' produced in this way have a precarious stability and need to be constantly 'maintained' lest they fall apart and produce what Durkheim called a state of *anomie*. Society must, therefore, find ways to legitimate its culture, that is, to give it objectivity. This in the past, says Berger, has been the task of religion which has legitimated social structures and, much else besides, by 'bestowing upon them an ultimately valid ontological status'. Religion does this, says Berger, by locating social structures within a sacred cosmic frame of reference, but in so doing, whilst providing a bulwark against *anomie*, at the same time, and in direct proportion to its capacity to fulfil this function, also produces 'false consciousness' and a sense of 'alienation', and religion does this because it imposes a 'fictitious inexorability upon the humanly constructed world'.[73]

However, mindful of the limitations which he has placed on himself qua sociologist, he immediately adds that it is, of course, 'impossible within the frame of reference of scientific theorising to make any affirmations, positive or negative, about the ultimate ontological status of this alleged reality [of religion]'.[74] Viewed from the perspective of the sociology of knowledge religion can be seen only as the product of human activity and human consciousness, and rigorous brackets have to be placed around the question whether these projections may not *also* be something else or, more accurately, refer to something other than the human world in which they originate.

However, in a later work, *A Rumour of Angels* (1969), Berger, writing not as a sociologist, but as a Christian thinker, took off the sociological–phenomenological brackets and openly raised the question whether the fact that human beings felt compelled to produce religions indicated that this was, perhaps, because they corresponded to something in the structure of reality, a question which he now answered in the affirmative. Berger had, in fact, hinted as much towards the close of *The Social Reality of Religion* where he had suggested that just as Marx, under the influence of Feuerbach, had, in the interests of an empirical understanding of human affairs, reversed the way that Hegel had understood human affairs, so the time might have come to reverse this state of affairs and stand Marx on his head – just so long as one understands that this takes place in a different frame of reference – and see the fact 'that man projects ultimate meanings onto reality because that reality is, indeed, ultimately meaningful and because his own being (the empirical ground of these projections) contains and intends these same ultimate meanings.' This, he further suggests, would be an interesting ploy on Feuerbach – the reduction of theology to anthropology would end in the reconstruction of anthropology in the theological mode.[75]

This is not the place to discuss Berger's exploration of the rediscovery of the supernatural in the modern world and the 'signals of transcendence' which he discerns, for this belongs properly to the philosophy of religion and this is not a book on the philosophy of religion. The relevance of what he has to say to our own enquiry lies rather in his realisation that when he has done all that a sociologist can do to show the human origins of religion, there are still questions that lie beyond the scope of sociological enquiry, for despite the fact that from the perspective of sociology religions must be regarded as social constructs, the issue of their truth or falsity remains. And, for Berger, this further enquiry is also, initially, an empirical one – Berger's own term is 'inductive' – for, as he argues in his book *The Heretical Imperative*, contemporary exploration of the truth claims of religion can begin only with an examination of the totality of claimed religious experience – a task which, Berger claims, has only just begun.[76] The only rider I would add to this is to repeat the remark that I made at the conclusion of my chapter on religious experience, which was that, as all experience is interpreted experience, such an enquiry can take place only within the context of a renewed programme of a natural theology which will give due consideration to all aspects of human experience – so that the notion of 'religious' experience is widened to include, hopefully in an integrated world-outlook, the whole range of human responses to the world – intellectual, moral and aesthetic. This, as I shall suggest in my conclusion, will, in the global village which is now coming into being and in which religions and naturalistic understanding of the world are beginning to interact and to compete with each other, be more of a collective than an individual enterprise. On a global scale the argument between competing understandings of the world has only just begun.

– NOTES –

1. *Marx and Engels Complete Works* (hereafter MECW), London: Lawrence & Wishart, 1975, Vol. 1, p. 18.
2. MECW, Vol. 1, p. 30.
3. MECW, Vol. 3, p. 137.
4. Ibid., p. 175.
5. Ibid., p. 175.
6. Ibid., p. 176.
7. Ibid., p. 176.
8. Ibid., p. 179.
9. MECW, Vol. 5, p. 38.
10. MECW, Vol. 3, pp. 305–6.
11. MECW, Vol. 5, p. 9.
12. Ibid., p. 7.
13. Ibid., p. 8.
14. For example, in *Capital*, Vol. III, Harmondsworth: Penguin Books, p. 259.
15. John Plamenatz, *Ideology*, London: Macmillan, 1971, p. 87.
16. MECW, Vol. 3, p. 333.
17. Ibid., p. 332.
18. Preface to 2nd edn of *Capital*, Vol. I, pp. 102–3.
19. MECW, Vol. 3, p. 276.
20. Ibid., pp. 304–6.
21. Plamenatz, *Ideology*, p. 77.
22. Norman Birnbaum, 'Beyond Marx in the Sociology of Religion?' in Charles Y. Glock and Phillip Hammond (eds), *Beyond the Classics? Essays in the Scientific Study of Religion*, New York: Harper & Row, 1973, p. 9.
23. MECW, Vol. 3, p. 333 (my italics).
24. Ibid.
25. C.f. *Capital*, Vol. I, pp. 303–4
26. J. S. Dunne, *The City of the Gods*, London: 1974, p. 217.
27. MECW, Vol. 3, p. 337.
28. I have sought to answer this question at length in my book *Marxist–Leninist 'Scientific Atheism'*, Berlin: Mouton de Gruyter, 1983, pp. 35–43, and the reader is referred to that discussion.
29. Bhagavadgita, IV. 13.
30. Helmut Gollwitzer, *The Christian Faith and the Marxist Criticism of Religion*, Edinburgh: St Andrew's Press, 1970, pp. 90–1.
31. MECW, Vol. 5, p. 44.
32. Ibid.
33. MECW, Vol. 5, p. 45.
34. Delos B. McKown, *Classical Marxist Critiques of Religion*, The Hague: Martinus Nijhoff, 1975, pp. 10–13.
35. Engels, *Anti-Dühring*, London: Lawrence & Wishart, 1975, p. 438.
36. Ibid., p. 440.
37. *Marx and Engels Basic Works*, London: Lawrence & Wishart, 1953, p. 247.
38. Ibid., pp. 443–4.
39. Ibid., p. 439.

RELIGION: THE CLASSICAL THEORIES

40. Leszek Kolakowski, *Marxism and Beyond*, London: Paladin Books, 1971, pp. 31–2.
41. V. Gardavsky, *God Is Not Yet Dead*, Harmondsworth: Pelican Books, 1973, p. 28.
42. Peter L. Berger, *Facing Up to Modernity*, New York: Basic Books, 1977, p. 69.
43. Durkheim, *The Elementary Forms of the Religious Life*, trans. J. W. Swain, London: Allen & Unwin, 1915, p. 69.
44. W. S. F. Pickering (ed.), *Durkheim on Religion*, London: Routledge, 1975, p. 251.
45. Durkheim, *Elementary Forms of the Religious Life*, pp. 2–3.
46. Durkheim, *Rules of Sociological Method*, trans. by W. D. Halls, London: Allen & Unwin, 1982, p. 259.
47. Durkheim, *Elementary Forms of the Religious Life*, p. 37.
48. Ibid., p. 44.
49. Ibid., especially pp. 415–47. However, the qualifications which Durkheim introduces into his argument at this point should be noted, for it is in the conclusion that he allows that religion serves functions other than that of simply representing society to itself.
50. Frank Parkin, *Durkheim*, Oxford: OUP, 1992, p. 50.
51. Durkheim, *The Elementary Forms of the Religious Life*, pp. 429–31.
52. Weber, 'Science as a Vocation', in Peter Lassman and Irving Velody (eds), *Max Weber's 'Science as a Vocation'*, London: Unwin Hyman, 1989, p. 30.
53. Thus, for example, in the first sketch for what would become his most famous work, *The Protestant Ethic and the Spirit of Capitalism*, which he published in the journal *Archiv für Sozialwissenschaft und Sozialpolitik* for 1904–5, he wrote of 'the unprecedented loneliness of the single individual' deprived of 'salvation through the Church and its sacraments', and from whose world magic had been almost totally eliminated. C.f. Benjamin Nelson, 'Weber's Protestant Ethic; Its Origins, Wanderings, and Foreseeable Futures', in Glock and Hammond, *Beyond the Classics*, p. 75.
54. Weber, 'Science as a Vocation', p. 18.
55. Ibid., p. 30.
56. Weber, *The Protestant Ethic and the Spirit of Capitalism*, London: Allen & Unwin, 1930, p. 181.
57. Ibid., p. 182.
58. Weber, *Sociology of Religion*, trans. Ephraim Fischoff, Boston: Beacon Press, 1964, p. 117.
59. So Gerth and Mills in their introduction to H. H. Gerth and C. Wright Mills (eds), *From Max Weber: Essays in Sociology*, London: Routledge & Kegan Paul, 1948, pp. 61–2.
60. Weber, *The Protestant Ethic*, p. 183.
61. Weber, *Sociology of Religion*, p. 46.
62. Talcott Parsons, *The Structure of Social Action*, New York: The Free Press, 1937, p. 662.
63. Ibid., p. 663.
64. Theodore M. Steeman, 'Max Weber's Sociology of Religion', *Sociological Analysis*, vol. 25 (1964), p. 53.
65. Parsons, *The Structure of Social Action*, p. 663. Weber discussed Nietzsche's theory of resentment in 'The Social Psychology of World Religions'. This essay can be found in Gerth and Mills, *From Max Weber*.
66. Peter L. Berger, *The Social Reality of Religion*, London: Faber & Faber, 1970, p. 100. This work was published in the United States as *The Sacred Canopy*. All references here are to the UK edition.
67. Ibid., p. 87.
68. Ibid., p. v.

69. Peter Berger and Thomas Luckmann, *The Social Construction of Reality: A Treatise in the Sociology of Knowledge*, London: Allen Lane, 1966.
70. Ibid., p. 13.
71. Ibid., pp. 69–70.
72. Berger, *The Social Reality of Religion*, p. 48.
73. Ibid., pp. 85–95.
74. Ibid., p. 100.
75. Ibid., pp. 180–1.
76. Peter L. Berger, *The Heretical Imperative: Contemporary Possibilities of Religious Affirmation*, London: Collins, 1979, p. 127.

CHAPTER 9

Conclusion: What is Religion?

I shall begin to draw this short survey of the classical theories of religion to a close by briefly rehearsing the answers given to the question 'what is religion?' by those whose theories we have considered. These range from the claim that religion is a response to the revealed word of God (Judaism, Christianity and Islam), that it is a way of life founded on 'the word' heard by the sages of old showing the way to final release from the eternal round of birth and rebirth (Hinduism and, in a qualified way, Buddhism), that it is the path to the existential realisation of the soul's identity with God or to union with God or Ultimate Reality (a variety of Indian and Western thinkers), to the claim that it is a primitive and now outmoded way of seeking to explain, predict and control events in the world (Tylor, Frazer and, in a qualified way, Horton), a roundabout way in which human beings have talked about themselves (Feuerbach and, in a qualified way, Berger), the fantastic realisation of the human essence in a world where the human essence has no true reality and an ideology legitimating the status quo (Marx), the revenge of the weak on the strong (Nietzsche), a regression to an infantile trust in a 'father-figure' in the face of the harsh realities of the world (Freud), a societies' celebration of itself (Durkheim), or a way of reconciling human beings to their fate (Weber and Malinowski).

The first thing that will strike anyone surveying these answers will be their sheer number and variety, the second will be the realisation of how little, if anything, these answers have in common and the third, at least to those with some knowledge of the data of the comparative study of religions, will be the realisation of how culture bound the majority of these answers are. The big divide, of course, as I stated at the outset of this survey, is between those who see religion as a genuine response to a transcendent 'Other' and those who do not and who seek, therefore, to explain religion as a wholly human construct. Yet even among those who see religion as a human construct there is no agreement as to what it is in human nature that leads human beings to spin the web of religion out of themselves. This does not necessarily mean that someone looking for a naturalistic theory of religion has to choose between a number of competing theories. The implication is rather that any naturalistic theory which stands a chance of winning support today will have to find a way of combining the insights of Marx, Freud, Nietzsche, Durkheim, Weber, and a host of others beside, just as any theory which seeks to substantiate the claims of religion to be a valid response to a transcendent reality will have to combine insights from a number of differing religious traditions. Whether a naturalistic or a religious theory can best combine the insights of both of these two main ways of explaining religion remains an open question.

Robin Horton, seeking – as so many historians of science have done – an answer to the question why science and technology took off in the way in which they did in the seventeenth century in Europe and not in any other part of the world, lists two main features of European society which might account for the success of European science – belief in cognitive progress and inter-theoretic competition.[1] In the postscript to his collected essays *Patterns of Thought in Africa and the West*, he adds a further factor, 'world-view universalism'.[2]

The belief in cognitive progress, which Horton, drawing on the work of Toulmin, Medewar, Sklair and Webster,[3] sees as preceding the scientific enterprise of modern Europe was, he argues, a powerful influence on the progress of science. Of itself, however, it would have been insufficient without the second factor to which he draws attention – inter-theoretic competition. Rejecting the view of the way in which scientific advance proceeds put forward in Thomas Kuhn's *Structure of Scientific Revolution*, and doing so on the strength of recent work in the history of science,[4] Horton notes that what this recent work suggests is that the growth of knowledge depends on healthy competition between the supporters of rival theoretical frameworks and he cites as examples of such competition the fact that from its earliest beginnings the Copernican/Galilean astronomical model developed in healthy competition with its Ptolemaic rival and that Newtonian dynamics grew and flourished in intense competition with the alternative systems of Hobbes and Descartes. He also points out that it was in England, where Newtonian dynamics enjoyed unchallenged allegiance, that it ceased to grow and develop.

The third factor – world-view universalism – perhaps needs more explication. What Horton means by this can best be illumined by contrasting it, as he himself does, with what he calls 'world-view parochialism'. 'World-view parochialism' is that outlook on life which sees each local community and its environment as governed by a distinct set of forces. In such a situation, says Horton, confrontation with a neighbour's alien world-view is unproblematic – in other words, inter-theoretic competition is virtually ruled out. By contrast 'world-view universalism', which insists that the entire world is governed by a single set of underlying forces, makes every confrontation with an alien world-view a challenge to one's own view. It, therefore, he says, 'greatly *encourages* inter-theoretic competition'.[5]

If this is the way that the great body of Western science grew, then this might offer hope to anyone frustrated by the variety of theoretical models which, as we have seen, abound in the study of religion, for the contemporary world is at the beginnings of a new period in the relationship between religions in that, today, religions are beginning to interact on a scale which is unprecedented, and this not just in the Western world, but world-wide. Never before in the history of the human race have the conditions existed for inter-theoretic competition between differing religious understandings of the world as they are beginning to do today. The repercussions for claims to religious knowledge are inestimable. The coming inter-theoretic competition will not, however, be only between the various religions of the world. It will, as is becoming evident, also involve competition between naturalistic and religious understandings of the world and will further involve discussion of the scope and limits of scientific explanation.

Peter Berger, another thinker whose views have figured predominantly in our account of theories of religion, predicts a similar scenario in his book *The Heretical Imperative: Contemporary Possibilities of Religious Affirmation*. In this book Berger foresees and welcomes what he calls 'the coming contestation of religions' for this is just, he believes, what religion needs if it is to develop or, indeed, survive. 'What is just about unique,' he writes, 'about the modern situation is the *sheer availability* of ... accounts and reports of the multiform religious experience of mankind.'[6] But over and above the availability of accounts, there is also the fact that people in many parts of the globe – not just in the Western world – live and interact, in our increasingly multi-faith and multi-cultural societies, with adherents of almost the whole gamut of religious and cultural traditions. What this portends for religious traditions and their associated world-views, whose adherents, until very recently, lived, in almost total isolation from each other, even in countries where there are adherents of a number of faiths, is hard to predict. Certainly few sociologists at the end of the 1990s have the certainty, which their colleagues had a generation ago, that the result will be the inevitable secularisation of the planet. This article of modernist faith has given way to post-modernist caution, if not to a post-modernist celebration of diversity. However, the latter trend has some disturbing features, for it can involve the shelving of difficult epistemological and ontological questions. If the irrationalism which seems to be sweeping over late twentieth-century Western culture is not to triumph, then what must be reasserted is that, in the growing competition between world-views, argument, based upon a belief in a common and universal rationality, must be given its due place. The alternative would be either to retreat into the ghetto or give up serious thinking altogether.

The issue between naturalistic and non-naturalistic understandings of reality is today more evenly balanced than it was even a generation ago and, hopefully, a book surveying theories of religion written at the end of the third millennium will give a less diverse series of answers to the question 'what is religion? than is possible in one written at the end of the second millennium.

– Notes –

1. Horton, 'Tradition and Modernity Revisited', in his *Patterns of Thought in Africa and the West*, Cambridge: CUP, 1994, p. 317f.
2. Horton, *Pattern of Thought in Africa and the West*, pp. 379–81.
3. Horton cites Stephen Toumlin and Joan Goodfield, *The Discovery of Time*, London: Hutchinson, 1965; Peter Medewar, *The Hope of Progress*, London: Methuen, 1972; L. Sklair, *The Sociology of Progress*, London: Routledge & Kegan Paul, 1970; and C. Webster, *The Great Instauration*, London: Duckworth, 1975.
4. Horton cites P. Feyerabend, *Against Method*, London: New Left Books, 1975; I. Lakatos and A. Musgrave (eds), Criticism and the Growth of Knowledge, Cambridge: CUP, 1970; I. Lakatos, 'Falsification and Methodology of Scientific Research Programmes', Lakatos and Musgrave's *Criticism in the Growth of Knowledge*; L. Laudan, *Progress and Its Problems*, Berkeley: University of California Press, 1977.
5. Horton, *Patterns of Thought in Africa and the West*, p. 379.
6. Berger, *The Heretical Imperative: Contemporary Possibilities of Religious Affirmation*, London: Collins, 1980, p. 35.

Index

Following the convention established by Professor John Hinnells, editor of the *New Dictionary of World Religions* (Oxford: Blackwells, 1995), I have eschewed the use of diacritical marks in the text but, for those who find them useful, have included them in the index.

Main references are indicated in **bold**.

Adams, John, 143
African Traditional Religion, 120–2
alienation, 54, 85, 130, 163–4, 166, 167–8, 170, 170–3
Anderson, Bernard, 16
Apocrypha, 23
Aquinas, Thomas, 28
Aristotle, 84
Arkoun, Muhammad, 32
Arnold, Matthew, 77
Athanasius, 10
Augustine of Hippo, 22
Australian Aborigines, 105, 106, 184, 186
Ayer, A. J., 67

Bacon, Francis, 133–4
Baillie, John, 28, 57
Barth, Karl, 24, 25–7, 41, 87
Beattie, John, 121
Becker, Ernest, 134
Bellah, Robert, 186
Berger, Peter, 1, 21, 49, 147, 161, 182, **194–8**, 202, 204–5
Birnbaum, Norman, 170
Braithwaite, Richard, 77
Buddha, 39, 156
Buddhism, 34, 35, 39–40, 64, 154, 180, 202
al-Bukhārī, Muḥammad, 30, 32
Burckhardt, Jacob, 152

Campbell, Joseph, 155
Carlyle, Thomas, 96
charisma, 20, 192–3

Christianity, 10, 16, 17, 18, 33, 38, 54, 75, 77, 82, 104–5, 136, 140, 142, 149, 165, 175, 180, 202
Cicero, 96
civil religion, 186
Clement of Alexandria, 42
Clements, Keith, 51, 52, 53
Codrington, R. H., 107
Communism, 11, 173
Confucianism, 42, 54
Cornford, F. M., 112
cosmological argument, 52
Critias, 94–5

death, 115–16, 172
Deism, 53, 96, 97
Democritus, 94
D'Holbach, Baron, 96
Dodds, E. R., 9
Donovan, Peter, 69
Dostoevsky, F., 1
Douglas, Mary, 12, 105, 117, 118
Dunne, J. S., 172
Durkheim, Émile, 40, 108, 109, 115, 126, **183–8**, 191, 202, 203

Eckhart, Meister, 67, 69
Engels, Friedrich, **161–79**, 183, 192
Enlightenment (*Aufklärung*), 53, 76, 80, 96, 99, 100, 132, 136, 138, 143, 149
ethics, 20, 77, 79, 80
Euhemer, 96, 127
Evans-Pritchard, E. E., 101, **117–19**

Existentialism, 142

faith, 27–8
Farmer, H. H., 57
Farquhar, J. N., 42
Feuerbach, Ludwig, 61, **126–35**, 140, 141,
    156, 157, 162, 163, 164, 165, 166–7,
    168, 169, 171, 194, 198, 202
Firth, Raymond, 121
Flood, Gavin, 34, 36, 37
Forward, Martin, 32
Foucault, Michel, 142
Frankfort, Henri, 12
Frazer, James, 2, 99, **101–5**, 106, 109, 113,
    114, 115, 117, 118, 119, 121, 136,
    144, 184, 185, 202
Freud, Sigmund, 2, 4, 40, 104, 120, 132,
    134, 140, **143–50**, 151, 152, 156, 157,
    183, 203
Fukuyama, Francis, 138

Gardavsky, Vitezslav, 181
al-Gazzālī, Abū Ḥāmid, 3
Glick, Leonard, 114
Glover, T. R., 97
Goethe, J. W., 2
Goldziher, Ignaz, 17
Gollwitzer, Helmut, 174
Gore, Charles, 16–17, 18, 19
Greeks, 9, 93–7
Gross, Otto, 151
Gunton, Colin, 42
Guthrie, Stewart, 133
Guthrie, W. K. C., 111

Ḥadīth, 30
al-Ḥallāj, 68
Hampshire, Stuart, 143–4
Harnack, Adolf von, 25–6
Harvey, Van A., 128, 133
Hebblethwaite, Brian, 41
Hegel, G. F., 3, 17, 54, 75, **80–8**, 126, 130,
    136, 141, 163, 166, 167, 168, 169,
    170, 171, 172–3, 182, 194
Heine, H., 148
Herbert of Cherbury, 97
Hick, John, 5, 41, 43, 57
Hinduism, 54, 173–4, 180, 202

history, 84, 85, 86, 87, 127, 164, 175,
    180–2
Hook, Sidney, 133
Horton, Robin, **119–22**, 187, 202,
    203–4
Hourani, Albert, 18
Humanism, 66, 130–1, 142–3, 170
Hume, David, 54–5, 60, 77, 81, 112–13,
    127
Huxley, Aldous, 49, **66–71**

ideology, 119, 165, 167, 173–4, 182
Ijtihād, 31
Indian religious tradition, 10, 20, 34–41
Irenaeus, 42
Islam, 10, 11, 16, 17, 18, 29–33, 38, 41, 54,
    82, 202
Ismāʿīlīs, 32
Ithna-ʿasharīyya, 31

Jabneh Academy, 21, 22
Jaeger, W., 96
Jainism, 35
James, William, 3, **61–6**, 82
Jeffreys, Richard, 68
Jerome, 22
Jesus, 16, 20, 25, 30, 41, 43, 50, 54, 77–8,
    156
Jevons, F. R., 102
Judaism, 10, 17, 18, 20, 38, 82, 149, 180,
    202
Jung, Carl Gustav, 143, **150–7**

Kant, Immanuel, 50, 51, 52, 53, 55, 60–1,
    76–80, 81, 132, 137, 162, 182
Kaufmann, Walter, 139
Kierkegaard, S., 190
al-Kindi, Abū Yūsuf Yaʿqūb ibn Isḥāq, 33
Kolakowski, Leszek, 5–6, 131–2, 180
Kraemer, H., 41
Kuhn, Thomas, 203

Laing, R. D., 70
Lang, Andrew, 106, 108
Leach, Edmund, 113, 120
Leary, Timothy, 70
Lee, R. S., 148
Legge, James, 42

Leibnitz, G. W., 66
Leo XIII, Pope, 27
Lessing, G. E., 82
Leuba, James H., 63
Lévy-Bruhl, Lucien, **108–12**, 118, 120
LSD, 69, 70
Luckmann, Thomas, 21, 195–6
Lucretius, 127, 134
Lukacs, Georg, 190
Lyall, A. C., 102

Mackintosh, H. R., 49
McKown, Delos, 176
Madhva, 38
magic, 13, 15, 102–4, 112, 113–14, 115,
    116, 185
Malcolm, Norman, 26
Malinowski, Bronislaw, 12, 13, 108, 112,
    113–16, 202
Marcel, Gabriel, 59
Marcion, 23
Marett, R. R., 107–8, 110
Martin, C. B., 71–2
Martin, Nicholas, 142
Marx, Karl, 2, 4, 40, 104, 126, 130,
    161–76, 183, 184, 191, 192, 198, 202,
    203
Marxism, 179, 181–2, 190
modernity, 1–2, 9, 204
Momen, Moojan, 31
monism, 38, 55, 84
Moses, 19, 21
Muḥammad, 16, 17, 29, 30, 32, 156
Müller, Friedrich Max, 64, 87, 107
Muslim, ibn al-Ḥajjāj al Qushayrī, 30
Myers, F., 64
mysticism, 66–72

Nagel, S. F., 116
Nanak, Guru, 40
National Socialism, 11, 153, 155
'natural religion', 174–6
Neusch, Marcel, 134, 135
New Age, 156
Newton, Isaac, 203
Nietzsche, Friedrich, 1, 2, 4, 126, 132,
    135–43, 148, 151, 157, 165, 189, 191,
    202, 203

Nock, A. D., 62
Noll, Richard, 151, 156
Nüdling, Gregor, 128
Numinous, The, 58–60

Oepke, Albrecht, 28
Oldenberg, H., 102
Origen, 42
Otto, Rudolf, 18, 49, 52, 55, **56–61**, 62,
    67, 107
Owen, Robert, 170

pan-en-hen-ism, 68
panentheism, 87
Pannenberg, Wolfgang, 27
pantheism, 64, 87
Parkin, Frank, 186
Parsons, Talcott, 192, 193
Paton, H. J., 61
Perennial Philosophy, The (Philosophia
    perennis), 66–7, 69
Perry, Willard, 62
Philips, Dewi, 26
Pietism, 49–50, 76, 77, 161
Plamenatz, John, 167, 170
Plato, 13, **74–6**, 95
Platonism, 136, 137, 140
Plotinus, 75
pluralism, 1, 10, 41–4, 93–4, 204–5
Polybius, 96
polytheism, 149
Post-Modernism, 119, 121, 204–5
Pragmatism, 65
primal religion, 9, 10–15, 187
Prodicus of Ceos, 94
prophet, 9, 10, 13, 15–20, 139, 186, 192;
    see also Shaman
Protestantism, 23, 24–5, 62, 82, 137, 189,
    190–1
Pruyser, Paul, 147

Qur'ān, 29, 30, 31, 33

Radcliffe-Brown, A. R., 116–17
reductionism, 3, 71, 82, 88
religion, definition of, 4–6
Richardson, Alan, 42–3
Ricoeur, Paul, 4

Roman Catholic Church, 23, 25, 26, 27–8, 62, 82, 106
Romanticism, 50, 82
al-Rummani, 33

Sandmel, Samuel, 21
Sartre, Jean-Paul, 142
Saul, 15–16
Schelling, F. W. J. von, 82
Schenk, H. G., 50
Schlegel, Friedrich, 50
Schmidt, Wilhelm, 106
Schleiermacher, Friedrich, 18, **49–55**, 56, 62, 67, 68, 81, 82, 87, 131, 146, 161
science, 100–1, 103, 104–5, 109, 111, 114, 118, 119, 120–1, 132, 138, 148–9, 183, 187, 189–90
Scripture, 21–1
    Buddhist, 40; Christian, 21, 22, 23–5, 28, 32; Jewish, 19, 21–3, 32; Hindu, 34–9, 67, 68; Muslim, 29–32; Sikh, 40
secularisation, 1–2, 204
Segal, Robert, 13
Semitic religious tradition, 15–33; *see also* Christianity; Islam; Judaism
Sen, Keshab, 44
Seneca, 97
Sextus Empiricus, 94
shaman, 13, 14, 15, 18, 186
Shankara, (Śaṇkara), 37, 38, 84, 86
Sharpe, Eric J., 4–5, 62, 103–4
Shiʿa, 31–2
Shruti (Śruti), 34, 35
Siculus, Diodorus, 113
Sikhism, 34, 35, 39, 40–1
Singh, Guru Gobind, 41
Smith, Wilfred Cantwell, 11, 42, 122
Smith, William Robertson, 101, 184
Smriti (Smṛti), 34, 35
Socrates, 13
Sophists, 93–6, 97, 195
Spinoza, Benedict de, 53, 68

Stace, W. T., 67, 68
Starbuck, 62
Stern, J. P., 138, 139
Stoicism, 64, 79, 94, 96–7, 190
Strauss, David, 135, 161

theism, 38, 51, 52, 60, 64, 68
theology, 53, 60–1, 65, 66, 82, 121, 129, 130, 134, 191, 198
Thomas, Keith, 13–14, 111
Tillich, Paul, 53
Tocqueville, Alex de, 138
Torah, 19, 21, 22
totemism, 184–5
Trent, Council of, 23, 27
Troeltsch, Ernst, 41
Tylor, Edward, 2, 12, **99–101**, 109, 117, 118, 119, 120, 121, 136, 144, 177–8, 185, 202

Veda, 34–5, 37
Vedānta, 36, 38, 39, 49, 62, 68, 75, 86
Vico, Giambattista, 127
Vivekananda, 63

Wagner, Richard, 135
Walls, A. F., 10
Ward, Keith, 12, 18, 42, 43, 51, 52, 79–80
Watt, W. M., 33
Weber, Max, 20, 111, 126, 138, **188–94**, 202, 203
Weitling, W., 170, 174
Winch, Peter, 121
Wittgenstein, L., 4, 5, 26
Wordsworth, William, 68

Xenophanes, 93, 127

Zaehner, R. C., 68, 70
Zakkai, Rabbi Jonathan ben, 21
Zeno of Citium, 97